AN INTEGRATED APPROACH TO BUSINESS STUDIES

An Integrated Approach to Business Studies

BRUCE R JEWELL

MSc, MA, BSc (Econ)

Lecturer in Business Studies and Economics, Weald College, Harrow
Joint Chief Examiner, 'A' Level Business Studies (London Board)

Pitman Publishing

PITMAN PUBLISHING
128 Long Acre, London, WC2E 9AN
A Division of Longman Group UK Limited

© Bruce R Jewell 1990

First published in Great Britain 1990
Reprinted 1991 (twice), 1992 (twice)

British Library Cataloguing in Publication Data
Jewell, Bruce R.
  An integrated approach to business studies.
  1. Business studies
  I. Title
  658

ISBN 0-273-03249-6

Typeset 10/12 pt Ehrhardt by ⩗ Tek Art Ltd, Addiscombe, Croydon,
Surrey

Printed in England by Clays Ltd, St Ives plc

Contents

Preface

The popularity of Business Studies as a GCE subject is seen in the growth in the numbers of examination candidates and in the proliferation of examination syllabuses both at 'A' and 'AS' level. This book will be of use to students of all syllabuses, although given the variations in both syllabus content and form of assessment it is difficult to serve all schemes equally well.

Each chapter in this book is followed by a variety of case studies and questions, exercises and examination questions. Where indicated, they have been taken from past AEB and Cambridge Syndicate papers and are reproduced with the kind permission of the Boards. Non-attributed questions were devised by the author to reflect the question style of various boards. The exercises should be seen as an integral part of the text and conscientious students will systematically work their way through them. Most exercises cover material from more than one chapter. This was a deliberate attempt to force the reader to see the inter-relationship between topics within the syllabus so as to develop the integrated approach emphasised both in the title of this book and in the examination syllabuses.

To succeed in this subject it is essential to develop:
- a knowledge of the subject matter, the concepts and the terminology
- an awareness of current trends in the business world
- an ability to interpret and analyse data, applying basic principles in an intelligent way
- an imaginative approach to problem solving
- an ability to present a case in a logical, coherent and appropriate manner.

The text is designed to provide a base of knowledge and exercises are designed to develop the skills required. To achieve a good grade it is necessary to consult other books which might provide additional information, a different slant and/or a different depth of analysis. It is also important to consult the 'quality' newspapers and the growing number of magazines in the field of business and finance.

As you embark on your 'A' or 'AS' level course I wish you good luck and ask you to remember that the more you put into an enterprise, the more you get out of it. Hence an active approach by taking responsibility for your learning produces dividends in terms of examination grades.

Acknowledgements

I wish to thank the following organisations and the editors of the named publications for kindly allowing me to use copyright material in this book:

Associated Examining Board
University of Cambridge Local Examinations Syndicate
Marketing Week
The Economist
Farmers Weekly
Financial Times
Financial Weekly
Euro Business
The Guardian
The Times
HMSO
Bank of England Quarterly Bulletin
Paterson Zochonis.

I am indebted to Larry Hunter (of Sunderland Polytechnic) for his encouragement. I thank the staff at Pitmans, especially Dominique de Buys, Liz Hartley and Catriona King, for their encouragement, advice and editorial skills.

Mrs Linda Windsor deserves special thanks for her skill and efficiency in typing the manuscript. Finally, I wish to thank my wife Jenny for her help, support, advice and encouragement.

I wish to dedicate this book to Jenny and to the memory of my brother Brian.

CHAPTER 1
An Introduction to Business Studies

The opening chapter of this book will focus on the philosophical basis behind the subject. Other 'A' Level subjects are bounded by specific techniques of analysis or by a clear definition of the subject matter. Our subject focuses on the theme of decision-making within an organisation surrounded by an environment.

OBJECTIVES

1 To understand the twin themes of decision-making and the environment.
2 To understand the importance of objectives and constraints in the decision-making process.
3 To appreciate the inter-relationships between functional areas within the organisation.
4 To understand the importance of information as the basis for decision-making.

What is Business Studies?

When teachers of Business Studies are asked to define or describe their subject there is a great temptation to say that it involves a 'little of this and a little of that'. Business Studies incorporates material from a wide range of other subjects, especially economics, accounting, psychology, management, marketing, sociology, statistics and communications. However, to say that Business Studies is merely a hybrid subject does it a great disservice and acts to undermine its legitimacy. Moreover, by presenting the subject as a series of discrete sections it makes it difficult to develop an understanding of the integrated nature of the subject. **Integration** is a key word in the syllabuses of the examination boards. Candidates are required to develop an understanding of the inter-relationship between the various components. The forms of assessment used (i.e. case studies, projects, and data response questions) demand that candidates adopt an integrated approach to the subject.

Integration is achieved through the two themes that constitute the essence of Business Studies.

The first theme is the relationship between the business organisation and the environment in which it operates. The environment can be defined as the forces and agencies external to the firm which impinge upon it. The firm has to be sensitive to changes in the environment and to respond in an appropriate manner. Economists tend to assume that only economic factors (income, interest and exchange rates, the level of employment) are important. In our subject the environment takes other forms: social, legislative, technological and political.

The second theme developed in Business Studies is the process of decision-making within an organisation. We develop a model of the decision-making process to understand a process which is not unique to private sector firms (or even to large bureaucracies) but which has universal validity. The model can be applied to all functional areas within the business.

The twin themes of Business Studies are illustrated in Fig 1.1. The large rectangle which represents the firm is surrounded by various components of the environment. Within the rectangle are the functional areas common to all business organisations. In a sole proprietor firm,

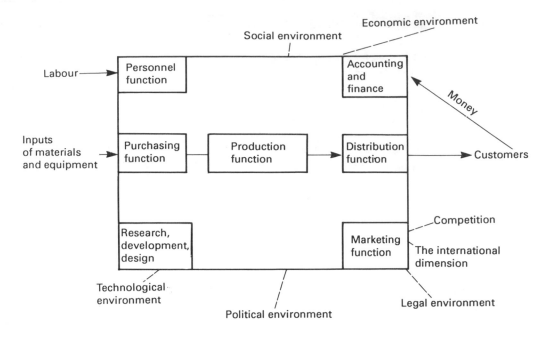

Fig 1.1   The organisation in its environment

all the functions may be undertaken by a single person whereas in a large organisation it is likely that there will be separate functional departments dealing with each area. However, large or small, the functional areas are common in all businesses.

1 The PERSONNEL function deals with the acquisition of labour or human resources. All management activities related to employees' pay, welfare, conditions of employment can be grouped under the personnel function.

2 The FINANCIAL AND ACCOUNTING function deals with the money aspects of business. Accounting involves the collection, recording, presentation and analysis of financial data. The financial side concerns the raising of finance for business operations and decisions on how the money should be spent.

3 The PURCHASING function deals with the acquisition of non-human resources (e.g. supplies of raw materials).

4 The RESEARCH, DESIGN AND DEVELOPMENT function (R and D) deals with the development of new products and processes. In a dynamic and competitive market, product development is essential for the long-term survival of the organisation.

5 The DISTRIBUTION function relates to the movement of goods and services to customers.

6 The PRODUCTION function (or operations function in a service firm) deals with the making of goods and services. If the marketing function deals with what is made, the production function deals with how it is made. Matters relating to techniques of production, scheduling, stocks of goods and quality control all come under production and operation management (POM).

7 The MARKETING function is seen by many people as the heart of the business organisation. Business organisations prosper by serving the market with goods and services that are demanded. Marketing (which must not

be equated with selling) is concerned with identifying and responding to the needs of the customer. In a market-orientated organisation, marketing provides the integration within the organisation since all decisions relating to the other functional areas are made with the market in mind.

Decision-making

Decision-making is the basic task of all managers in whichever functional area they operate. Obviously, we all make countless decisions in the course of a day, but managerial decisions are designed to influence the actions of other people. Hence, a change in the pay structure of employees is designed to alter work practices to achieve an increase in productivity (output per man-hour). A change in the price of the product is designed to influence the buying behaviour of customers. Since managerial decisions are designed to affect others, we should see the decision-making process within the environment.

Constraints

The environment acts as a constraint on the decision-making. For instance, the decision to expand the firm's operations is constrained by the financial and real resources at the disposal of the organisation. Possible resistance by employees will reduce the room for manoeuvre for management interested in implementing change within the organisation. In the external environment customer demand affects the ability of the firm to achieve its profit or sales targets.

Objectives

Before making rational decisions it is necessary to consider aims and objectives. In choosing 'A' Level subjects, the sensible students will have considered, among other factors, their long-term plans. 'A' Level Business Studies may be a good choice

of subject for many students, but not for those whose aim is to study medicine at university.

Business organisations have aims and objectives which should be clearly understood by all. Objectives give the organisation a sense of purpose and direction. They provide a motivation and a 'yardstick' by which performance can be measured, especially if the objectives are expressed in a quantitative manner. In economics, very simplistic assumptions are made about the objectives of private enterprise firms. Traditional theory is based on the assumption of profit maximisation. In Business Studies we replace the idea of a single objective with a hierarchy of objectives (*see* Fig 1.2). The principle of the hierarchy can be illustrated with reference to the Second World War. The mission or purpose was to make the world safe for democracy. The overall objective was to defeat the fascist powers. The 1944 strategy was to open a 'second front' in Europe. Tactics included seaborne landings in Normandy.

Aim, Purpose or Mission embody general ideas about what the enterprise is trying to accomplish. They are indefinite and refer to intention rather than specific goals. The mission of the privatised water companies is to supply safe, reliable water at an economic price. Strategic objectives are broad statements of what the organisation intends to achieve. This is likely to be expressed in terms of:

(*a*)   survival;
(*b*)   the level of profits;
(*c*)   growth of sales;
(*d*)   sales revenue;
(*e*)   market share; and
(*f*)   productivity or efficiency.

Tactical objectives are more detailed statements of targets for individual departments or sections within the organisation. If they are expressed in numerical terms with a time frame they are known as **budgets**. As shown in Fig 1.2, the higher order objectives are set by directors and top management, whereas the tactical objectives are set lower down in the organisation.

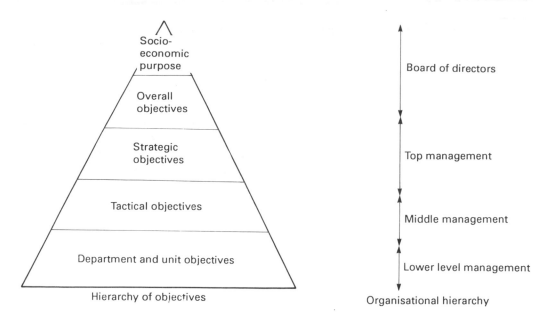

Fig 1.2   Relationship between objectives and the organisational hierarchy

Information collection and analysis

Animals, including human beings, collect informa-tion through their senses. Human beings have highly developed powers of analysis and interpre-tation of the information provided: rational deci-sions must be based on information.

Quantitative information is more objective and verifiable than information in the form of words. There are a variety of techniques available to process, analyse and interpret the data. The use of statistical analysis enables us to judge the validity of data based upon a sample of popula-tion. Decision trees (*see* pages 170–1) aid the process of decision-making by taking into account both expected outcomes and the likelihood of achieving that outcome. Network analysis enables planners of complex multi-stage operations to identify critical activities (whose delay would postpone the completion of the task) and thereby aid decision-making on the deployment of resources.

One of the deficiencies of quantitative analysis in business is that the future remains uncertain. No matter how sophisticated the analytical tech-nique, it remains based on assumptions about future trends. It is, therefore, important to disting-uish between verifiable facts (about past and present trends) and facts and data based upon assumptions about the future. All profit or cash flow forecasts used in business documents are based on a view about the future course of events. If these assumptions are not correct in practice, the forecast will also be incorrect. To complement quantitative information, the decision-maker requires qualitative information.

Choice

Decisions invariably involve a choice from a number of possible courses of action. Should the firm choose machine tools from one firm or more expensive but superior tools from another firm? Should a manufacturer of electrical goods buy-in specific components or establish production facili-ties itself? Should the firm increase output by taking on more workers or employ existing workers on overtime? The various alternatives have to be identified and clarified in the minds of the decision-makers. They have to consider the advantages and disadvantages of particular courses of action. In the final analysis a choice has to be made. We should see the quantitative techniques as an aid to decision-making, but the decision-makers have to base the decision on qualitative as well as quantitative information. This requires judgement.

Implementation

Once the choice is made, the decision has to be implemented. This will require planning to ensure that resources are available to put the decision into operation. There must also be a control mechanism to ensure that the planned activity is guided towards the goal. Deviations from the standard set should be reported so that adjustments can be made.

Evaluation

The final stage in the process is to review progress to see if the objective has been reached. If it has not, the reasons for failure to achieve goals should be analysed. The evaluation process thereby provides data for the next cycle of decision-making.

Decisions can be classified in two ways. First, we can distinguish between strategic decisions and tactical decisions. Strategic decisions concern the broad objectives, policies and plans of the organisations and as such are taken at a high level within the organisation. Tactical decisions are concerned more with day-to-day operations. They fill in the details of the strategic decisions and are more concerned with how objectives are to be achieved than what is to be achieved.

The second distinction is between programmed decisions and unprogrammed ones. The former are routine, repetitive and handled by a definite procedure. The latter are unique and non-repetitive with the result that no procedure is established. Like the strategic decisions these will be taken by the higher levels of management especially if high risks are involved.

Conclusion

After looking at the two themes of our subject (the concept of the environment and the process of decision-making) we will now look at the environment in greater detail. Then in the second part of the book we will look at decision-making in the functional areas of the organisation.

EXERCISE ● ● ●

● 1   This first exercise is designed to encourage you to investigate simple business issues. Remember, there are no 'correct answers' and that how you tackle the exercise is more important than the answer itself.

Sarah has a fondness and aptitude for looking after cats and dogs. For the last three years she has worked as receptionist and veterinary nurse at a local veterinary practice. Sarah recently inherited some money and this has rekindled in her mind the idea of establishing her own business. She is particularly keen on setting up a 'pets' hotel' to look after pets when their owners are away. Sarah realises that she needs a partner to contribute part of the finance and to share the work load. She therefore invites you to join her in the enterprise. You are tempted but, being cautious, seek further information.

Undertake an investigation of this business proposal for your own particular area. In particular, you should find out:

(a) the extent of the market and competition for this type of enterprise;

(b) the type of services required by pet owners and the features they look for in a well-run 'pets' hotel';

(c) the legal formalities required for establishing such a business in your area and the insurance that it is advisable to take out;

(d) the most effective ways of advertising the service taking cost into account;

(e) the problems associated with this form of business;

(f) related business activities that could be developed alongside the 'pets' hotel'.

2   Mr Khan is considering buying one of two newsagency businesses. Shop A has a low floor space and no room for expansion but has a good location close to a commuter railway station. This ensures a good trade in newspapers, magazines, cigarettes and confectionery. Unfortunately, there is no room for other goods.

Shop B is in a small shopping area on a housing estate. The premises have three times the floor space allowing a greater range of goods such as cards and toys. However, under the lease for shop B he would be committed for a longer time period and would have to invest in considerably more stock.

(a) Identify possible constraints on Mr Khan's decision-making.

(b) Advise Mr Khan on (i) the quantitative and (ii) the qualitative information he should seek before arriving at his decision.

(c) Suggest various objectives (apart from profit maximisation) which should be used as the basis for his decision.

FURTHER READING

GENERAL WORKS

J CLIFFORD *Decision Making in Organisations* (Longman)

J GRAY *Business Organisation* (NCC)

D LOCK AND N FARROW (ed) *The Complete Manager* (Wildwood House)

D NEEDLE *Business in Context* (Van Nostrand Reinhold)

M FRAMPTON, R NORRIE, A REES AND B WILLIAMS *Organisations at Work* (Pitman)

S HAMMOND *Business Studies* (Longman)

D DYER AND I CHAMBERS *Business Studies: an introduction* (Longman)

R STEFANOU *Understanding Industry Now* (Heineman)

M W BUCKLEY *Structure of Business* (Pitman)

CASE STUDIES

JOSEPH CHILVER *Introducing Business Studies* (Macmillan)

SHEILA RITCHIE (ed) *Case Studies in Management* (Elm Publications)

PETER CHISNALL *Small Firms in Action* (McGraw-Hill)

G D GREEN *Case Studies in Industrial Relations* (Pitman)
SHEILA MAY *Case Studies in Business* (Pitman)
I SPURR, J FORRESTER, H SHAW, *Business Case Studies* (Pitman)
I SPURR AND J FORRESTER *Case Studies in Marketing* (Pitman)

REFERENCE WORKS

R LAMMING & J BESSANT *Macmillan Dictionary of Business and Management* (Macmillan)
J BLAKE AND P LAWRENCE *The ABC of Management* (Cassell)
M STEER *Dictionary of Business Studies* (Pitman)
T KEMPNER (ed) *A Handbook of Management* (Penguin)

CHAPTER 2
Business Enterprise

This chapter focuses on the nature of business enterprise, the role of the entrepreneur and the relevance of size to our understanding of business organisations.

OBJECTIVES

1 To understand business as an input-output system.
2 To analyse the role of the entrepreneur.
3 To understand the main types of business organisations.
4 To analyse the advantages of large scale organisations.
5 To identify the role of small firms in a dynamic economy.

Human beings, like other animals, have wants which they seek to satisfy. At the basic level there are physiological needs which have to be satisfied to sustain life (e.g. the need for food, warmth, shelter). As human beings progress they develop other needs which are satisfied by the acquisition and consumption of goods. Unfortunately, nature does not provide a ready supply of most of the goods we require. Therefore, people have to engage in production to obtain them. We could engage in subsistence production by producing everything for ourselves but this usually results in a low standard of living. Our present high standard of living is due to a large extent to the process of specialisation and exchange in which we engage. Instead of trying to produce everything ourselves, we specialise, by exchanging the product of our specialisation with that of others. Most of us sell our labour to business organisations, and in return we receive a money income which enables us to purchase goods and services. Some people are not content with offering their labour and instead establish business enterprises to produce goods and services to sell to other people. In this chapter we will investigate the nature, legal form and size of business organisations.

Business organisations engage in resource conversion. Inputs are combined together to create an output which could be a physical object (goods) or something intangible (services). The essential resources for all production are known in Economics as the **factors of production**. Natural resources such as minerals, soil and timber are essential. Despite their intelligence, human beings cannot create anything – they merely convert natural resources into a man-made or manufactured product. These natural resources are the gift of nature but we have a duty to look after them. Some natural resources are non-renewable and their depletion threatens the future of human life on this planet. Soil and timber are renewable but require careful handling.

These natural resources are combined with labour and other resources used in production and we make no distinction between manual labour and intellectual labour. Although many automated factories have economised on labour, it is not yet possible to eliminate it altogether. The word 'capital' frequently causes problems. In ordinary speech capital refers to finance used in the establishment and expansion of a business. In economic theory it refers to man-made resources used in production. This includes machinery, plant, buildings such as factories, and vehicles that assist in the movement of goods. To avoid confusion it is useful to distinguish between financial capital (money tied up in the business) and real capital (the man-made resources themselves).

The fourth factor of production is known as **enterprise** or **entrepreneurship**. The entrepreneur is the active ingredient in the productive process. The other factors remain dormant unless galvanised into action. The entrepreneur initiates the productive process and in so doing risks the finance put into the enterprise. This is because most production occurs in advance of sales. There is no guarantee that the goods will sell in the quantities that were produced. Even production to order (as in bespoke tailors, shipbuilding or civil engineering) carries some risk. The entrepreneur has to invest in capital equipment and acquire a workforce before orders can be obtained. Given the uncertainty of the market, risk-taking is a feature of entrepreneurial life.

The Austrian Economist, Joseph Schumpeter, placed greater stress on the entrepreneur's role as innovator. Successful entrepreneurs are not content to produce the same products as existing firms. Instead, they are motivated to devise new goods and services and to adapt existing products for new markets. Successful entrepreneurs who epitomised Schumpeter's concept include Anita Roddick (Body Shop) and Richard Branson (Virgin Group), and less well known is Roger McKechnie who, with three colleagues, developed a range of exotic snacks sold under the *Phileas Fogg* brand name.

In return for risk-taking, the entrepreneur enjoys two substantial rights. First, under the private enterprise (or capitalist) system of production, the risk-taking entrepreneur is entitled to make decisions regarding the running of the business. Supporters of the system would argue that by risking their finance in a business venture entrepreneurs' minds are more concentrated to make sound business decisions. All decisions ultimately are made by the owners who risk their finance, although, obviously, they may choose to delegate decision-making powers to paid, professional managers.

Second, entrepreneurs enjoy the profits of the business enterprise. In the private enterprise system profits play a key role. Profits motivate the entrepreneur. The prospect of profit encourages innovation. Profits not only provide the signal indicating lines of expansion, they also provide the finance for expansion. The reinvestment of past profits has traditionally been the way in which British business has grown. Moreover, the successful firm will find little difficulty in raising external finance for expansion. Finally, profits provide the incentive for supply to respond to demand. Business is responsive to the needs of the customer since profits are derived from the satisfying of those needs.

Types of business organisation

When establishing a business, consideration must be given to the choice of legal form. There are three forms of private enterprise organisation:

- sole trader
- partnership
- joint stock or limited liability company.

The choice will be influenced by the financial needs of the business, considerations of owners' liability and the degree of personal control sought by the founder who is the entrepreneur in the widest sense of the word.

Sole traders

This is a form of business organisation which is commonly found in trades where only small amounts of finance are required and where there are few advantages of large-scale production. Sole owners may employ others as wage labourers but alone provide the permanent finance and bear the risks. In return they retain full control and enjoy all the profits of the business.

The sole trader enjoys distinct advantages:

- freedom and flexibility
- personal satisfaction
- secrecy. There is no need to disclose business affairs except to the tax authorities and to creditors when seeking loans
- personal control with no requirement to consult
- personal contact with staff and customers
- enjoyment of all profits
- absence of legal formalities when establishing the business.

Against these advantages there are major drawbacks:

- limited sources of finance
- restricted growth
- limited scope for economies of scale
- success depends on the owner's energy and continuing fitness
- the constraint of the lack of time and specialisation
- full personal responsibility for decisions and for the debts of the business
- no continuity of existence with the business dying with the owner.

Partnership

To overcome some of the problems inherent in the sole trader form of business, a partnership might be formed. The law defines a partnership as the relationship which subsists between persons carrying on a business in common with a view to profit. A partnership is an association of individuals and is not a legal entity in its own right. Consequently it cannot sue or be sued in its own name but instead each of the partners has to be named. Each partner is responsible for the debts of the partnership. Moreover, every partner, when acting on behalf of the firm, acts as an agent of the partnership and can thus bind his or her fellow partners. In simple language, the individual partner can be personally sued and held liable for all decisions made, and debts incurred, by other partners provided these people were acting with the authority of the partnership. Therefore, one should choose business partners very carefully and draw up a legal agreement on the rights and responsibilities of each partner.

Where one of the partners contributes a disproportionate amount of the finance, it is doubly important to draw up a written agreement. This is because the 1890 Partnership Act lays down that, except where there is a specific agreement to the contrary:

1 all partners are entitled to an equal share of profits;
2 each partner is entitled to participate in the management of firm;
3 decisions are settled on a majority basis except that any change in the nature of the business requires unanimous agreement.

As a business form, partnerships enjoy certain advantages over the sole trader form of business:

- additional sources of finance
- sharing of responsibilities
- specialisation
- sharing of losses.

In addition partnerships enjoy greater privacy and fewer legal formalities compared with the company form of organisation.

However, the attractiveness of the partnership form of organisation is reduced when it is remembered that each partner is fully responsible for decisions and debts. The problems associated with this form of organisation and the ease by which companies can be formed reduces its popularity. It is most commonly found in the professions where the rules of the appropriate professional association (e.g. the Law Society) preclude the translation of the business to the company form. Outside the professions, there is a preference for the joint stock company form of organisation.

Joint stock companies

During the 18th and early 19th centuries, companies were treated with great suspicion. This was partly because historically companies were equated with monopoly privileges (e.g. the East India

Company had a monopoly of trade with Bengal), but also because, following the South Sea Bubble of 1719–20, companies were associated with swindle and fraud. Despite these reservations about the company form of organisation, the capital requirement of canal and railway building necessitated the formation of companies with substantial numbers of shareholders. The extension of the joint stock company principle followed in the mid-19th Century when companies could be formed by the process of registering under the Companies Act.

Like a partnership, a company is owned by a number of people but the important distinction is that the act of incorporation creates a new legal entity independent of the shareholders. This has important implications in the separation of the affairs of the business from those of the people who own shares in it. Companies can make contracts, they can sue and be sued. All actions taken by the company, including the contracting of debt, are actions of the company rather than actions of individual owners. Unlike the business forms described earlier, the legal position of a company is completely unaffected by the death (or retirement) of one of the shareholders.

Shareholders enjoy the privilege of **limited liability** which means that they are liable to meet the debts of the business only to the extent that they have invested in the business. Hence, if the shares they own are fully paid-up, no further claim can be made on the shareholder. Limited liability (seen by early Victorians as an attempt to evade responsibility for the debts of a business) is regarded as essential in overcoming the reluctance of people to purchase shares in a business. Although the company is fully liable to meet its debts, the individual shareholder is liable only to a limited extent. However, it should be pointed out that when granting a loan, creditors often insist that shareholders in a small private company (or directors in a larger one) accept some personal responsibility for the debt.

The advantages of company status are:

- limited liability for shareholders
- continuity of existence
- legal identity
- increased opportunities to raise finance for expansion.

Against these advantages there is a price to be paid. First, the privilege of limited liability is accompanied by the obligation to disclose information about the business to the Registrar of Companies. This is done in the interests of creditors, investors, suppliers and customers, both present and prospective. Second, there are various legal formalities which have to be followed. These include the drawing up of a Memorandum of Association which establishes the company and determines the objects of the business. It is possible to seek a court order to declare contracts outside these objects as *ultra vires* (beyond the powers of the directors) and therefore void. For example, if you buy shares in a company owning a chain of hairdressing salons you might not approve of a move into another market. The Articles of Association deal with the internal rules governing the conduct of the company (e.g. method of electing directors). With these documents drawn up, the founders will seek to register the company with the Registrar who will grant a Certificate of Incorporation. In the case of a private company this completes the process and the company can commence trading. There are additional requirements in the case of public companies. Before we look at the process of 'going public' we should understand the distinction between the two types of company.

In late Victorian times many businesses were converted from partnerships to joint stock companies. This was partly to raise additional finance for expansion or for investing in new technology. However, it was also to acquire the privilege of limited liability. Many family firms remained unchanged in ownership and control but took advantage of Victorian legislation which allowed the formation of companies by registration. The law was amended in 1907 to recognise the distinction between private and public companies. The fundamental distinction between the two types of companies is that a private company cannot issue a prospectus and therefore cannot appeal to the public to subscribe to a share issue. It must sell its shares by private negotiations with interested individuals. Moreover, there are restrictions on the transfer of shares from existing shareholders to outsiders. A public company, on the other hand, is permitted to issue a prospectus inviting the public to subscribe to a share issue. Shares in a public company can be transferred freely on the Stock Exchange.

'GOING PUBLIC'

The great advantage of 'going public' is the greater availability of finance for public companies. However, there are problems that should be considered. First, when shares are freely transferrable the company is vulnerable to take-overs. Unless the founders retain more than 50 per cent of shares they could lose control of the company. Shareholders are interested in dividends (a distribution of profits) and/or capital gain from their investment. The directors will have to satisfy shareholders if they are to retain their position. Even though shareholders' control by means of voting at the annual shareholders meeting is generally ineffective, shareholders can exert power by threatening to 'vote with their feet'. Second, public companies are required to make extensive disclosure of information. The requirements are more relaxed in the case of private companies.

Because public companies invite the public to subscribe to a share issue, they are subject to a greater degree of scrutiny than are private companies. Initially they have to satisfy the Stock Exchange Council. The Stock Exchange is in effect a market for 'second-hand shares', but nevertheless plays a crucial role in raising capital. Shareholders will require assurance that shares in public companies can be re-sold (or transferred). The Stock Exchange Council aims to protect investors against the kind of fraud that characterised the South Sea Bubble. Hence, it will ensure that companies seeking a quotation on the Exchange are properly constituted and are soundly managed. This does not, however, mean a guarantee against the normal business risks that

are inherent in any venture. Once the Council is satisfied, it will grant a quotation on the Exchange. The Registrar of Companies will also require assurance that the company has raised sufficient finance to be able to undertake the project with a reasonable chance of success. Only when the Registrar is satisfied will a Certificate of Trading be issued which permits the public company to commence trading.

The overwhelming majority of companies are private companies and many of these are husband-and-wife or father-and-son businesses. Conversion to a public company is not worthwhile unless the business needs to raise a very large sum of money. Not only is a public share issue complicated and expensive, we have seen that 'going public' creates new problems for a business.

Economies of large-scale production

To understand the nature of economies of scale it is necessary to distinguish between the short- and long-run. The short-run is defined in economics as a period of time in which at least one factor of production is in fixed supply. Hence, firms can increase output by hiring additional quantities of the variable factors (e.g. labour and raw materials) and combining them with a fixed quantity of the remaining factor (i.e. capital). It is possible to achieve lower costs in the short-run by spreading the fixed costs (or overheads) over a greater volume of output. If variable costs are £1 per unit and fixed costs amount to £1000, the average cost of producing each of 1000 units is $£1000/1000 + £1 = £2$. When output rises to 2000, average (or unit) costs are $£1000/2000 + £1 = £1.50$.

A good example of 'spreading the overheads' is newspaper production. The first copy off the press costs thousands of pounds to produce, but successive copies are produced at very low cost. The more copies printed, the lower the average cost of producing each copy. The process of spreading the overheads is likely to reduce unit costs only over a limited range of output. As we approach full utilisation of the fixed factor, it becomes more difficult and more costly to raise output. For instance, to increase output further it might be necessary to employ labour on overtime rates of pay and, as a result, unit costs start to rise. Consequently there is a limit to the fall in average costs in the short-run.

Economies of scale on the other hand refer to the advantages of increasing the scale of production and are as such a long-term phenomenon. The long-run is a period of time in which all factors of production are variable so that the firm is able to acquire additional capital equipment to complement the additional labour and materials. The economies are usually categorised as follows.

1 TECHNICAL ECONOMIES. These include the access to large and often indivisible equipment.

2 RESEARCH ECONOMIES. Large firms are better able to finance research and development to extend and improve their product range.

3 MARKETING ECONOMIES include the cost advantages of bulk buying, access to costly but effective advertising and economies in distribution.

4 MANAGERIAL ECONOMIES relate to specialist, functional managers and delegation of detail.

5 FINANCIAL ECONOMIES enable large firms to obtain finance from a variety of sources and at lower rates of interest than those charged to small firms.

6 RISK-BEARING ECONOMIES. Large firms with a diversified product range sold in a variety of markets are less exposed to risk and are better able to withstand losses.

Growth in the size of the firm may take the form of an increase in the size of the plant (the generic name for factory, works, workshop, etc.) or an increase in the number of plants owned and managed by the company. Technical economies are available only through an increase in the size of the plant. The other economies of scale are available to firms that grow both by increasing the size of the plant and by the acquisition of more plants.

Economists also identify so-called diseconomies of scale which are in effect the managerial problems associated with large scale production. In large firms decision-making can be delayed because of the need to consult: control is more difficult and the organisation becomes rigid and bound by procedures (i.e. bureaucratic). Labour relations often deteriorate with an increase in the scale of the organisation. However, diseconomies of scale are related to the quality of management and should not be seen as inevitably raising unit costs. Moreover, it is incorrect to envisage economies of scale up to a certain scale of production followed by diseconomies. Instead, every increase in scale should generate both economies and diseconomies. Whether average costs rise or fall depends upon the balance between economies (advantages) and diseconomies (problems) of the increase in scale. For many in business the economies of scale argument is very persuasive and this led to a 'big is best' mentality. Firms have grown in size or mergers have been arranged in the belief that an increase in the scale of production would enable them to compete more effectively in world markets.

The growth of businesses

The growth of firms can be accomplished in one of two ways.

1 INTERNAL OR AUTONOMOUS) GROWTH involves the expansion of the existing firm. It can be seen as a natural outcome of business success in a system which rewards the successful but punishes the unsuccessful. The profitable firm is able to finance expansion by re-investing profits. Moreover, with a record of success it will be relatively easy for a firm to obtain additional loan or equity finance. Supporters of the market system see this as one of its great virtues. Financial and real resources are easily acquired by those with a proven record of success. With additional resources the firm can grow.

Internal growth is a slow process but it can take place without disturbing the organisational structure. This is organic growth which is easy to manage and to absorb.

2 EXTERNAL GROWTH involves the acquisition of other firms by merger or take-over. The distinction between the two is frequently blurred but merger implies an element of voluntary agreement whereas a take-over implies that a predator firm swallows up another firm. Public limited companies are always open to take-over since there are no restrictions on the transfer of shares within the company. This vulnerability is increased if shareholders are dissatisfied with the performance of the company or if it is under-capitalised. A complete merger results in the creation of a new company and an exchange of shares. More common is the purchase by one company of a controlling interest in another with both legally remaining separate. Mergers are categorised as:

(a) *Horizontal* – a merger of firms at the same stage of producing a product, e.g. British Airways' take-over of British Caledonian Airways.

(b) *Vertical* – a merger of firms at a different stage in the chain of production. The acquisition of a firm at an earlier stage is known as backward integration whereas if it is at a later stage it is known as forward integration. The acquisition of public houses by brewers is an example of vertical integration.

(c) *Lateral* – merger of firms using similar techniques to produce related but not identical products, e.g. British Aerospace's acquisition of the Rover Group.

(d) *Conglomerate* mergers involving firms of a diverse nature, for example, Sky (TV), 20th Century Fox and News International which are all owned by Rupert Murdoch.

An increasingly important category that should be added is the international merger to produce a **multinational** company.

The major advantage of external acquisition over internal growth is that it results in an instant expansion of the firm. Not only does it acquire existing plant and equipment, it also acquires a labour force, expertise, products, brand names and patents. Conversely there are often problems of adjustment. The acquisition might not be easy to digest in the short-run and this frequently contributes to disappointment immediately following the merger.

It is a common error to confuse merger (a change in ownership and control) with integration (reorganisation following a merger). It is sometimes believed that the new, merged firm enjoys economies of scale immediately but in practice there are few economies of scale deriving from a mere change of ownership. When management and communication problems of a large undertaking are added, it is not surprising that performance of the combined firm is often disappointing. It is also quite common for post-merger reorganisation plans of top management to be frustrated by middle management. In the case of conglomerate mergers there are additional problems if specialist expertise does not reside in the controlling firm. Contrary to the assumptions in economic theory, some take-overs or mergers are ill-thought out and prompted more by the desire for power and prestige.

The underlying motive for any take-over (or merger) is the belief that it will prove profitable. More specifically this can be for a number of reasons. The first eight reasons listed below are acceptable reasons for merger and will be used in defence in any Monopolies and Mergers Commission investigation:

1 to obtain economies of large scale production;
2 to improve service to customers;
3 to eliminate middlemen;
4 to defeat foreign competition;
5 to gain a more secure base by diversification;
6 to secure additional finance for research and development or expansion. There are examples of small firms which have sought to be taken over because of difficulties of raising finance for internal growth;
7 to gain the advantage of product specialisation by plant;

8 to rationalise the industry. This involves a merger followed by some plant closures. The aim is to create a 'leaner but fitter' industry.

The remaining reasons are less acceptable and would not be a suitable defence against criticism:

9 to achieve market domination;
10 to control suppliers or market outlets;
11 to control the development of rival industries;
12 to acquire the patents of rivals;
13 to evade Restrictive Practices legislation which is more strictly enforced than monopoly policy;
14 to engage in asset stripping. Where assets such as land or buildings are worth more than the share capital of the company, the firm is acquired not as a going concern but to sell off assets. This has been described as the 'unacceptable face of capitalism' (Edward Heath).

Small firms

In the past, small firms were frequently ignored by governments and economists. Belief in economies of scale led to a widespread acceptance of the benefits of large-scale production and the idea that 'big is best'. Britain's failure to compete was often attributed to the small size of British manufacturing firms in relation to competitors abroad. Consequently, in the 1960s and 1970s, governments promoted industrial mergers to create large scale firms. Small firms were seen in a rather negative light as firms that through lack of finance, drive, ability and market opportunity failed to grow.

Belief in the advantage of large-scale production was subject to critical scrutiny in the 1970s for two reasons. First, the performance of large and recently merged firms such as British Leyland was disappointing. Second, people came to appreciate the attractions of working in small scale, human-sized units of production, especially after the publication of Ernst Schumacher's influential book *Small is Beautiful*. Small firms are now seen not as failed large firms but as organisations in which people can be fulfilled. In the 1980s, the Thatcher Government viewed them as a source of new products, investment and employment. A healthy economy requires a continual stream of new small firms to fill gaps in the market and to replace old and declining firms.

We can explain the continued existence of small firms in both positive as well as negative ways:

- Small firms satisfy new market needs;
- In a growing, dynamic economy new opportunities arise;
- There is a continual supply of would-be entrepreneurs;
- Small firms enjoy advantages such as good relations with customers and staff;
- Small firms provide a flexible, personal service;
- Small firms satisfy needs in a specialised or fragmented market;
- There is often a complementary relationship between large and small firms. Components for complex products are often produced by small firms in a relationship known as **vertical disintegration**;
- In certain industries and trades (e.g. personal services such as hairdressing) there are few economies of scale;
- In some cases the market remains small;
- In other cases there are limitations on the supply side (e.g. difficulties of raising finance, limitations of the owner-manager).

Despite the advantages to society of a healthy and prosperous of small firm sector they face major problems. Some of the problems are natural and inherent; others reflect the way in which the economic system (and financial institutions) discriminate against small firms:

- Absence of economies of scale;
- Lack of specialist expertise, e.g. design;
- Small product range;
- Dependence on limited number of markets;
- Limited access to city institutions;
- Reliance upon bank loans;
- Less favourable treatment from banks;
- High gearing, which increases a firm's vulnerability.

Government assistance to small firms is an attempt to redress the balance. The Labour Governments of the 1970s made some attempt to help the small firm sector, mainly in various forms of tax relief. The Royal Commission on Financial Institutions, chaired by former Prime Minister, Harold Wilson (1977–80), also made recommendations concerning help for small businesses. These included tax reforms, a loan guarantee scheme, and the establishment of the **Unlisted Securities Market**.

The USM was established in 1980 to enable existing small firms to raise limited sums through a share issue. The requirements for a quotation on the USM are less onerous than for a full Stock Exchange Quotation. This aids established small and medium-sized firms but is of little use for new enterprises.

Assistance for the smallest of firms was extended by the Thatcher Government and comes in the form of advice from the DTI's Small Firms Service, Local Enterprise Agencies, the Training Agency (formerly the Manpower Services Commission) and bodies such as the Council for Small Industries in Rural Areas. Under the Enterprise Allowance Scheme the unemployed are encouraged to establish their own businesses by a £40 per week allowance. Applicants are required to invest £1000 of their own (or borrowed) money in the business. Various forms of tax concessions are also available for small firms, for example, small companies are subject to a lower rate of corporation tax. Under the Business Start Up Scheme, which was later transformed into the Business Expansion Scheme, shareholders in new, small companies could gain tax relief. The Loan Guarantee Scheme is designed to reduce banks' reluctance to lend to the marginal borrower. The Government does not lend money but instead underwrites loans of up to 70 per cent on payment by the firm of a three per cent premium.

The final area of assistance is in keeping with the supply-side economics that is espoused by the Thatcher Government. 'Supply-siders' believe that the greatest contribution a Government can make is to reduce the legal and bureaucratic constraints on enterprise. An early (and limited experiment) in getting the Government 'off the back' of business was the 1980 Enterprise Zone Scheme. Designed to assist the regeneration of designated inner city areas, firms in the Enterprise Zone were granted exemption from local rates (for ten years) and Development Land tax and enjoyed 100 per cent capital allowances and a relaxation of planning controls. Critics of the Enterprise Zone idea argue that it merely encourages firms to move within the inner cities and does not encourage the establishment of new businesses.

'Lifting the Burden' was the title of a Government White Paper on removing the unnecessary burden of form-filling on business. It is argued that completion of statistical returns takes a disproportionate amount of time in small firms. Laws have also been relaxed to help the small entrepreneur. Under the Employment Act 1980, small firms are exempted from various requirements relating to industrial tribunals, maternity rights and unfair dismissal procedures. The Companies Act of 1981 relaxed the rules on disclosure for small firms.

Conclusion

This chapter has been concerned with the related issues of entrepreneurship, the legal form and size in business. There is always risk in business since investment and most (but not all) production occurs in advance of sales. Changes in the environment can lead to unsold goods and wasted investment. Fortunately for the health of the private enterprise system, there is a neverending stream of would-be entrepreneurs. Not for them the relative security of a wage packet and a company pension. Instead they seek the challenge and the rewards of entrepreneurship, but they must be prepared to accept the consequences of failure.

The search for funds additional to those that entrepreneurs can raise personally results in a compromise. Absolute control is sacrificed as partners (or shareholders in a company) are taken on. Further growth, undertaken in the belief that 'big is best', can result in a separation of ownership from control. Professional managers are appointed to make decisions because of their expertise. Ultimate control remains with the shareholding owners of the business but they delegate powers to the managers.

The other issue addressed in this chapter was size. We can use an analogy from natural history. The stronger and bigger fish eat the small fish in a pond. If we believe that 'big is best', we should not be surprised at this chain of events (although we might be concerned about its implication for monopolistic hold over the market). If we believe that 'small is beautiful' we can take comfort in the ability of a neverending stream of newly hatched fish to use their greater flexibility and ability to adapt to the pond, to remain in existence and even prosper.

CASE STUDY 1
The Virgin management buy-out

The privatisation of the National Freight Corporation in 1982 was unusual in that, rather than offering shares for public purchase, the company was bought by its management and staff backed by loan capital from financial institutions. This is an example of a trend in the 1980s towards management buy-outs. Its supporters see management buy-outs as a reaction against the disappointing mergers of the 1960s and 1970s, as they represent the remarriage of ownership and control to sustain smaller, more autonomous units.

An interesting management buy-out of recent years was the repurchase by Richard Branson of the Virgin Group in 1988. Branson started a mail order record business in 1970 and achieved rapid growth in the following decades through record sales, record outlets, nightclubs, video and films, as well as his Virgin Atlantic Airlines. Despite his success Branson sought expansion into the American and Japanese markets. It has also since been revealed that he wanted to launch a takeover and break up bid for Thorn EMI (*Business*, November 1989). His expansion plans required additional capital which would only be available by a public issue of shares.

With the exception of the airline and Branson's holiday interests, the Virgin group became a public company in 1986. However, the share issue was not as successful as Branson hoped. 'We had 60 000 small shareholders, the largest of any offering outside of a privatisation, but it was not underpinned by institutional support', Branson is quoted as saying. The Stock Market crash of 1987 meant that Virgin shares, at one time 20p above the issue price of 140p, fell to 83p: moreover he told stock market analysts that it might be years before the US operation showed a profit. This sent his shares down further and put an end to any idea of taking over Thorn EMI.

The rationale behind the original floatation now disappeared. Moreover, Branson became increasingly frustrated with city institutions which seemed to prefer short-term profit to Branson's long-term strategy. Hence, in 1988 Branson, with the aid of £182 million syndicated loan, bought the Virgin Group back from its shareholders. With Virgin once again a private company Branson can reassert control over his empire without interference from city institutions with their short-term mentality.

1 What are the advantages to the Government of privatisation by management buy-out?
2 What are the likely consequences for staff and for the performance of a company following a staff buy-out?
3 Why was the Virgin Group floated on the Stock Exchange in 1986?
4 Suggest reasons why Virgin Atlantic Airlines was not included in the floatation?
5 Explain Branson's statement: 'it was not underpinned by institutional support'.
6 Why did the Stock Market Crash end his idea of taking over Thorn EMI?
7 Explain what is meant by short-termism and why did Richard Branson become irritated by city institutions?
8 Does reversion to private company status mean the end of Virgin's expansion plans?

Saga family in bid to go private

Mark Milner

SAGA, the tour operator for the over sixties, may soon follow in the footsteps of the likes of International Leisure Group and Richard Branson's Virgin Group by going private.

The De Haan family, which owns 63 per cent of the travel to financial services company, said it was considering an offer to buy the remainder of the shares at about £3 each.

At that price the whole company, which came to the stock market 11 years ago, would be valued at just over £54 million. Saga shares jumped 66p to 293p after news of the approach.

A bid would be subject to the family raising the £20 million needed to finance the purchase of the shares it does not already own, but Mr Roger De Haan, who is leading the bid approach, said discussions were already under way with a bank and he was confident the money would be available.

Mr De Haan, who is also chairman of Saga, said the group could not enjoy one of the most important advantages of being publicly quoted – using its shares to fund acquisitions – because the family was determined not to dilute its controlling interest.

The company was founded by Mr De Haan's father and two of his brothers also work for the group.

"We built it up, it is our baby," he said, adding that if the family allowed its interest to fall below 50 per cent it would risk being taken over by a hostile bidder. "We just don't want to be in that position."

As a result "we have not been able to take advantage of what the City has to offer."

On the other hand, however, Mr De Haan said the company had to put up with what it regarded as disadvantages of being publicly quoted.

There were occasions, for example, when the board felt a conflict between the need to distribute profits to meet the short term aspirations of the City and making medium and longer term investments in the business.

"We think it would be better as a private company, without that pressure", said Mr De Haan, though he said the move did not reflect any disenchantment with the City.

Mr De Haan said the original reason for going public was his father's concern that as a private company, with no market in its shares, the family might one day be faced with the prospect of having to sell the entire business to meet death duties.

The group got underway as a holiday company when Mr De Haan senior, who owned a Folkestone hotel, began arranging holidays for pensioners in the "off season". Since then it has widened its scope considerably, with packages ranging from the traditional fortnight at an English seaside resort to treks through the Himalayas and month-long tours in South America. It is believed to sell about 250,000 holidays a year.

In recent years it has added to the services it provides for the retired to include financial services, retirement homes and magazine publishing.

In the six months to the end of July the group made a profit of £1.18 million – 4.4 per cent down on the same period last year.

Saga has about 1,500 shareholders, with institutions accounting for around half the shares not held by the family and the remainder held by private investors.

Mr De Haan said a £3 a share offer would represent a 25 per cent compound annual growth for investors who had bought shares when the company first came to the stock market. "We believe it is a fair and generous price."

The three-independent directors on the Saga board said last night that they had noted the possible offer, adding that discussions "are at an early stage" and a further announcement would be made "as soon as practicable". In the meantime shareholders were advised not to take any action.

(Source: *The Guardian*, 20 December 1989)

1 Explain the difference between a private and a public company.
2 Why could Saga 'not enjoy one of the most important advantages of being publicly quoted'?
3 What are the disadvantages of being publicly quoted?
4 Why is there a growing market for 'holidays for pensioners in the 'off season''?
5 What is meant by:
   (*a*) independent directors;
   (*b*) institutional shareholders.
6 In the article it is stated that the De Haan family is considering an offer to buy shares at £3. The current price is 293p.
   (*a*) Why is the family willing to pay 7p extra for the shares?
   (*b*) Why would anyone be willing to sell at 293p?
   (*c*) Why did share prices 'jump' 66p to 293p?

EXERCISE ● ● ●

1 In the journal *Small Business Economies* (January 1989) Brock and Evans argued that a number of factors in the environment have shifted the balance of advantage towards the small firm. In particular, they identified:
   (*a*) new technology;
   (*b*) the turbulence of the modern economy (e.g. exchange rates);
   (*c*) demographic and social changes favouring people who desire to set up their own business;
   (*d*) the break up of homogeneous mass markets; and
   (*e*) the worldwide trend towards deregulation.
   Investigate these issues and explain why small firms are likely to benefit from these trends.
2 What conclusions can be drawn from the disappointing performance of many firms following a merger?
3 Examine the consequences for businesses of the separation of ownership from control.
   How, despite their weakness in the annual meeting, can shareholders affect decision-making?
4 'Our objective in encouraging small business enterprise is to tap the potential for creating new wealth in the economy which resides in the talents and enthusiasm of people who are prepared to take risks in business. This is an essential part of the government's action of redressing the economy in favour of business and industry with control of inflation as the main priority.' (John MacGregor).
   Explain what is meant by 'creating wealth' and 'risk in business'. Why does the free enterprise Thatcher Government consider it necessary to assist small businesses?
5 Study the following account which is adapted from an article by Clive Woodcock, published in *The Guardian* (December 11th 1989) and then answer the subsequent questions.

   Small firms struggle with the 'people gap'
   The ability of small firms to continue the past decades rapid growth into the 1990s could suffer from increasing problems with what is now being called the 'people gap'.
   The importance of the 'people factor' in bringing the small business sector's share of the UK's economic activity up to that of other advanced countries is a theme which the Small

Firms Minister intends to pursue. The reason behind the emphasis is an admission that not enough has been done to help the small, growing company and a belief that a key element in the failure of many growing enterprises to expand beyond a certain size is the lack of links with the right people to provide help in the major decisions faced at that stage . . .

Their (small firms) plans for growth are threatened by their apparent inability to find, retain and manage key staff – in fact, they rate the problem higher than the level of interest rates.

Unfortunately research reveals a tendency for them to recruit the wrong people . . . A failure to recognise the implications of demographic change for the labour market is a further factor which could seriously affect the competitive position of smaller businesses . . . Small firms in the past have tended to recruit younger people . . . The corporate (larger firm) sector is developing policies to meet potential labour shortages, such as career break and return-to-work schemes for women as well as creche facilities, attractions with which small firms find it difficult to compete . . .

The trend seems likely to force small firms to compete with the large corporate sector on pay, training and fringe benefits, putting further pressure on their ability to cope with the strains of growth.

(a) Can you reconcile the Thatcher Government's support for the free market with help to small firms?

(b) What problems, other than the 'people gap', are faced by small firms?

(c) Suggest reasons why small firms find it difficult to 'find, retain and manage key staff'.

(d) What are the 'demographic changes' hinted at in the article?

(e) Explain why small firms will find it more difficult to compete with the corporate sector.

(f) Why is it important to bring the 'small business sector's share of UK economic activity up to that of other advanced countries'?

EXAMINATION QUESTIONS ■ ■ ■

■ 1   What contribution can small business enterprises make to the economy? Evaluate the strengths and weaknesses of small business in making this contribution.

(AEB, June 1983)

■ 2   (a) What is a 'small' firm and why do such firms exist?

(b) From a *human* perspective, what problems and opportunities might such firms present?

(c) What effect might an increase in the proportion of small firms have on the UK economy?

(Cambridge, June 1985)

FURTHER READING

BUSINESS ENTERPRISE

P BURNS AND J DEWHURST *Small Business and Entrepreneurship* (Macmillan)

K GLAISTER *The Entrepreneur* (Heinemann)

T T JONES AND T A J COCKERILL *Structure and Performance of Industries* (Philip Allan)

S HUGHES *The Structure of Industry* (Collins)

S RITCHIE (ed) *Case Studies in Management* (Elm)

P CHISNALL *Small Firms in Action* (McGraw-Hill)

CHAPTER 3
The External Environment

Business organisations do not operate within a vacuum but within a multi-faceted environment. The external environment includes all those forces and agencies that impinge on the firm. Literally, anything outside the firm can be included in the environment since it has the potential to have an impact on the firm. Moreover, the environment is never stable. The organisation needs to understand the environment in which it operates and the changing nature of the environment. It must be willing and able to respond to these changes: failure to adapt ultimately results in the failure of the business. In this chapter we are concerned about the nature of the environment and the ways in which businesses respond.

OBJECTIVES

1 To explain the changing nature of the environment.
2 To analyse the social, legal, political and technological environment.
3 To analyse the ways in which the environment affects business organisations.
4 To analyse how organisations respond to the changing environment.

The environment can be categorised in terms of the extent and the frequency with which the particular force impinges on the firm. We can make a two-way division between the proximate (immediate) environment and the general environment. A business organisation is a resource conversion system where inputs are combined together to create output. Hence, the proximate environment is concerned with the acquisition of the various resources and the way in which the system distributes the resulting output. Included in the proximate environment are customers, suppliers, the labour force, financial institutions, competitors and shareholders. These groups impinge on the organisation directly and frequently. The general environment refers to those forces in the background that occasionally, irregularly or indirectly impinge on the firm. It includes social, cultural, political, legal and technological factors. All have the potential for directly impinging on the firm.

A second way to categorise the forces in the environment is functionally in terms of the nature of the force. The most frequently used classification can be summed up by the word 'SLEPT', which is shorthand for the social, legislative, economic, political and technological environment. In dealing with each, we should bear in mind the previous distinction between the proximate and general environment.

Social environment

The most obvious component of the social environment concerns the size of the country's population. The study of population trends is known as **demography** and business organisations should be sensitive to demographic changes. We are not just concerned with the total size of population but also with changes in the composition of the population. A growing population is beneficial to firms in terms of increasing the size of the potential market and the available supply of labour. Slow population growth will act as a constraint on the firm both in terms of markets and available supplies of labour. Britain has experienced slow population growth for a number of decades but until recently employers have benefitted from plentiful supplies of young people joining the labour force. In the immediate future that supply of additional labour will decline in size, and this is forcing firms to be more receptive to the employment of older workers, to value younger workers more and to invest in training to maximise the benefit from scarce resources.

As well as the overall number of people, business organisations should study trends in the age composition of the population. Trends in the birth rate are crucially important for firms such as Mothercare or Early Learning Centres. They will investigate demographic trends before opening a new branch. At the other end of the age scale we have a growing number of retired people. Many of these people are fit and enjoy a comfortable lifestyle as a result of occupational pensions. Consequently, there is a growing number of firms that concentrate on this niche in the market: Saga Holidays, for example, specialise in off-peak holidays for older people. There has also been a considerable boom in the construction of retirement flats for pensioners who move into smaller homes. For building firms it also has the added advantage of fitting more dwellings into each acre of ground since local authorities insist on less car parking space for each flat if it is intended for retired people than if it was intended for the public in general. Firms catering for senior citizens have prospered as a result of the increase in the number of older people who are both active and comfortably off.

Changes in society are not confined to changes in the size and age composition of the population. Lifestyles, values and beliefs, the ethnic or religious background of society or socio-economic classes are also subject to change. These changes are of significance to business organisations because of their impact on the pool of available labour and on the purchasing behaviour of people in society.

The 20th Century has seen a decline in the size of the traditional 'cloth-cap' working class, but a rise in the skilled manual and clerical classes. One consequence of these trends is the closing of some marketing opportunities and the opening up of new opportunities. These social changes have brought a change in the character of public houses away from the 'sawdust on the floor' of old to a modern establishment selling a variety of drinks and food. The home improvement industries and the financial service section have also benefitted from this change in nature of the working class.

Changes in lifestyle can bring about changes in the market. The modern concern for fitness and health has provided great opportunities for firms supplying sports equipment and leisurewear, but others have suffered. Cigarette consumption has declined in the UK and may in time disappear. Tobacco companies have been forced to diversify into new products and to new markets. It is a matter of concern to people interested in the health of people in the Third World that tobacco companies have chosen to target the Third World to compensate for loss of sales in the developed world.

Our attitude to animal welfare has changed significantly in the 20th Century. Practices that were once accepted as normal and natural are now condemned. The fur trade, for example, has suffered major and probably irreversible decline because of changes in attitudes to fur products.

There are also changes in family life that should be noticed. The working wife, combined with widespread possession of a car and a freezer has been a major factor in the rise of the large, out-of-town shopping centre. In our society there is a growing number of one-person households, which also presents a challenge to business as these people seek small-sized packets rather than large family-sized packets. The customer-orientated firm will supply goods in packets of varying sizes to suit the needs of households.

Social responsibility

The villain of the film *Wall Street* started a speech

with the words, 'Greed is good'. The most charitable explanation of this sentiment was that it was a reaffirmation, in crude terms, of Adam Smith's economic philosophy. Smith argued that the pursuit of self-interest in a competitive market would ensure the common good. However, it is doubtful if the villain of *Wall Street* was thinking of the common good. He ruthlessly sought power and wealth and was prepared to trample on anyone who got in his way.

Should self-interest be the sole objective of business or should there be an acceptance of business organisation's responsibility to society? Right-wing economists from Adam Smith to Milton Friedman reject the notion of a business organisation's responsibility to the community. They argue that all we should expect from business is efficient, profitable production, creating jobs and providing goods and services at the price and quality customers desire. As profits are derived from efficient production, any reduction of profits in pursuit of social objectives leads to a decline in economic efficiency. Moreover, under company law, directors and managers are required to serve the interests of shareholders.

The belief that business organisations should act in a socially responsible way comes from those who believe that with economic power comes economic and social responsibility. Firms do not exist in isolation, but within the community. The actions of all firms, but especially large firms, have an impact on society (pollution, job losses, prosperity or poverty) and, therefore, firms should consider the impact on the community in their decision-making. It would be naive to believe that firms always behave in a socially responsible way, but it is cynical to believe that they are incapable of behaving in such a manner.

The major test of social responsibility relates to issues of:

- the environment
- the treatment of employees
- the treatment of customers
- relationships with other firms
- the welfare of disadvantaged groups
- the arts and education
- ethical issues.

The natural environment is now a matter of great concern. Nature has given us valuable resources, some of which are non-renewable. It is the duty of each generation to ensure that resources remain available to future generations. Even the renewable resources (e.g. the soil, rivers, fish stocks) have to be carefully looked after. It would be an act of gross irresponsibility if selfish behaviour by the present generation jeopardised the future of later generations.

Firms have traditionally been judged in terms of efficiency and profitability. Data on the commercial performance of a firm is recorded in its profit/loss account and balance sheet. A social audit extends the accounting principle into the social sphere. Different interest groups in society will judge firms in different ways:

1 Shareholders judge a firm in terms of return on their investment.
2 Employees judge firms in terms of working conditions, pay, supervision and fairness as an employer.
3 Customers judge firms by reference to price and quality of goods and services.
4 Creditors judge in terms of credit worthiness and the promptness of repayment of debt.
5 Suppliers judge by promptness of payment.
6 Society assesses firms in terms of their concern for and respect of the community and the environment.

A social audit will highlight those areas of the firm's activities which harm the environment as well as those activities beneficial to the environment. In this way it is hoped that all firms will behave in a socially responsible manner.

In part, socially responsible behaviour is a form of enlightened self-interest. Support for the arts is good for publicity. Moreover, leaders of commerce and industry realise that self-regulation reduces the danger of legislative action. But the truly socially responsible firm accepts that as it takes from society it has a duty to make a contribution to society.

The legal environment

Business organisations work within a legal framework which resolves disputes and regulates behaviour for the benefit of the community. Business relations usually involve a contract promising the delivery of goods or services or the payment of money some time in the future. It is, therefore, important for there to be a clear understanding of the rights and obligations of both parties to a contract. These rights and obligations are defined in Contract Law which also provides for remedies for failure to perform duties under the contract. It is difficult to see how the complex system of exchange in a modern economy could function smoothly without this framework of contract law.

The business organisation's contracts with (*a*) consumers and (*b*) employees (dealt with in Chapter 13) are subject to special laws. This is because it is felt that, in the absence of special protection, consumers and employees would be in a vulnerable position. Consumers are unable to fully evaluate the product before purchase. Many goods that we buy are packaged to prevent us seeing the goods until we get them home. We are required to trust the supplier to provide the goods as promised. Petrol is an extreme case. The motorist rarely sees the product and has to accept that the pump supplies petrol to the quantity and quality required. Complex goods such as cars or washing machines cannot be fully tested by the purchaser until after the purchase has been made. In these circumstances it would be unjust if the principle of *caveat emptor* (buyer beware) applied. In view of the weak position of the consumer it was necessary to develop a body of law more detailed than normal contract law. By protecting the consumer, the law places a constraint on business limiting what it can do, and raises its costs. The main areas of recent consumer law are summarised in Table I.

Table I   The main areas of consumer legislation

1968	*Trade Descriptions Act*	Creates offences relating to mis-description of goods and/or services, accommodation and facilities.
1971	*Unsolicited Goods Act*	Unsolicited goods become the property of the recipient if sender does not retrieve them within 30 days of notice (or 6 months without notice). Illegal to demand payment for goods not ordered.
1973	*Fair Trading Act*	Established the Office of Fair Trading to deal with unfair and restrictive trade practices. The Act seeks to encourage self-regulation through Codes of Practice but could be replaced by a 'general duty to trade fairly'.
1973	*Supply of Goods (Implied Terms) Act*	Introduced implied terms into the contracts of hire purchase similar to those implied into contracts of Sale of Goods by the Sale of Goods Act. Implied terms are not specifically and mutually agreed at the time of making the contract but are assumed to exist.
1974	*Consumer Credit Act*	Introduced a comprehensive licensing system. Creditor as well as supplier may be liable if there is a breach of contract or misrepresentation. Introduced detailed requirements on documentation, for example, true rate of interest (APR) to be displayed.

Table I/cont'd

1977	*Unfair Contract Terms Act*	Introduced detailed controls on the use of exclusion and limitation clauses.
1979	*Sale of Goods Act*	Introduced implied terms into all contracts for the sale of goods. Goods are to be of merchantable quality, as described and fit for their purpose. Consolidated previous law.
1987	*Consumer Protection Act*	1 **Product liability**. Implemented EC Directive. Strict liability for any defective goods causing damage. Purchaser no longer has to prove negligence. 2 **Consumer safety**. Offence to supply any goods failing to satisfy general safety standard. Consolidated existing legislation. 3 **Pricing**. Creates a general offence to give a false or misleading price indication, backed by a statutory Code of Practice.

A related area of law designed to protect the consumer concerns the abuse of monopoly power. Most economists see monopoly situations as undesirable. Monopolists can fix prices and produce inefficiently in the absence of competition. Since the Second World War there has been a series of Acts of Parliament on monopolies and restrictive practices. The 1973 Fair Trading Act consolidated the earlier laws and gave powers to the Office of Fair Trading. Dominant firm situations (defined as 25 per cent of the market) or proposed mergers involving 25 per cent or more of the market can be referred to the Monopolies and Mergers Commission. The Commission can conduct an investigation to consider whether or not the monopoly or merger is in the public interest. The MMC has no power to act, but can recommend to the Secretary of State for Trade that monopoly be broken up or the proposed merger be disallowed. It is generally acknowledged that monopoly and merger policy is ineffective in the UK. Legislation on restrictive practices, however, is more effective. All price fixing and similar agreements between firms are illegal unless they confer significant benefits on the community. The Restrictive Practice Court was established to deal with these issues.

The ownership, control and conduct of business organisation is regulated by the Companies Acts and the Partnership Act (1890). The Companies Acts evolved in the 19th Century to protect the interests of:

(*a*) creditors, who made loans to organisations whose owners enjoyed limited liability; and

(*b*) shareholders.

The law requires the Company to clearly state in the Memorandum and Articles of Association the constitution, the names of directors and the objectives of the company. All action outside these objects can be declared *ultra vires* (beyond the powers). Disclosure of information is a further obligation on companies, especially public limited companies.

A further area of the law of concern to businesses deals with the relationship of the organisation with the wider community. Where business activities cause an offence or nuisance or could lead to disorder, they are subject to regulation and licensing (sale of alcohol, places of entertainment). Growing concern over the environment has led to controls on certain industrial activities. Planning laws also act as a constraint on business. Whereas in the 19th Century landowners could do whatever they wanted with property, today there are restrictions designed to limit the nuisance caused to the community. For instance, planning authorities look carefully at proposed new shopping developments: large hypermarkets affect traffic flows and, therefore, permission is sometimes granted on the condition that the developer finances road improvements in the vicinity of the development. This practice, known as a **planning gain**, adds to the cost of development, but is seen as protection for the community.

The Government and the political environment

Despite recent privatisation, Britain still possesses what economists call a mixed economy. There is a mixture of privately owned and government-owned enterprise. Private enterprise sells goods and services in the market place and responds to the needs of the customers because of the profit motive. The public sector is the government sector of the economy and consists of a number of component parts. Central government provides services such as defence while local authorities provide services such as education and council housing. Also included in the public sector is the National Health Service and the remaining nation-alised industries such as the nuclear power industry. Parts of the public sector operate in the market place. For instance, the nationalised industries sell their services and are required to be commercially efficient. Conversely, many govern-ment and local government services are provided free to consumers but are paid for out of taxation. Whatever the method of paying for and distribut-ing services the important point is that the State is a major provider of goods and services.

The State performs other roles in the economy. Not only does it supply goods and services, it is also a buyer of goods and services. Many private sector firms rely heavily on public sector contracts; for example, manufacturers of military equipment are very dependent upon the government and therefore any cut in defence spending could have harmful consequences for these firms. There are many firms that supply materials to schools and colleges. One problem that confronts such firms concerns the size and nature of the school and college budget. The bulk of education expenditure is committed to the payment of teachers' salaries. Like other workers, teachers have legal rights when it comes to redundancy, consequently it is not possible to make an immediate saving on the educational budget by cutting the teaching force. The surest and quickest way to cut educational spending is to reduce purchases of furniture, textbooks and stationery. These are the easy targets but it creates problems for the firms in the educational supply industries. Consider also the firms that rely on NHS contracts. Opticians and pharmaceutical firms, for example, are affected by any change in NHS funding and policy.

As well as providing and purchasing goods and services, the State acts to regulate, encourage and guide the private sector of the economy. This may take the form of cash subsidies or tax concessions to encourage desirable trends, legislative controls to curb the excesses of the unregulated market or changes in interest rates to correct macro-economic problems. It is important to remember that much of what the State does acts as a constraint upon, rather than giving assistance to, private enterprise. Consumer and employee pro-tection legislation was passed to help consumers and workers rather than to help business organ-isations. Consequently, the role of the State in regulating and guiding the private sector is a matter of great controversy. To understand the differing philosophical views on the correct role of the State let us look at three stereotypical views.

1 THE *LAISSEZ-FAIRE* OR INDIVIDUALIST VIEW Supporters of *laissez-faire* believe in the market forces of supply and demand and in the virtue of individual initiative. Self-interest is seen, not as a vice contrary to the common good, but as the motivating force resulting in the creation of wealth. Supply responds to demand because of the profit motive operating in a competitive market. Not only does the market solve economic problems but State intervention is seen as

destablising. In the *laissez-faire* view, the correct role for the State is one of minimal interference. It should be confined to the provision of a framework of law, order and stability in which competitive private enterprise should be allowed to flourish.

2 THE RADICAL VIEW

The radical view is derived from Marx's analysis of the capitalist system. In such a system economic and political power is derived from the private ownership of the means of production. Invariably there are inequalities of income, wealth and power. These inequalities inevitably result in conflict leading to the collapse of the capitalist system and its replacement by a socialist system of production. Radical Marxists do not favour State intervention to guide or control the private enterprise system. Instead they look to the inevitable collapse of capitalism.

3 THE REFORMIST (OR PRAGMATIC VIEW)

This is the consensus view which takes in people across a wide political spectrum. There is an acceptance of the basic features of private enterprise capitalism, namely individual initiative, the profit motive and market forces. However, as the system also has undesirable features (known to economists as market failures) some degree of State intervention is considered necessary.

The defects of the private enterprise system are:

(*a*) The failure of the market to provide certain goods (e.g. law and order services) or to provide others in adequate quantities (e.g. education) or a satisfactory quality (which was the argument for the municipalisation of water supply in the 19th Century).

(*b*) Inequalities of income and wealth.

(*c*) Market domination by one, or a small number, of firms. It should be noted that all arguments in support of private enterprise are based on the assumption that it operates in competitive markets. Even the *laizzez-faire* economists of the 19th Century accepted State intervention to control private monopoly.

(*d*) The existence of external costs (pollution, noise, etc.) which are often ignored by private entrepreneurs in their search for profit but inflicted on the rest of society.

(*e*) The exploitation of consumers who, in our increasingly complex world, are unable to make a full evaluation of the products they purchase until they have taken them home. Consumer protection legislation is an attempt to redress the balance of power between supplier and customer.

(*f*) Fluctuations in the level of economic activity resulting in macro-economics problems such as unemployment, inflation and balance of payments deficits.

Reformists would argue that if the market creates problems (or at least fails to solve them) it is necessary for the State to intervene to solve them. Intervention by the State has increased over the years (or at least until 1979). Even in the mid-19th Century, which is usually depicted as the age of *laissez-faire*, there were state controls over working conditions, the quality of food, the urban environment and railways. Reforming governments in the 19th and 20th centuries took on more roles for the state. This process is often compared to a ratchet. Reforming or socialist governments took on more powers and functions but in-coming Conservative governments rarely reversed the trend.

The arrival of the Thatcher Government reversed this trend with the stated objective of 'rolling back the State'. Privatisation (the sale of public enterprises) has been accompanied by deregulation to free private enterprise from constraints imposed by previous governments. Perhaps the ratchet will, in the future, work in reverse with Thatcherite governments reducing State intervention but incoming Labour governments accepting many of the free market measures of the previous government.

The technological environment

The technological environment in which the business operates is also subject to change, providing both opportunities and threats. As with the other aspects of the environment, the successful organisation is the one that is willing and able to adapt to these environmental changes.

The most obvious way in which technology affects business is in terms of demand for the firm's products and the production processes it employs. An example of this is shown in the record industry where the development of the compact disc presented new market opportunities to firms supplying electrical goods and to the record companies which proceeded to re-release some of their classic older material in the new form. On the other hand it presented a threat to firms engaged in supplying materials and equipment for the manufacturers of tapes, traditional records and sound equipment.

Another industry affected by technology is satellite television which presents opportunities for more businesses to supply television broadcasts but poses a problem to advertisers because the proliferation of media reduces the audience for particular television channels. Firms enjoying monopoly powers in the market may be tempted to stifle technological developments which threaten their traditional product range or traditional methods of operation. However, the force of competition will stimulate the process of change. Each firm realises that if it fails to engage in technological development it will lose out to rivals.

Changing technology also affects businesses in other ways. The number and type of employees changes in response to changing technology. In some instances, for example computerisation of the office, new technology economises on the number of staff, but places a greater emphasis on the skills and quality of staff. In other instances, for example automation in factories, new technology has reduced the skill element in work. Pessimists see new technology as destroying jobs and replacing them by fewer and inferior jobs. The optimistic view of new technology points to the experience of history. Despite the fears of the 19th Century Luddites, new, better paid and more interesting jobs have been introduced to replace those which are disappearing. They also point to international comparisons of unemployment and

the use of robots. The countries with the lowest unemployment (e.g. Japan) have the highest proportion of robotic equipment to labour.

The newspaper industry provides an interesting example of technological development where new technology has led to a newspaper revolution. Computer links have enabled publishers to disperse printing to regional centres. The change in technology has reduced the work force required and has reduced the circulation required to break-even. This has facilitated the introduction of new papers such as the *Independent* and *Today*.

Conclusion

We live in an age of change and uncertainty and, although it sounds somewhat hackneyed, the pace of change is accelerating. The mediaeval peasant lived his life in a way little different from his forefathers. The same will not be said of us. Whether you are middle-aged or an eighteen-year-old student, the fact is that you have seen more change than in any other period of history of comparable length.

Some of the changes take the form of dramatic shocks which become headline news, for example, a revolution in Eastern Europe, a rise in interest rates, a new government introducing sweeping new laws, or a technical breakthrough. However, most changes are not dramatic and will not appear in the headlines. Instead, they are trends which become apparent over the years and decades (a change in family life, growing consciousness of environmental issues and growing concern over the welfare of other species that inhabit this planet). The 'trends' are not dramatic but are pervasive.

Whether the change takes the form of a 'shock' or a 'trend' it is part of the turbulent background against which business operates. The pessimist will perceive the challenge of the turbulent environment as a threat. The entrepreneur will seek to convert the challenge into an opportunity.

CASE STUDY 1
The Metro Centre

Out-of-town shopping centres developed in the 1970s and 1980s as a result of changes in the social and economic environment. Expansion of demand for retail services coupled with problems in town centre sites forced retailers to look to new and in many cases green field sites.

An early example of a hypermarket outside the town centre was the Carrefour Hypermarket in Eastleigh, Hampshire. To allay fears that it would undermine the position of traditional retailers, Eastleigh Borough Council produced a report arguing that expansion of demand coupled with attraction of custom from outside the borough would enable existing retailers to prosper as Carrefour expanded.

These early out-of-town centres have been followed by the large regional centres such as Brent Cross in north-west London, and more important still, the Metro Centre in Gateshead (Tyneside). The Metro Centre is built on derelict land that was included in the Tyneside Enterprise Zone in 1981. Firms in enterprise zones are granted the following concessions:

(a) automatic planning permission for most activities

(b) free of rates for ten years
(c) capital costs set against tax

The developers, Cameron Hall Developments Ltd, considered using the area for discount retail warehouses but decided that returns on investment would be greater in the case of a large, comprehensive shopping centre.

The success of large shopping developments in part hinges on the ability of developers to attract big-name stores. Consequently, the decision by Marks and Spencer to acquire premises was important to the success of the Metro Centre.

The Centre now contains a Carrefour Hypermarket, major chain stores (BHS, House of Fraser, etc.), leisure facilities, a hotel, specialist attractions and space for 9000 cars. The weak pound and the high cost of living in the Scandinavian countries has contributed to Metro Centre's attraction to people abroad. Metro Centre's supporters would therefore claim it has placed a significant part in reviving an area usually associated with unemployment and despondency.

1 Suggest changes in (a) the social environment; and (b) the economic environment which encourage the development of out-of-town shopping.
2 Why are local authorities keen to attract new firms into their area?
3 Explain the statement 'capital cost set against tax'.
4 Why is it important to attract the 'big stores'?
5 Suggest concessions that developers might give to attract big names into retail centres.
6 Explain the significance of the weak pound and the cost of living in Scandinavian countries to the Metro Centre's success.

CASE STUDY 2
Candleford

Candleford is a large town on the west coast of England which prospered as a port, with related port industries, in the 19th Century. However, in the late 20th Century it declined, a victim of the changing pattern of UK trade. Subsequent decay and dereliction in the area made it unattractive to new enterprise.

In 1980, under Mrs Thatcher's first government, Parliament established the Candleford Docklands Development Corporation to initiate a programme of renewal and regeneration in the dockland area of Candleford. Parliament established its objectives as:

1 to improve rapidly the image of Docklands by undertaking programmes of physical works throughout the area, and by creating confidence in the continuing improvements to come;
2 since the amount of public money available to the CDDC is small in relation to the size of the task, to use this money primarily as a lever to attract private investment;
3 where vacant and under-developed sites are not being suitably redeveloped by their owners, to acquire as much of such land as money permits in order to undertake the necessary reclamation and essential basic work, followed by sale or lease.
4 to undertake a major programme of environmental improvements.
5 to publicise and to market the opportunities in Docklands.

Although the CDDC is a public sector organisation, it was obligated to revive the area in partnership with the private sector. Moreover, at a time of severe controls on government spending, there was a limited budget to finance its various activities. Its first priority was to improve the environment and the infrastructure to attract private enterprise.

1 Why was Candleford a victim of the changing pattern of UK trade?
2 What factors do firms look for in a good site and how will improving the environment and infrastructure attract private enterprise?
3 What marketing strategies should the CDDC employ to attract the private sector?
4 To what extent is the CDDC (a) compatible with; and (b) contrary to the philosophy of the Thatcher Government?

CASE STUDY 3
Japanese investment in the UK

In an article in *Eurobusiness* (January 1990), Christopher McCoocy and Tim Hindle analysed Japanese investment in the UK. Britain is the favourite 'destination for Japan's direct investment in Europe, and likely to remain so throughout the 1990s'. They report that the Mitsui Bank considers that the UK has seven main advantages:

- A stable government and economy. No longer the sick man of Europe, 'Britain is seen as less restrictive and more enterprising than other European countries'.
- Labour force and labour costs. 'Investors are actually attracted to the UK by its industrial relations ... (and) by the relative cheapness of the labour force, its willingness to retrain and its higher productivity'.
- The English language. The Japanese are 'comfortable' with English as the international business language and with the English legal system.
- A life-style and manners comparatively easy for the Japanese to absorb. One hundred years ago, Victorian Britain was characterised by economic energy, commercial competition, entrepreneurial risk-taking, hard work, self-discipline, faith in technology and optimism for the future. Japan, just emerging from isolation, looked to Britain as a model ...
- A wide variety of facilities and incentives.
- Good sea and air communications and the Eurotunnel link.
- The positive stance of central and local government authorities, for example, 'the way in which the British government stood up for Nissan when the French were arguing about the local content of British-made Nissan cars'.

1 What is meant by Japan's direct investment?
2 What is meant by Britain being less restrictive and more enterprising?
3 Explain why there is apparent surprise about Britain's labour relations.
4 What is meant by:
   (a) productivity;
   (b) retraining;
   (c) entrepreneurial risk-taking?
5 What incentives are given to attract inward investment?
6 Why was 'the local content of British-made Nissan cars' a controversial issue?

CASE STUDY 4
Football league clubs

Football league clubs are in fact limited companies. Most are private limited companies although, a few, such as Tottenham Hotspur, are public companies with their own shares quoted on the Stock Exchange. As companies they have financial objectives like any other business. The question is: do the people who run league clubs seek financial success in order to achieve footballing success, or do they seek success on the field to achieve a better financial return? Clearly the two types of success are inter-related. A club cannot win the league unless it survives and it will only survive if the money flows in in sufficient quantities. At the same time, financial success is aided by a good performance on the football field.

Like all businesses, league clubs are subject to the turbulence of the environment. This might take the form of a (relatively) sudden shock such as:

- a change in direct or indirect taxation;
- the exclusion of English clubs from European competition in the late 1980s;
- legislation to force a membership scheme on reluctant clubs;
- the arrival of satellite television to compete with BBC and ITV for television rights.

It might take the form of social trends such as:

- movement of people to the suburbs;
- greater mobility of the population;
- economic and demographic decline in some of the formerly great footballing towns of the north;
- the rise of the modern father and husband who prefers to be with the family at weekends.

1 Use the hierarchy of objectives concept to identify levels of objectives of football clubs.
2 What are the sources of income for football clubs other than receipts at the gate?
3 Suggest three reasons why people become major shareholders in football clubs.
4 Why was the membership scheme expected to reduce gate receipts?
5 How do clubs in the lower divisions benefit from the transfer system?
What would be the effect of an imposition of a maximum (e.g. £100 000) on transfers?
6 If all league clubs receive a share of television rights, what will be the result of:
(a) continual exclusion from Europe?
(b the formation of a 'Superleague' separate from the Football League?
7 How has greater mobility affected
(a) the big clubs?
(b) the small clubs?
8 Suggest other environment factors which have had an impact on the finances of football clubs.
9 In what ways has football recently adopted a more modern marketing approach?

EXERCISE ● ● ●

● 1 The Refuge Assurance Company has recently moved from their headquarters in central Manchester. This was a large and imposing Victorian building close to Oxford Road station which is one of Manchester's main commuter stations. The new headquarters is on a 'green field' site in the Cheshire suburb of Wilmslow, some 15 miles from Manchester.

Identify and analyse the factors in the changing environment that may have contributed to the decision to move.

● 2 In advertisements designed to encourage companies to settle in the town, Livingston Development Corporation claimed that it has everything needed to help in-coming companies 'make it big in Europe'.

In particular, Livingston:
- has immediate access to the motorway network;
- is 20 minutes from Edinburgh, 'Europe's second financial centre';
- has a skilled and adaptable workforce;
- has Scotland's foremost high technology park;
- has advance factory and warehouse units, greenfield sites and customised premises;
- access to Government financial assistance;
- provides a home based in a united Europe.

(a) Explain why each of the claims made by Livingston is important to firms contemplating relocation.
(b) What locational disadvantages is the advertisement trying to combat?
(c) In the light of claims made in the advertisement, what type (or types) of business are they trying to attract?

● 3 Study the data below and answer the questions following the table.

UK demographic changes 1985–2025.

Year	Working age population	Retired population	Aged Dependency Ratio (retired population as % of working age population)
1985	61.2	18.0	29.4
1995	60.6	18.2	30.0
2005	60.5	18.3	30.2
2015	60.4	20.2	33.4
2025	57.9	22.3	38.5

Source: Government Actuary's Department.

(a) How can statisticians predict the age structure of the population in the year 2025?
(b) What market opportunities and threats are presented by this changing age structure?
(c) What are the likely consequences for the NHS and government finances of these predicted trends? What will be the 'knock on' effects for private sector firms?
(d) The working age population is expected to stagnate in absolute terms but decline as a proportion of the total population. Consider the consequences for labour recruitment and suggest strategies to enable firms to overcome labour supply problems.

4 Read the extract below, taken from an article in the *Financial Times*.

GREEN consumerism has the briefest of histories in Britain, but there are signs that it is entering a new phase – one in which businesses will have to take greater care to substantiate their claims before wrapping their products in a green label.

The Government this week signalled that it is losing patience with manufacturers which plaster their wares with unjustifiable claims of eco-virtue in an attempt to cash in on the environmental band-wagon.

On Tuesday ministers unveiled plans to amend the Trade Descriptions Act to prevent goods from being falsely labelled as "environmentally friendly." They also announced their support for a European Community labelling scheme. That would require products to be vetted by an independent body before they could carry the proposed EC eco-label.

Ironically, the Government appears to be preparing to act just as the more blatantly false environmental claims are becoming a thing of the past. This is thanks largely to pressure from environmental groups such as Friends of the Earth and from consumer organisations like the Consumers' Association.

Ms Sian Morrissey, a researcher on environmental issues for the Consumers' Association says: "We are not saying that companies are telling blatant lies – the Trade Descriptions Act could deal with those – but they are still misleading people."

Which? the association's magazine, published an article on green labelling this month which called for the banning of general claims, such as "environmentally friendly," and of claims that are not explained, such as "environmentally friendly pulp."

Companies' green labels may be seen as a half-way house before the adoption of a statutory scheme. Sainsbury, which like Procter and Gamble, says it backs the Government's plans, explains: "We support a strong government-backed labelling system. We regard our labelling system as an interim one until the Government comes up with a standard labelling system."

In fact, some companies which helped to pioneer environmental consumerism have already evolved more subtle labelling.

For example, Varta, the West German-based batteries group, took market share from its competitors when it described a mercury-free battery as "green" in 1988.

Last year, it went one better by introducing a cadium-free battery, but also revised its labelling, describing its batteries as "environmentally friendlier." Mr Chris Ash, Varta's UK marketing director, explains: "We realised that we had been implying an absolute standard which is impossible for any product."

The first set of part-opportunistic, part-naïve, responses by companies to environmentalism may be coming to an end.

Still unclear is the impact of the Government's latest intervention on business attitudes.

On the one hand, ministers appeared to embrace a tough attitude by suggesting that they would clamp down on loose terms such as "environmentally friendly" and that products would not qualify for the proposed EC eco-label unless they were environmentally benign from their production through to their disposal.

On the other hand, the Government was studiously vague about the timetable for amending the Trade Descriptions Act or for the official eco-label. The Environment Department said yesterday that it would introduce an eco-label in Britain only after agreement on an EC-wide system.

Environmental labelling is likely to remain an area ripe for confusion and bitter argument in the meantime.

(Extract from an article by David Thomas in the *Financial Times*, 30 December 1989)

(*a*) What is meant by Green consumerism? Why are businesses anxious to be seen as being green?

(*b*) Investigate;
   (i) the provisions of the Trade Descriptions Acts (1968);
   (ii) the work of the Consumers' Association; and
   (iii) methods used by environmental pressure groups.

(*c*) What is meant by 'part-opportunistic, part-naive responses' of companies and why is this phase coming to an end?

(*d*) What is wrong with the term 'environmentally friendly'?

(*e*) What is the distinction being made in the article between a 'green label' and an 'eco label'?

(*f*) Why will it be difficult to satisfy the standards for the proposed EC eco label?

EXAMINATION QUESTIONS ■ ■ ■

■ 1 A company's production processes are regarded by a pressure group as polluting the environment. Discuss how the company might be affected by the actions of the pressure group in this situation.

(AEB, June 1984)

■ 2 Discuss the view that modern technological innovations such as microprocessors are a mixed blessing in that such innovations will create new systems and new products but will also create unemployment.

(AEB, June 1980)

■ 3 Legislation such as that concerned with employee and consumer protection and the regulation of potential monopolies cause the loss of international competitiveness. This is too high a price to pay.'

To what extent do you agree?

(AEB, June 1989)

■ 4 Discuss the proposition that government legislation does little for business except hinder its growth and reduce its profitability.

(AEB, June 1987)

FURTHER READING

THE EXTERNAL ENVIRONMENT

R H BARBACK *The Firm and its Environment* (Philip Allan)
B RICHARDSON AND R RICHARDSON *Business Planning: An Approach to Strategic Management* (Pitman)
G GREENLEY *Strategic Management* (Prentice Hall)
G DONNELLY *The Firm in Society* (Pitman)
J TILEY AND S BAILEY *Business Law* (Longman)
D KEENAN AND S RICHES *Business Law* (Pitman)
T REGAN *The Politics of Privatisation* (Longman)
B DICK *Privatisation in the UK: The Free Market v State Control* (Longman)
B HURL *Privatisation and the Public Sector* (Heineman)
T BURDEN, R CHAPMAN AND R STEAD *Business in Society: Consensus and Conflict* (Butterworth)
D LITTLER *Technological Development* (Philip Allan)

CHAPTER 4

The Economic Environment

People involved in managing business organisations need to be sensitive to the economic environment which, like other elements in the environment, is continually changing. We live in a dynamic or changing economy. A knowledge of economics does not guarantee success in business but it does provide a way of interpreting and analysing trends in the economic environment.

OBJECTIVES

1 To explain microeconomic theories of demand, supply and price.
2 To explain the concept of elasticity.
3 To derive lessons from economists' theory of the firm.
4 To analyse macroeconomic problems and government policies.
5 To explain the current controversies in macroeconomics.

Economics is conventionally divided into microeconomics and macroeconomics. The former involves the study of a small part of the market (a single firm or product) whereas macroeconomics deals with the whole, inter-related economy. We will look first at microeconomic theories of prices before proceeding to outline macroeconomic theory.

Demand

In economics, demand refers to the desire to purchase a good or service backed up by an ability and willingness to pay for the product. Mere desire is insufficient: only when both conditions (desire and ability to pay) are met is demand said to be effective. Ability to pay is clearly related to income and the other claims on our income. The desire to acquire the product is related to an assessment of the benefit or pleasure expected to be derived from the product compared with the sacrifice of money (and therefore other purchases) in acquiring the

good. Consumers are assumed to be rational. They make decisions which aim at maximising the pleasure (known in economics as **utility**) gained from their purchases: the rational consumer will only purchase goods if the pleasure expected from consuming them is at least equal to the sacrifice of money in purchasing the goods. Although the theory is unprovable it does have a common sense appeal: for example, it would be folly to buy a chocolate bar priced 25 pence if you did not expect the equivalent amount of satisfaction.

If we consume up to the point where price and expected pleasure are equivalent, then any reduction in price will result in an increase in the quantity of the good that we purchase. This is the basis behind the downward sloping demand curve. Table II shows a demand schedule. At a high price (e.g. £10), the quantity demanded is low (100 000 tonnes). As price falls to £7 there is an increase in the quantity demanded to 130 000 tonnes. This principle is adopted intuitively by market traders or ticket touts outside a rock concert. When faced with a surplus, especially of a highly perishable product, they will reduce price

Table II   A demand schedule

Price	Quantity demanded (000 tonnes)
10	100
9	110
8	120
7	130
6	140
5	150

to 'clear' the market. The data in the demand schedule can be plotted on a graph (*see* Fig 4.1). The downward sloping demand curve informs us that quantity demanded is inversely related to price.

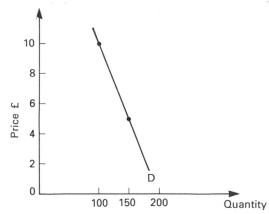

Fig 4.1   A demand curve

Economists make a number of assumptions which, although somewhat divorced from reality, enable us to concentrate on the variable we wish to study. In this case it is the impact of price on demand for the product. Hence, the demand curve is drawn on the assumption that other factors remain unchanged. This causes dismay to students new to economics who rightly point out that other things never remain unchanged in a dynamic economy. However, by holding other factors constant we can focus on the impact of the single variable (price). In this respect the economist is

adopting an approach similar to that of a chemist conducting laboratory experiments.

When other factors do change there is a change in demand: for instance, a rise in income will lead to an increase in demand with the demand curve shifting outwards to the right. At each price level more is demanded than before (*see* Fig 4.2). A shift of the demand curve is caused by a change other than price, such as a change in taste or fashion, a change in population, a successful advertising

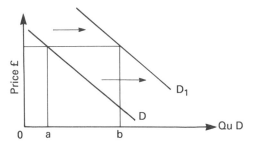

D_1 represents demand after a rise in income

Fig 4.2   A shift of the demand curve

campaign, a change in the price of complementary goods or a change in the price of substitute goods. Complementary goods such as petrol and cars or film and cameras are jointly demanded. We derive little benefit from a car unless we can obtain petrol. Hence, a rise in the price of petrol may deter some people from purchasing a car and may encourage others to purchase a more economical car. Substitute goods, as the name suggests are rival products, such as butter and margarine or tea and coffee. They perform similar functions and, if we assume that some people are prepared to drink both tea and coffee, a rise in the price of coffee is likely to encourage some switching to tea drinking.

We can now summarise demand theory by stating that demand is a function of (i.e. related to) a number of factors:

Quantity Demanded = f (price, income, price of complements, price of substitutes, taste, population).

If other things are held constant then demand is a function of price. The relationship is inverse so that as price falls, quantity demanded increases. A movement along the demand curve is caused by a change in the price of the good and to avoid confusion it is called an extension or contraction of demand (*see* Figs 4.3 and 4.4). A shift of the demand curve is caused by something other than price and is called an increase or decrease in demand (*see* Figs 4.5 and 4.6).

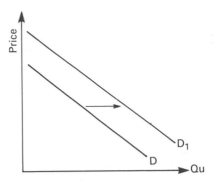

Fig 4.5 An increase in demand caused by: *(a)* a rise in income; *(b)* a favourable change in taste; *(c)* a fall in the price of a complement; *(d)* a rise in the price of a substitute; *(e)* a rise in population.

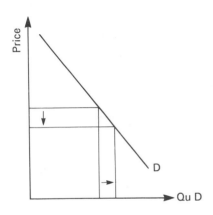

Fig 4.3 An extension of demand caused by a fall in price

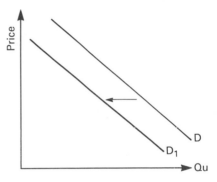

Fig 4.6 A decline in demand caused by: *(a)* a fall in income; *(b)* an adverse change in taste; *(c)* a rise in the price of a complement; *(d)* a fall in the price of the substitute; *(e)* a fall in population.

Elasticity of demand

The enquiring student should be thinking at this stage that there are some things we buy almost irrespective of price. The smoker is not discouraged by a rise in the price of cigarettes; the rock music fan may be willing to pay inflated prices to see his or her favourite band. These facts can be accommodated within demand theory through the concept of elasticity of demand. Elastic stretches whereas other products do not. Consequently,

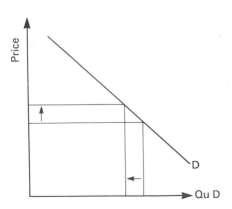

Fig 4.4 A contraction of demand caused by a rise in price

what economists mean by elasticity is sensitivity or responsiveness of demand to changes in price.

As an exercise, construct a list of those products where a demand is very sensitive to price changes and another list of products where demand is less sensitive to changes in prices. As a general rule we can conclude that demand tends to be inelastic (unresponsive) where:

- the product is a necessity (e.g. bread)
- there are no close substitutes (e.g. electricity)
- the product is habit forming (e.g. tobacco)
- the product is inexpensive in relation to income.

Demand tends to be elastic (sensitive) if the product:

- is a luxury item (e.g. foreign holidays)
- has close substitutes (e.g. going to the cinema or watching a video)
- is expensive in relation to income.

Demand for the product of a particular firm is likely to be more elastic than demand for the product in general. For example, most couples want a professional photographer to take pictures at their wedding. Hence, demand for the services of a photographer is likely to be inelastic. However, photographers are in competition with each other. If one photographer raises his/her prices, he or she is likely to lose custom unless he/she has some distinctive advantage in other aspects of the marketing mix (e.g. a reputation for the high quality of the service). Firms with distinctive advantages may be able to retain custom even if they raise prices.

There is a simple formula for calculating **price elasticity of demand**:

Price elasticity of demand

$$= \frac{\% \text{ change in quantity demanded}}{\% \text{ change in price}}$$

EXAMPLE

Suppose a price rise from £1 to £1.25 was followed by a fall in quantity purchased from 100 tonnes to 80 tonnes. Assuming that the price rise caused the fall in quantity sold (an assumption which could be difficult to prove), calculate price elasticity of demand.

Quantity demanded falls by 20 tonnes or 20%
Price rose by 25p   or 25%

Therefore price elasticity of demand
is $\frac{20\%}{25\%}$ or 0.8

It should be noted that the elasticity is less than one, that means it is relatively inelastic (price insensitive). If elasticity exceeds one, demand is said to be **relatively** elastic (price sensitive). If the resulting number is exactly one, we say that elasticity is **unitary**.

The calculation of elasticity is difficult in the real world but some notion of price sensitivity is important for a firm considering altering its price. A price reduction would produce little benefit for the firm if demand is insensitive to price. On the other hand, a firm considering a price rise may suffer a serious loss of trade if demand is sensitive to price. The relationship between elasticity and the firm's revenue after a price change can be illustrated in the following example.

Price	Quantity demanded	Total revenue (price × quantity)
£	(Tonnes)	£
10	200	2000
9	240	2160
8	290	2320
7	320	2240
6	330	1980
5	340	1700

A price rise from £5 to £6 results in an increase in revenue (although as we know nothing about costs we cannot comment on profits). However, a rise from £9 to £10 causes a fall in the firm's revenue. A task for the reader is to calculate price elasticity of demand for both price changes.

It is convenient at this point to mention two other elasticities of demand. Income elasticity of demand refers to the responsiveness of demand to changes in income. For most goods, a rise in income is likely to be followed by an increase in demand (a rightward shift of the demand curve). This increase is likely to be greatest in the case of luxury goods such as package holidays abroad. It is likely to be low in the case of a basic necessity such as bread. It is possible for income elasticity to be negative. This applies to a situation in which a rise in income results in a fall in demand. Such products are known as inferior goods but this should not be taken to mean sub-standard or 'shoddy'. Public transport might be considered an inferior good if bus travellers switched to travelling to work by car following a rise in income.

The formula for calculating income elasticity of demand is:

$$\frac{\% \text{ change in demand}}{\% \text{ change in income}}$$

Cross elasticity of demand is the least well known elasticity of demand. It refers to the effect on demand for one product of a change in the price of another. The formula is:

$$\frac{\% \text{ change in the demand for Product X}}{\% \text{ change in the price of Product Y}}$$

Consider two very different examples. In the first a 20 per cent rise in the price of coffee results in a 10 per cent rise in the demand for tea.

Cross elasticity is $\frac{10\%}{20\%}$ or $\frac{1}{2}$

As both percentages refer to rises we should state that cross elasticity here is positive (a plus divided by plus).

In the second case, a 50 per cent rise in the price of video recorders results in a 20 per cent fall in the demand for video tapes.

Cross elasticity is now $\frac{-20\%}{+50\%}$ or $\frac{-2}{5}$

The simple conclusion we can draw is that in the case of substitute products cross elasticity is positive. In the case of complementary products cross elasticity is negative.

Demand, supply and price

The counterbalance to demand is supply which refers to the quantity offered to the market at each price level. The higher the price, the greater the quantity offered in the market. Hence, the supply curve slopes upwards (*see* Fig 4.7). Once again the graph is drawn on the assumption that other factors remain unchanged. These other factors mainly concern the cost of producing the goods. Clearly a fall in the price of inputs will increase the attractiveness of supplying goods to the market with the result that at each price level more is supplied. This is illustrated by an outward shift of the supply curve (S_1). Economists distinguish between an extension/contraction of supply caused by a change in price and an increase/decrease caused by something other than price.

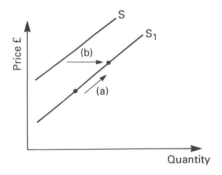

Fig 4.7 A supply curve

Price elasticity of supply refers to the responsiveness of supply to changes in price. Supply tends to be inelastic in the short run. A rise in price will encourage firms to supply more but unless they possess spare capacity or can acquire additional inputs of labour, machinery and raw materials, they will be unable to respond immediately. In the long run supply is more elastic. The formula for calculating price elasticity of supply is similar to previous elasticities:

$$\frac{\% \text{ change in quantity supplied}}{\% \text{ change in price}}$$

If the result exceeds one, supply is said to be

elastic. If it is less than one, supply is said to be inelastic.

By combining supply and demand on the same graph we can determine the equilibrium or market price (*see* Fig 4.8). At equilibrium price the amount that buyers wish to purchase is exactly equal to the amount that suppliers are willing to offer to the market. At all other prices there is disequilibrium. At price OA, demand exceeds supply. Competition between buyers forces price up. At price OB, supply exceeds demand. Competition between sellers forces price down. Only equilibrium price (OE) is sustainable in the long run.

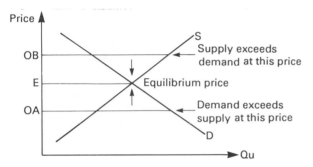

Fig 4.8   Equilibrium price

This suggests that price is determined in the market with the firm having little control over price. It has to accept the market price but decides whether or not it is worthwhile competing in the market at current prices. We will see in the later sections that a firm's discretion over price depends upon (*a*) its degree of monopoly power, and (*b*) its ability to offer something distinctive in terms of other aspects of the marketing mix.

The theory of the firm

The theory of the firm is a rather abstract area of economic theory which we do not need to explore in detail. However, the theory does provide some important lessons which enable us to understand the firm in its market environment.

In the theory of the firm, economists outline and investigate a number of market structures of which the ideal is known as **perfect competition**. In such markets there are numerous buyers and sellers with no single firm able to influence price. Customers make decisions on price alone since each firm sells a product which is identical in all respects to that of its rivals. (In effect this means that the non-price elements in the marketing mix are fixed and inoperative.) The perfectly competitive firm is a price taker – it has no control over price but must accept the price determined in the market. Economists assume that the firm seeks to maximise profits. As it cannot control price it will maximise profits by producing at the profit maximising output.

Exactly the opposite situation is known as **pure monopoly**. This refers to a single seller of a product with no close substitute. For instance, we might think that British Gas enjoys a monopoly position in the market. It is true that it has a monopoly in the supply of gas piped to households. However, it faces competition from suppliers of rival services, most notably the electricity suppliers. The monopolist has some discretion over price and can be seen as a price maker rather than a price taker. But even a monopoly firm has to accept the logic of the demand curve. A rise in price is likely to be followed by a contraction of demand. A common error is to assume that a monopolist can fix both price and quantity. In fact they can fix price or quantity but not both.

Between the two extremes we have various forms of imperfect competition. In many markets there is some competition but it involves a handful of firms rather than hundreds or thousands. This market structure composed of a small number of large firms is known as **oligopoly**. The oligopolist realises that any decision made will have a direct impact upon rival firms which are likely to retaliate. The benefits of reducing price will be lost if rival firms follow suit. Consequently oligopolistic firms may prefer not to compete directly over price. There is a natural tendency for them to collude over prices even though most forms of collusion are illegal under Restrictive Practice Law. Price leadership, however, represents tacit collusion and is a common feature of oligopolistic markets. Here the recognised leader (perhaps the largest or most efficient firm) sets prices which the others follow. No agreement is necessary. The pattern develops that when the leader raises prices the others will follow. The leader can safely raise prices in the knowledge that others will follow. Occasionally these tacit arrangements break down with price warfare developing. This involves competitive price cutting to destroy rivals but is a dangerous and, in the short run at least, damaging strategy. It is only successful when the aggressive firm is efficient or has large reserves to enable it to sustain temporary losses. On the surface it might seem as though price warfare acts in the interest of customers, but where it results in the elimination of rivals, it is in fact harmful to them.

If oligopolistic firms are reluctant to compete over price they will concentrate on competing in other ways, e.g. product, packaging, promotion, after sales service and product variations. Economists refer to this as **non-price competition** but this is because price is central to economists' view of the market. In marketing, however, it is accepted that price is but one element in the mix. Hence, the theory of oligopoly suggests that oligopolists may decide to suspend competition in one element but concentrate on other elements in the mix. There is one very good reason for concentrating on these non-price elements. The more distinctive the oligopolist makes his product, the greater his freedom of manoeuvre. In fact, with a distinctive product perceived to be superior to that of its rivals, the oligopolist might be able to raise the price without losing sales to rivals.

The macroeconomy

Macroeconomics involves the study of the whole economy with particular emphasis on the level of employment, inflation, balance of payments and the rate of growth in the economy. In Business Studies we are not concerned about these variables for their own sake but for the way in which they have an impact on business firms. However,

before we can fully understand the macroeconomic impact on business we need to investigate the theory.

Mention was made earlier of the different philosophical approaches to the market. There are those who believe that the market solves all problems and that government interference is unnecessary and destabilising. There are others who believe that the government has a positive role to play in correcting problems thrown up by the market. In macroeconomics this distinction is illustrated by the controversy between two schools of economic thought: the **Keynesian** and **Monetarist** schools.

In the 19th Century, unemployment was not considered to be the concern of the government. Unemployment was the result of excess supply of labour at existing wage rates. The solution was a reduction in the price of labour which would make it more attractive to take on more workers. Unemployment was seen as a purely temporary problem until wage cuts returned the economy to a state of full employment. Inflation would be eliminated by tight control of the money supply which, in the 19th Century, was achieved by maintaining a fixed relationship between gold held in reserve in the Bank of England and the note issue. The gold standard also provided an automatic, if somewhat painful, mechanism to solve balance of payments problems. Countries experiencing a trade deficit would lose gold and banks would be forced to raise interest rates, thereby reducing the volume of lending. This in turn would reduce spending and bring about a decline in imports. Economic growth was also left to market forces. In this supremely optimistic age it was believed that the freeing of trade from all restrictions would open up market opportunities and provide the stimulus for economic growth in Britain. In all aspects of the macroeconomy the market was assumed to solve all problems and therefore there was no need for government to take corrective action.

The slump of the 1920s undermined this belief in market forces. Cambridge economist, John Maynard Keynes, argued that free market forces could not be counted upon to solve the problem of

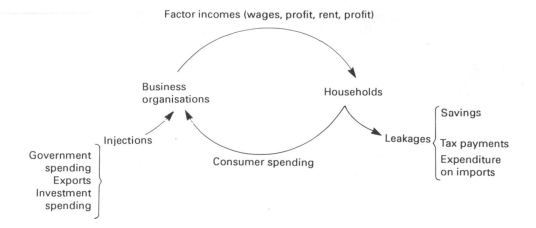

Fig 4.9 The circular flow of income

unemployment. First, trade unions resisted wage cuts which were regarded by governments as the solution to unemployment. Second, and more important, Keynes pointed out that wage cuts would further reduce demand for goods and, therefore, for labour. Rather than solving the problem of unemployment, wage cuts would aggravate the problem.

The theoretical model is illustrated by the circular flow of income (*see* Fig 4.9). Business organisations hire labour and other resources from households. In turn households are rewarded with income (wages, rents, profits, interest). Households return this income to businesses when they purchase goods and services. Income flows around the system in a circular fashion. However, not all income is spent on British goods and services. In Fig 4.9 some of the income leaks away in the form of:

- tax payments
- money spent upon imported goods and services
- savings (which economists define simply as income not spent).

Leakages reduce the demand for goods, services and, therefore, for labour. On the other hand, there is some spending on British goods and services undertaken by agencies other than households. These are known as **injections** and they

add to demand and assist the process of job creation. The injections are identified as:

- government spending
- purchases by foreigners of British exports
- investment spending by British firms.

The model is useful in that it enables us to identify those factors which boost aggregate demand and those which reduce it. Anything which increases the size of injections or reduces the size of leakages increases aggregate demand. Keynes used the circular flow model to explain why the free market could not be relied upon to guarantee full employment. Like earlier economists, Keynes accepted that the economy was always moving to a balanced or equilibrium state, but, unlike his predecessors, Keynes believed that this equilibrium did not involve a particular level of employment. The macroeconomy is in equilibrium when the leaks are balanced by injections so that the amount of income flowing around the system remains unchanged. It was possible for the economy to be in a state of equilibrium when a deficiency of demand would lead to persistent unemployment. If the market could create a situation of persistent unemployment it was the duty of the government to act. The action took the form of fiscal and monetary policies designed to manage the level of demand to achieve the government's objective of full employment (usually regarded as 2.5 per cent unemployment).

Unemployment

The unemployed are defined in government statistics as those people who are seeking work but are unable to obtain a job and who are registered as unemployed. In theory, a high level of unemployment should increase the reserves of labour available to business. Firms seeking additional labour for expansion will benefit from the availability of labour. Moreover, excess supplies of labour will weaken the resolve of union to seek high pay rises and/or improved conditions. In this way unemployment might be seen as beneficial to business organisations. Life, however, is never quite as simple. It is possible for high unemployment to co-exist with shortage of particular types of labour or shortages in certain geographical areas. To solve the problem of unemployment it is always necessary to combine policies of boosting aggregate demand (such policies are called reflationary) with measures designed to assist the movement of labour into shortage trades and areas.

In terms of demand for goods and services, unemployment is harmful to business. The higher the unemployment the lower the demand for goods and services and consequently the greater the problems involved in selling goods. These difficulties are likely to be most acute in the case of non-essentials which are the first items we economise on as our income falls. However, it should be remembered that, although unemployment is painful, it actually affects only a minority of people. It is quite possible for the majority to enjoy higher living standards at a time of high unemployment.

Table III summarises the main types of unemployment and their remedies.

Table III   Unemployment: Keynesian Analysis

Type	Description and cause	Remedy
Demand – deficiency unemployment	A shortfall in aggregate demand	Raise the level of demand by reflation.
Frictional	Job changing unemployment	Improve the flow of information about job vacancies.
Seasonal	Seasonal fluctuations in activity	Diversification in the local economy.
Structural/regional	Long-term decline of major industries.	Retraining. Regional policy.
Technological	Labour saving technology causes job losses.	Retraining.

For thirty years after the Second World War, British governments adopted Keynesian macroeconomic policies to manage the level of demand in the economy. Unemployment and inflation were seen as opposite problems suggesting that they could not coexist. It was accepted wisdom that a 'trade-off' existed between unemployment and inflation. Therefore, the lower the unemployment, the greater the pressure on prices to rise. On the other hand, price stability was only possible at high levels of unemployment. The task of the Government was to manage the economy to achieve a satisfactory combination of inflation and unemployment. The major policy weapons can be summarised as follows:

	Reflation (to combat unemployment)	Deflation (to combat inflation)
Government spending	Increase	Reduce
Taxation	Reduce	Increase
Interest rates	Reduce	Increase

Confidence in Keynesian remedies was undermined by the co-incidence of heavy unemployment and high inflation in the 1970s. This led to a revival of pre-Keynesian economic ideas. The Monetarist School, led by the American Milton Freidman, urged governments to concentrate on tackling the problem of inflation. He dismissed Keynesian reflation as futile except in the short run. There is a natural rate of unemployment in the economy and this is linked to what economists call 'imperfections' in the market. These imperfections act as barriers to people obtaining jobs or establishing new enterprises. They include employment legislation (which discourages firms employing labour) trade unions (which price labour out of work) and rules on entry to trades. Monetarists do not attempt to reduce unemployment by fiscal or monetary policy. In fact, they do not believe in 'managing the economy'. Instead, they believe in letting market forces solve the problem.

The Thatcher Government did not attempt to reduce unemployment by reflation. Instead, the emphasis was placed on microeconomic policies. Retraining schemes have been devised to enable the unemployed to fit into the available jobs. Enterprise has been encouraged, not by giving positive help, but by relaxing and even eliminating some of the barriers on enterprise. The Thatcher Government reduced the levels of direct taxation, not to increase demand in the Keynesian fashion, but to stimulate the supply-side of the economy. Controls on capital movement were abolished soon after Mrs Thatcher became Prime Minister. Controls on planning and trading regulations were also relaxed to stimulate enterprise.

Inflation

Inflation is a rise in the general level of prices. The UK inflation rate is expressed in terms of the Index of Retail Prices which reflects a weighted average of price rises over the previous twelve months.

Economists attribute inflation to one of three causes:

(a) Excess demand in conditions of full employment (known as **demand pull** inflation).
(b) An excessive rise in the money supply (**monetary** inflation).
(c) Monopolistic forces pushing up prices and wages (**cost push** inflation).

Inflation, except of the mildest kind, is regarded as undesirable by all economists. As some groups in society gain (e.g. debtors) while others lose (e.g. savers, creditors, those on fixed incomes, those in non-union trades) inflation has the effect of redistributing purchasing power. Business might suffer if their customers experience a decline in their real incomes. Moreover, if the inflation is one of costs rather than prices, profit margins will be squeezed. Conversely, inflation caused by excess demand may lead to an increase in profit margins.

The most damaging aspect of inflation from the business point of view is that it makes planning for the future difficult. Assessing future investment projects is made more complicated by uncertainty about future prices. Budgetting of future spending is also more difficult. Making provision for the replacement of equipment as it wears out is more difficult when the replacement cost is higher than the initial (or historic) cost.

All economists accept that it is within governments' power to reduce inflation. The chosen solution, however, reflects the government's analysis of the cause of inflation, but all techniques to remedy the condition cause pain and discomfort to the patient. The most common form of policy to tackle cost push inflation was **incomes policy** and this was a feature of pre-Thatcher Britain. Here the aim was to secure agreement with both sides of industry to moderate pay and price rises. The ideal was that wages should rise by no more than productivity which meant that they were self-financing. Most incomes policies were successful in the short run, but disintegrated after three years. Even supporters of incomes policy accept that it only works with union co-operation. Critics argue that it fails to deal with the root cause of inflation and has the effect of distorting market forces. Wage differences (which tend to be reduced by incomes policy) are seen as essential for shifting labour from declining and into expanding firms and industries.

The Keynesian solution to demand pull inflation is deflation by means of cuts in government spending, increases in taxation and a rise in interest rates. The process is painful to businesses whose sales decline and to workers who are made redundant. The Monetarist solution is to control the growth of the money supply. In the early 1980s this meant reduction in government spending to eliminate the Government's borrowing requirement. The link between borrowing and the money supply is that governments in effect 'print money' to finance excess spending. By the late 1980s the government deficit was eliminated but inflation rates rose because of excessive private sector borrowing. Interest rates were raised to reduce borrowing from banks. Once again, the medicine harms the patient. High interest rates discourage investment, therefore, firms selling in the industrial goods markets find orders less forthcoming. As far as consumers are concerned there is little evidence that people are deterred from borrowing by high interest rates. However, a higher mortgage rate results in a decline in discretionary income and therefore in spending. Tight control over the money supply reduces spending and forces firms

to control costs. Failure to do so will lead to insolvency and closure. Monetarists argue that, although it leads to short-term misery, inflation is more damaging in the long run.

Business taxation

Business organisations are affected by taxation in one of a number of ways:

1 by reducing profits available for reinvestment and distribution to shareholders;
2 by reducing willingness as well as ability to expand;
3 by raising the price of goods, thereby causing a contraction of demand;
4 by reducing disposable incomes and therefore consumer spending.

The Thatcher Government has pursued a policy of reducing taxation, especially direct tax. These taxes on wealth and income act as a disincentive to enterprise and effort. As well as reducing income tax (especially the higher rates of income tax), the Thatcher Government has reduced the burden of **Corporation Tax**. This is a tax on company profits (the profits of sole traders are subject to personal income tax) and clearly reduces their ability and willingness of firms to re-invest profits.

A rise in tax on companies will add to their business costs, and a rise in tax on incomes and spending will reduce demand. In both cases industry will have to be more competitive to survive.

In the reform of local taxation, attention has been focussed on the introduction of the **Community Charge** to replace the Domestic Rate. The Community Charge is imposed on individuals and will reduce disposable and discretionary income. Business rates will remain, but will be fixed nationally as the National Non-Domestic Rate. As the rating system was much resented by the business community and led to firms favouring low-rated areas, the National Rate may work to the advantage of firms established in otherwise high spending local authority areas. The new business rate is nationally set (protecting businesses from high spending local authorities) *but* the revaluation of property has increased the rate burden on many businesses. The greatest increases in rateable value have been on businesses in the South of England. In effect, the new business rate will redistribute income from the south to the north of the country.

Taxes on spending are known as **indirect** taxes. Value Added Tax is a broad-based tax covering most goods and services. As an *ad valorem* tax, its rate is fixed as a percentage of the value of goods. The specific taxes on petrol, tobacco and alcohol are related not to value but to a physical measure such as weight. The effect of both is to raise the price of goods to consumers.

The other taxes that affect business are:
- Capital Gains Tax which is a tax on the capital gain from selling shares, land and buildings;
- Inheritance Tax which is a tax on transfers of wealth at death. This tax could pose a problem for the sole trader business.
- North Sea Taxes (royalties and the Petroleum Revenue Tax) are taxes on exploitation of North Sea Oil reserves; and
- National Insurance Employers Contribution which is, in effect, a payroll tax.

Economic growth

Economic growth has been an objective of government economic policy since the Second World War, although policies to promote growth have frequently been sacrificed in order to combat inflation and/or correct a balance of payments deficit. Until recently the desirability of growth was not questioned: politicians and economists might argue about how to achieve growth and how the fruits of growth are to be distributed, but most people accepted its desirability.

Growth involves an increase in output per head and, therefore, provides the means to achieve higher living standards for all. Growth is attractive to both Conservative and moderate Labour governments since it opens up the prospect of reducing (and even eliminating) absolute poverty without the necessity of income redistribution. This preference for growth rather than redistribution is even greater under the Thatcher Government. Income redistribution leading to a reduction in inequality is seen by Mrs Thatcher as undermining the incentives which are considered necessary to encourage hard work and enterprise. The final argument for growth is that it is the only way to increase the provision of public services (such as the NHS) without placing a heavy burden of taxation on the private sector.

Economic growth is obviously beneficial to private sector firms. New market opportunities will be created in an expanding economy. This provides scope for the birth of new firms as well as the expansion of existing ones. However, although market opportunities are greater in a growing economy compared with a stagnating one, there are no 'easy' or 'soft' markets. In a dynamic economy the market is continuously changing. Entrepreneurship is about identifying and responding to changing market opportunities.

The main debate about growth has tended to be about Britain's disappointingly slow rate of growth and how it is to be raised. Labour has traditionally favoured interventionalist policies to raise the rate of growth. These involve direct government investment and government channelling of private sector investment. The Labour Party in the 1970s proposed to nationalise major High Street Banks to ensure that sufficient funds were available for investment. This reflected a widespread belief by the 'Left' that city institutions have consistently 'failed the nation'. The Conservative Party under Mrs Thatcher rejected the state involvement that was a feature of earlier Conservative governments and favoured a policy of freeing the private sector from regulation and opening up the market to competitive forces. It is argued that private enterprise firms do not require government assistance but they require government regulation even less. Hence, alongside the policy of privatisation there has been a steady dismantling of controls.

The Green Movement has challenged the belief in growth. Greens argue that all existing parties from Conservative to Communist have one policy objective in common: the achievement of economic growth. Greens believe that growth which causes external costs (such as pollution) or threatens the precious natural resources of the planet has to be controlled in the interests of future generations. Even though the Green Party is only a minor party in British politics, many of the concerns of the ecology movement are shared by the wider public. Socially responsible private sector firms will have to adjust to a public which is increasingly concerned about their activities.

Conclusion

They say that if you laid all economists end to end you still would not reach a conclusion. President Roosevelt despaired of his economic advisors: 'Bring me a one-armed economist', he said, 'I am fed up with them saying on the one hand this and on the other that.'

The fact is that economics is not a precise science (and modern economists have the modesty to admit it). All economic forecasting is based on certain assumptions about environment and the behaviour of the participants in the economy. If those assumptions are incorrect the forecast will be incorrect. However, that does not mean we should give up trying to understand what is happening in the market and what can be expected in the future.

It is said that economics is too abstract and theoretical for the practical world of business. Now, it has to be admitted that price reductions do not always lead to increased sales in the way suggested by the downward sloping demand curve. Factors other than prices and incomes do influence behaviour. However, despite all its shortcomings, economics does provide us with an analytical framework by which we can understand and interpret the myriad of individual events in the market at both a macro and a micro level. The difficulties of predicting trends should not discourage us from the attempt.

CASE STUDY 1
A downturn in advertising

The Guardian (3.11.89) reported that the advertising industry was experiencing its first major reversal in its fortunes for a decade. The decline in consumer spending, the consequence of high mortgage rates, was now starting to affect advertising expenditure.

The downturn is likely to affect both the advertising agencies and the media that carries advertising. For instance, although newspaper advertising rose by 0.7 per cent overall in the first half of 1989, there was a five per cent reduction in advertising in Sunday newspapers. This was at a time when at least two new Sunday papers (*Sunday Correspondent* and *Sunday Independent*) were being planned.

One problem faced by both agencies and the media is that a high proportion of costs is fixed with labour (especially creative labour) taking up 60 per cent of agency costs. Although staff can be dispensed with (subject to the constraints of Employment Law) a reduction in staff could lead to a damaging loss of talent and therefore competitiveness. To remain as a major force in advertising a pool of creative staff with complementary talent is essential.

The problem is especially acute in the case of ITV companies which face the problem of a proliferation of television channels competing for advertising revenue. Moreover, with ITV franchises up for renewal in 1992, it is important to retain a creative staff rather than losing them to rivals for the regional franchises. Conversely, the Government's preference for auctioning franchises to the highest bidder (subject to guarantees on quality) places a premium on cost-cutting.

In both cases the dilemma is whether to cut costs to maintain short-term profitability or retain staff for the future.

1 Why should high mortgage rates affect:
   (*a*) consumer spending; and
   (*b*) spending by advertisers?
2 What do advertising agencies do?
3 Why is advertising revenue so important to newspapers?
4 What are the 'constraints of Employment Law'?
5 Why is the proliferation of TV a problem for:
   (*a*) the ITV companies; and
   (b) firms which advertise?
6 Why does the proposed franchise auction place a premium on cost-cutting?
7 Why are labour costs so high in advertising?

EXERCISE ● ● ●

● 1   The following demand schedule refers to product X.

Price	Quantity demanded per week
£10	2000
£11	1900
£12	1800
£13	1700
£14	1600
£15	1500
£16	1400
£17	1300
£18	1200
£19	1100
£20	1000

(a) Calculate price elasticity of demand as price
   (i) rises from £10 to £11
   (ii) falls from £20 to £19.
(b) At what price is revenue maximised?
(c) Over what price range is demand
   (i) elastic; and
   (ii) inelastic?
(d) It is noticed that following the reduction in the price of X from £20 to £19 the demand for product Y rises from 10 000 to 12 000 per week. Calculate the cross elasticity of demand. What can we conclude about the two products?
(e) Following a rise in real income, the demand for X at price £20 increases from 1000 to 1500 per week. If income elasticity of demand for X is 7, by what proportion has real income increased?

● 2 Study the article from *Farmers Weekly* and answer the questions that follow:

Big drop forecast in oilseed rape prices

OILSEED rape ex-farm prices will drop by £40 or £50 at next year's harvest, predicts Plant Breeding International's Mike Bearman.

Speaking at an oilseed rape conference organised by the Assocation of Applied Biology, Mr Bearman said that if all estimated plantings this autumn come to harvest with average yields, the 1990 crop could be as much as 5.5m tonnes. For every 1% of production over the maximum guarantee quantity – currently 4.5m tonnes – there is a 0.5% cut in the target price.

Such a price reduction would, said Mr Bearman, lead to "seesawing" once again, in which 1991 oilseed rape plantings may come down to 1988 levels and the whole low price, low plantings – high price, high plantings cycle begins again.

He hoped that the introduction of double-low varieties, leading to higher inclusion rates into animal feed and therefore increased usage, would persuade the EC to fix a higher MGQ in the future.

"Unfortunately the entrance of Spain and Portugal into the EC will lead to increasing interest in sunflower seed production," he said. "With the EC policy of helping the smaller and less affluent farmer, we may see pressure on the budget for sunflowers in the south – and against oilseed rape production in northern Europe."

Mr Bearman stressed that the industry's survival depended on oilseed rape being economically viable for the grower. "The price of oilseed rape has increased to 2.5 times that of wheat. That appears to be the ratio which the grower needs to compensate for the additional risks and costs incurred in growing a crop of rapeseed rather than wheat."

As soon as the gross margin of oilseed rape dropped to that of wheat, growers would switch back to cereals, he warned. "It has to be recognised that rapeseed is more risky to grow and more difficult to manipulate than cereals."

(Source: *Farmers Weekly*, 22 December 1989)

(a) Draw a sketch supply and demand graph to illustrate the effect of an unexpected good harvest on prices.

(b) Explain the following terms:
   (i) yield;
   (ii) maximum guarantee quantity;
   (iii) target price.

(c) In what way are sunflowers competitors to oilseed rape?

(d) Explain the 'low price, low plantings – high price, high plantings cycle'.

(e) Why is it important for farmers to receive a higher price for oilseed rape than for wheat?

3   Study the article on inflation from *The Guardian* and answer the questions that follow.

Warning over inflation battle

Larry Elliott
Economics Correspondent

THE GOVERNMENT was warned yesterday that a heavy-handed approach to curbing inflation could jeopardise Britain's chances of exploiting the opportunities provided by the creation of a barrier-free Europe in 1992.

The message from the influential backbench Treasury and Civil Service Committee came as the latest official figures provided further evidence of the economy grinding to a halt.

According to the Central Statistical Office, gross domestic product rose by 0.5 per cent in the third quarter of this year, but almost all the increase resulted from the recovery in North Sea oil production after the series of pipeline accidents in 1988 and early 1989.

Essentially, the economy was flat over the past six months, with the annual growth rate in the year to the third quarter 1.9 per cent, compared with 2.7 per cent in the year to the second quarter and 4.1 per cent at this time last year.

Meanwhile, money supply figures from the Bank of England showed that borrowing increased by £4.9 billion in November, the smallest monthly rise since February 1988.

In September, bank lending rose by more than £10 billion, but this fell to £5.2 billion in October. Mr John Shepperd, analyst with Warburg Securities said firms may have started to destock rather than continue borrowing at high rates of interest.

That would cause a sharp slowdown in the economy next year, but could also herald an improvement in the UK's record trade deficit. "The feeling in the market is that there could be a good trade figure in store," Mr Shepperd said.

The considerable scope for destocking – the main cause of the recession of the early 1980s – was highlighted by the CSO, which said industry had been building up inventories of unsold goods for two years. Officials estimate that supply has exceeded demand by £7.5 billion since the beginning of 1988.

Although the economy grew by 2 per cent over the year to September, the drain caused by the deterioration in the current account meant national wealth increased by only ½ per cent.

After increasing by 9 per cent in 1989, manufacturing investment is expected to rise by just 1 per cent next year as firms lower their growth expectations in the light of high interest rates and muted consumer demand, according to the CSO's investment intentions survey.

The Government's main fear for the coming year is that the economy will enter a period of stagflation, with minimal growth combined with stubborn inflationary pressures.

In its report on Nigel Lawson's last Budget earlier this year, the TCSC said the Chancellor was walking a tightrope, with inflation on one side and recession on the other. It said yesterday that Mr Major remained in the same predicament as his predecessor.

One important element of inflationary pressure – the level of wage settlements – has shown no signs of abating in recent months, according to the Confederation of British Industry's pay databank. Deals in manufacturing industry struck in the third quarter averaged 8.3 per cent, up from 7.6 per cent in the second quarter.

The TCSC was sceptical about the Treasury's forecast of inflation dropping to 3 per cent by 1992 given that official predictions have been wrong so often in the past. "Repetition in the face of failure has not added credibility to this forecast," the report noted drily.

It added that control of inflation was necessary, but it was important that "a reduction of a few percentage points in the headline inflation rate should not be achieved at a disproportionate cost in terms of income creation and employment."

(Source: *The Guardian*, 21 December 1989)

(*a*) Define and explain the following terms:
  (i) inflation;
  (ii) growth;
  (iii) money supply;
  (iv) trade deficit;
  (v) stagflation;
  (vi) recession.
(*b*) What is meant by 'destocking' and why was it the cause of the recession in the early 1980s?
(*c*) Why is investment expected 'to rise by just 1%?'

(*d*) Why is stagflation the Government's main fear? Why is it so difficult to solve?

(*e*) Why is the sharp 'slowdown' likely to 'herald an improvement in the UK's record trade deficit'?

(*f*) What is the significance of:
   (i) the October fall in bank lending?
   (ii) the level of wage settlements?

(*g*) If predictions have been wrong in the past, why continue with the practice?

4 Read the passage below which has been abridged from an article in *The Guardian* by Clive Woodstock, 2nd January 1989, and answer the following questions.

Prospects for small firms

'Expansion of the service sector has been a major factor in the growth of self-employment and the small business sector over the past decade, but the future for the small enterprise ... may be uncertain in the Nineties ... much of the growth (of small firms has been) among companies which supply and serve other businesses, reflecting both the growth of the economy and greater sub-contracting of services ...

The question now is whether the small enterprise element in the service sector can be maintained or increased ... Professor James Curran suggests that although service firms comprise the overwhelming majority of small businesses and underwent rapid growth in the Eighties, the economic structure of the Nineties may not provide an environment conducive to further expansion.

There may well be a rise in industrial concentration in the service sector as markets and products mature ... In areas where the service sector becomes more capital-intensive and where the product can be standardised, the smaller enterprise may be at a disadvantage in comparison with larger firms which have adopted new technologies ... systems with high fixed costs may not be open to the smaller firm, affecting their ability to compete and raising further barriers to entry for new firms ...

If the growth rate of the service sector slows during the Nineties, which could well happen after the dramatic expansion of recent years, the trend is likely to be towards restructuring and concentration.

Large capital will be looking for new and profitable markets, squeezing the smaller independents and absorbing them. Where cost reductions can be achieved in the provision of a service through use of new technology, small service firms could again come under pressure ...

(On the other hand) small service operators benefit in many areas from relatively low barriers to entry and where markets are fragmented ... Either way the smaller enterprise in the service sector faces turbulence in the Nineties which is likely once again to test its resilience'.

(*a*) Define and explain the following terms:
service sector; industrial concentration; capital intensive; restructuring.

(*b*) Explain why the height of 'barriers to entry' and the extent to which 'markets are fragmented' affects the size of the small business sector. Suggest some 'barriers to entry' into markets.

(*c*) What is meant by fixed costs and why do high fixed costs affect the ability of small firms to compete?

(*d*) Why do firms sub-contract out some services?

(*e*) In your own words explain the meaning of the last sentence.

5 The account that follows deals with a hypothetical industrial country. Read the account and answer the questions.

'The economy is currently experiencing a boom in production. Order books in the manufacturing sector are fuller than they have been for a decade with capacity utilisation at 88%, the highest since the boom of the late 1960s.

Domestic demand will receive a further stimulus as the tax reductions announced in the budget 'feed through' as increased disposable income. Household consumption will increase adding to the problems of satisfying demand. Investment will also be at a high level given the present high capacity utilisation and the profitability of investment. The yield on real capital investment is expected to be greater than that on financial investment.

Manufacturing companies are having to resort to additional shift working and overtime. Nevertheless, delivery times are lengthening. It is likely that these supply-side bottlenecks will lead to a slowing down in the growth of real output towards the end of the year. The other retarding influence will be the worldwide tightening of monetary policy which will reduce overseas demand for the country's exports'.

(a) Define the following terms:
     boom; capacity utilisation; disposable income; real capital investment; supply-side bottlenecks; monetary policy; real output.
(b) What evidence is there of upward pressure on prices?
(c) We are told that capacity utilisation is 88 per cent, suggesting some spare capacity. Explain why delivery times are lengthening.
(d) Analyse the consequences of the tax reductions from a Keynesian perspective.
(e) In your own words, explain why investment is likely to be at a high level.
(f) Give two reasons why exports could decline.

6 The following account is taken from an article by Ben Laurance and published in *The Guardian* (27th May 1989). Read the account and answer the following questions.

'Retailers are feeling the pinch. Just as the growth in consumer spending is slowing . . . retailers find themselves searching for customers to fill acres of new shopping space. Their costs are rising. The consumer boom is over. Shopkeepers are in a squeeze . . .

The problem is not that retail sales are falling . . . (but) that retailers were spoiled by the consumer boom which preceded the current squeeze . . .

Rents are a big worry. Between 1980 and 1986, the annual growth in shop rents rarely topped 10%. In 1987, they took off and last year the annual increase topped 40% . . . Rents are typically reviewed every five years. So while 1989 may see modest increases in rental rates, companies whose rents are reviewed this year face likely demands for large increases from freeholders trying to make up ground lost during the 1987–88 rental boom. Those huge increases will take a long time to work through the system: bad news for retailers such as Storehouse which trade largely from rented premises; less of a worry for the likes of Marks and Spencer which owns the freehold on most of its shops . . .

. . . The very nature of the shopkeeping business makes it highly operationally geared: a 10% rise in sales can be handled from the same selling area and using much about the same staff; profits go up by much more than 10%. The reverse is equally true: any sales fall has a disproportionate effect on the retailers return . . .

Britain's big high street chains are still struggling to throw off the legacy of three years of unbridled sales growth. When times were good, they dreamed up big and expensive store opening programmes. Those programmes are now coming to fruition. And although retailers now want to trim plans for future expansion, store opening programmes are like supertankers: they take a long time to get going but, once under way, they are hard to stop.'

(*a*) What is meant by:
    (i) consumer boom;
    (ii) 'the current squeeze';
    (iii) freeholders.
(*b*) Why do retailers choose to rent premises? What are the advantages and disadvantages of adopting the Marks and Spencer practice?
(*c*) Are there any advantages in favour of an annual review of rents?
(*d*) The article suggests that the five-year review can work against the retailer. Can you describe a situation in which it works to the benefit of retailers?
(*e*) Using your own words explain what is meant by 'highly operationally geared'.
(*f*) What conclusions can be drawn from the final paragraph about investment in large shopping centres.

7   Read the article below, taken from the *Financial Times* and answer the following questions.

BRITISH INDUSTRY was warned yesterday not to let "gloom-mongers" talk the economy into recession in 1990.

Sir Trevor Holdsworth, president of the Confederation of British Industry, acknowledged in his new year message that 1990 had been "designated a difficult year" but argued that there was "every ground for optimism."

He urged companies to invest in new capacity, innovation, the infrastructure "and above all in people" to ensure that gains in manufacturing productivity, the investment boom and the "cautious buoyancy" of exports all continued.

"The risks of confusing speculation with ownership and financial engineering with the real thing have never been greater. The UK is the foremost takeover target in Europe and the 1990s will belong to those who take the long view – not those looking for near-instant returns."

Only if British industry kept up the momentum of investment would it overcome the trade deficit and the "unacceptably high" level of inflation.

Sir Trevor called on companies, particularly small ones, to seek more export opportunities. He also urged the Government to ensure "a level playing field" for British business to compete on equal terms with its trading partners and rivals. "Subsidies are not the answer, nor is protectionism. Competition is the spur."

● In his new year message, Mr Peter Morgan, director general of the Institute of Directors, said he did not anticipate recession. "We expect economic activity to be no lower than in 1989, and we are confident businesses will take advantage of the many continuing growth sectors of the economy, particularly the improving climate for exports."

He also reiterated the IoD's call for tax cuts for businesses and individuals.

(Source: *Financial Times*, 30 December 1989)

(*a*) What is the Confederation of British Industry? What does it seek to do?
(*b*) Explain the following terms:
    (i) innovation;
    (ii) infrastructure;
    (iii) productivity;
    (iv) investment.
(*c*) What does Sir Trevor Holdsworth mean by confusing 'speculation with ownership and financial engineering with the real thing . . .'?
(*d*) Why is investment necessary to overcome the problems of a trade deficit and inflation?
(*e*) What does Sir Trevor mean by a 'level playing field'? Why is competition rather than subsidies or protection the answer?

(*f*) Why does the Institute of Directors favour tax cuts?

(*g*) Both the statements of Sir Trevor Holdsworth and Mr Morgan concern expectations. Why are expectations of the future so important in business?

8 The data below refers to the highest marginal tax rates paid by individuals and companies in eight major western industrial economies. In 1979 for instance those on the highest incomes in the UK paid 83 pence in every additional £1 of income above a specified level of income.

Top tax rates	Personal %		Corporate %	
Country	1979	1989	1979	1989
UK	83	40	52	35
Italy	72	50	36	36
USA	70	28	46	34
France	60	57	50	39
Australia	60	50	46	39
Japan	75	50	40	42
West Germany	56	53	56	56
Canada	43	29	46	28

(Source OECD)

(*a*) Using only the data above, can we conclude that the UK was the most highly taxed economy of the eight listed?

(*b*) Account for the widespread trend towards lower taxation.

(*c*) What are the benefits of lower taxation?

(*d*) Suggest three ways in which lower government spending (necessitated by lower taxation) harms business enterprise.

(*e*) Is there a correlation between tax rates and economic success?

(*f*) How will multinational companies react to the differences in corporate tax rates?

EXAMINATION QUESTIONS ■ ■ ■

■ 1   The extract below is taken from *The Times*, 19 November 1986. Read the extract and answer the questions that follow.

'RATE OF INFLATION RISES FOR FIRST TIME THIS YEAR'
(By David Smith, Economics Correspondent)

'The rate of inflation rose to 3 per cent last month, from 2.4 per cent in August. This was the first rise in the inflation rate this year, and the sharpest underlying increase for more than a year.'

'A big rise in petrol prices, dearer clothing and footwear, and higher prices for draught beer and a range of other products, pushed the retail price index up by 0.5 per cent last month.'

'. . . Excluding Budget price increases, Department of Employment officials said, last month's rise was the biggest underlying increase since May last year.'

'. . . Britain's inflation rate of 3 per cent last month compared with latest rates of 2 per cent in France, 1.6 per cent in the US, −0.2 per cent in Japan and −0.4 per cent in West Germany.'

(a) Given that the Retail Price Index stood at 385.9 in August 1986 and the inflation rate rose by 0.5 per cent in the month, calculate the Index for September 1986.

(b) Produce a bar chart to illustrate the inflation rates for the 5 countries mentioned in the article.

(c) What is happening to prices in
    (i) Japan; and
    (ii) the United States?

(d)   (i) Assess **two** ways in which inflation may be said to adversely affect a firm.
       (ii) Assess **two** ways in which inflation may be said to favourably affect a firm.

(e) Suggest **two** policy measures the Government could use to control inflation which would affect the demand for a firm's products.

(AEB, November 1988)

■ 2   (a) 'Marketing managers need to know about elasticity'. Why?
       (b) If the Bank of England introduced tighter monetary policy, what, in your opinion, would be the consequences of this for a firm producing video machines.

(Cambridge, June 1985)

■ 3   The Chancellor of the Exchequer in his *Budget*, proposes that tax *thresholds* should be lifted, rather than reductions made in *personal tax rates* for higher income earners.
       (a) What do the italicised terms mean?
       (b) How might a personnel manager evaluate these changes?
       (c) How would the marketing manager of a package holiday firm expect these changes to affect his business?

(Cambridge, June 1987)

■ 4   Examine the consequences for different businesses of the Uniform Business Rate introduced in 1990.

■ 5   'We will reduce the level of direct taxation and so increase the incentive to work' (Prime Minister: the General Election 1983). Do you think such a policy would achieve its objective?

(Cambridge, June 1985)

■ 6 Business benefits more by the removal of restrictions on enterprise than from cash subsidies and protection. Discuss.

■ 7 Examine how an enterprise might alter its plan if a prolonged period of heavy unemployment is predicted.

(AEB, June 1988)

■ 8 Discuss how economic and other constraints might influence the exploration and development policy of an oil company.

(Cambridge, June 1989)

■ 9 (a) Briefly explain how you would measure the rate of inflation.
  (b) Discuss the likely consequences for your company, a UK-based washing machine manufacturer, of a significant increase in the rate of inflation.
  (c) What policy measures might you expect a company retailing your products to adopt in reaction to this change?

(Cambridge, June 1988)

FURTHER READING

THE ECONOMIC ENVIRONMENT

D R MYDDELTON *The Economy and Business Decisions* (Longman)

A NEALE AND C HASLAM *Economics in a Business Context* (Van Nostrand Reinhold)

C HARBURY AND R LIPSEY *An Introduction to the UK Economy* (Pitman)

J F PICKERING AND T A J COCKERILL *The Economic Management of the Firm* (Philip Allan)

D SMITH *Mrs Thatcher's Economics* (Heinemann)

N BRANTON AND J M LIVINGSTONE *Managerial Economics in Practice* (Hodder & Stoughton)

N WALL *Controlling the Economy* (Collins)

F LIVESEY *Economics for Business Decisions* (Pitman)

CHAPTER 5
The Presentation and Processing of Data

There are substantial differences in the statistics content of 'A' Level Business Studies syllabuses. This chapter does not attempt to cover the whole field of quantitative methods. Instead, it outlines the methods of presenting data and introduces the student to some ways of processing the data.

OBJECTIVES

1 To become familiar with the terminology of statistics.
2 To investigate sampling methods.
3 To understand appropriate ways of presenting data.
4 To be able to interpret data.
5 To provide an introduction to normal distribution.

Introduction to Statistics

Statistical analysis involves:

1 the selection, collection and organising of basic facts into meaningful data;
2 the summarising of essential features and relationships of the data; in order to
3 determine patterns of behaviour, outcomes or future tendencies.

In the business context, data is used for decision-making (e.g. marketing research data is used in decisions about product, price, distribution and promotion), planning (data collection is a pre-requisite of planning for the future) and control (data on the production of defective items is essential to controlling quality).

Data collected and used in its original purpose is known as **primary** data. It becomes **secondary** data when it is used for a purpose other than that for which it was collected. Data relating to output and sales can be obtained from written records, and other data is obtained by observation (e.g. work study data) or by surveys (data on people's preferences). To reduce the cost of the exercise it is common to collect data from a sample of the total number of units under investigation. If we use a sample we have to decide (*a*) how the sample is chosen, and (*b*) how many units should be included. The sample has to be representative of the 'population' as a whole and should be sufficient in size to enable us to draw conclusions. The methods of choosing samples are summarised in Table IV.

The information that is collected has to be organised to enable us to make sense of it. Frequency is the number of times an occurrence happens and it can be shown in table form or by graphical representation. There are three important features of any distribution of frequency:

1 measure of central tendency (i.e. average)
2 measure of dispersion (the spread of the data)
3 skewness (lopsidedness)

Averages are summarised in Table V.

Table IV Types of sample

Type	Definition	Type	Definition
Random	Each item/person has an equal chance of being included.	**Cluster**	The population is divided up into clusters. Sampling takes place only within the selected cluster.
Systematic	Every nth. person/item.	**Multi-stage**	Random sampling of sub-units. When primary sample is completed it may be necessary to sub-divide further for more random samples.
Stratified	People/items divided into strata (mutually exclusive sub-groups). Within each stratum a sample is chosen. The purpose is to ensure that each sub-group is represented.		
Quota	A quota of people with specific characteristics is included in the sample.	**Sequential**	Rules are established for an early stop to interviews (if they are repetitive) or for further interviews for more clarification.

Table V Measures of central tendency (averages)

Type	Definition	Advantages	Disadvantages
Arithmetic mean	Sum of items divided by the number of them.	Uses all the data.	Distorted by an extreme value.
		Further statistical processing possible.	The resulting figure may not be a typical value.
Median	Middle value in order of size.	Not distorted by extremes.	Further statistical processing impossible.
		Can be computed from incomplete data.	
Mode	The most frequently occurring value in a distribution.	Represents a typical value.	Further processing not possible.
		Unaffected by extremes.	Does not use all values.

EXERCISE ● ● ●

● 1   Calculate (*a*) mean, (*b*) mode, and (*c*) median of the following numbers:
12, 15, 8, 25, 12, 32, 31
It is slightly more difficult when we are given a grouped frequency distribution:

Age groups	No. of people	Frequency × midpoint of the class interval
10–14	10	10 × 12 = 120
14–16	20	20 × 15 = 300
16–18	15	15 × 17 = 255
		675

The mean age of the 45 teenagers is 675 ÷ 45 = 15

The median is the value which divides the frequency distribution into equal parts. In the data above it is clearly the 23rd person who is the 14–16 age range. However, where is he/she within the range? If the 20 are evenly spread over the range then this person will be number 13 out of the 20 in the class. Multiply 2 years (the class interval) by 13/20 to get 1.3 years. The median age is 14 plus 1.95 equals 15.95 years.

Table VI   Some measures of dispersion

Measure	Description
Range	Distance from lowest to greatest
Interquartile	The gap between the top point of the bottom 25% and the bottom point of the top 25%
Standard deviation	Dispersion of the items around the mean
Variance	Square of the standard deviation
Mean deviation	Arithmetic mean of the absolute difference of each value from the mean

Presentation of data

After data has been collected it needs to be presented in a form which communicates the information and enables conclusions to be drawn.

As the purpose of the data is to aid decision-making and to report back results (to facilitate control) it is necessary to choose a means of presenting the data in a manner which is clear, accurate and appropriate. The recipient should be able to interpret the material and, therefore, draw conclusions. However, it is essential to look critically at the data, detect its limitations and not 'read into it' facts that are not present.

1 TABLES are a non-graphical way of presenting data. The data has to be processed and classified into specified categories. In the same way that a map must have a scale and a legend (key), a table must be dated, show sources and the measurement unit employed. Tables convey a mass of information accurately but lack the visual impact of graphical representation.

2 BAR CHARTS use bars of standard width (but varying heights) to represent magnitudes. They can be used to illustrate comparisons over time or between items. A compound bar chart divides the bar into sections representing component parts. Bar charts facilitate comparison by a clear visual impact but only relatively straightforward data can be shown. In the case of the compound bar

chart, only a few sub-sections can be shown and even then comparisons are difficult. Bar charts must not be confused with histograms.

3 PIE CHARTS are useful for depicting proportions, although once again there is a limit on the number of items that can be included in an easily-interpreted pie chart. Unless the proportions are written in each section it will be difficult to use a pie chart for anything other than gaining a general impression. To show change over time (as well as proportions) a second pie chart can be drawn. It is important to remember that the total size is illustrated not by the radius or diameter of the pie but its area.

4 PICTOGRAMS use pictures to represent data. Although visual impact is strong, only simple and limited data can be shown.

5 CARTOGRAMS combine a map with graphs, symbols and pie charts to present various data where location is considered important. It is more pictorial than useful.

6 HISTORIOGRAMS (or line graphs) are a useful way of showing relationships such as growth over time. The historiogram gives a sense of continuity which is lacking in a bar chart.

The independent variable (e.g. time) is shown on the horizontal axis while the dependent variable (e.g. output) is on the vertical axis. Historiograms combined with time-series analysis can be used to separate out:

(a) the trend (long-term change);
(b) fluctuations around the trend;
(c) random factors (*see* Fig 5.1).

7 STRATA CHARTS combine a line graph with component sections depicting relative importance.

8 SEMI LOG GRAPHS show rate of change rather than magnitude. If the graph is a straight line the data is changing at a constant percentage rate.

Fig 5.2   'Z' chart depicting sale

9 A 'Z' CHART is depicted in Fig 5.2. Note that, plotted against time, there is:
(a) the original data showing current position (monthly sales)
(b) cumulative total showing the position to date (cumulative monthly total)
(c) the moving annual total showing the trend. The moving annual total is obtained by adding a new month each time to replace a month from the previous year.

10 HISTOGRAMS are at the same time one of the most important graphs for depicting business information and yet widely misunderstood. Histograms display grouped data. The width

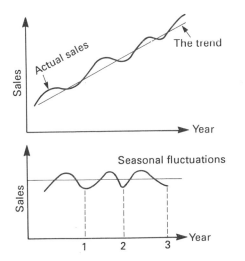

Fig 5.1   Analysis of time series to separate out (a) the trend; (b) fluctuations around the trend; and (c) seasonal fluctuations.

of the bar is proportional to the class interval. The magnitude for a particular class is shown not by the height of the bar but by its area. If class intervals are of equal length the histogram is similar to a bar chart but where class intervals are not equal the histogram is very different. This can be shown in the example below:

Income groups	No. of people	Class interval length	Frequency density per £1000
(£000)	(millions)		(millions)
10–11	1	£1000	1
11–12	2	£1000	2
12–15	6	£3000	2
15–20	5	£5000	1

When we produce a histogram depicting this information, the £12–15,000 group has a bar the same height as the £11–12,000 group. The explanation is simply that the class interval is larger. There are no gaps between histogram bars (*see* Fig 5.3).

If we join up the mid points of the tops of each histogram bar we produce a many-sided figure which is known as a **frequency polygon** (*see* Fig 5.4). When the many sides are 'smoothed out' the result is known as a **frequency curve** which tend to be of six types (*see* Fig 5.5):
- U-shaped
- J-shaped
- horizontal
- positively skewed (to the left)
- negatively skewed (to the right)
- normal

Normal distribution

This occurs in the case of naturally occurring phenomena and can be employed in sampling theory. The main features of normal distribution are:

1 it is continuous, symmetrical and bell-shaped;
2 the tails approach but never touch the horizontal axis;

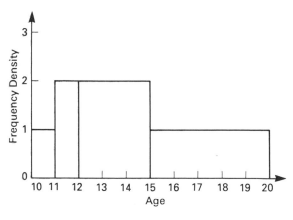

Fig 5.3   A histogram

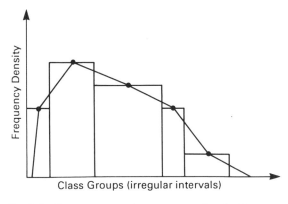

Fig 5.4   Frequency polygon – constructed by joining mid points of histogram blocks.

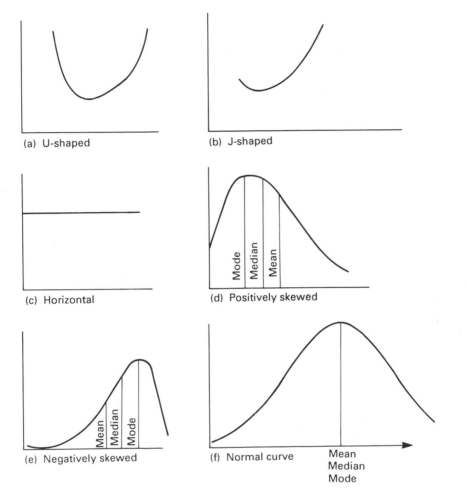

Fig 5.5 Typical frequency curves

3 it is unimodal with mean, mode and median passing through the peak; and

4 the width of the base is equal to six standard deviations. Standard deviation is a measure of the dispersion of values around the arithmetic mean. Normal distribution curves have the important characteristic that:

(*a*) 68 per cent of values are within one standard deviation of mean;

(*b*) 95 per cent are within two standard deviations of mean;

(*c*) 99 per cent are within standard deviations (*see* Fig 5.6).

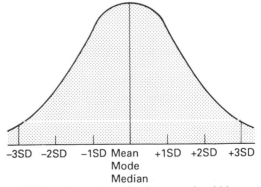

99.5% of the area under the curve is within 3 standard deviations of the mean

Fig 5.6 Curve of normal distribution

EXAMPLE

To see how this principle can be applied consider the following example. A machine is used to pack 'Georgie-Cat' biscuits into packets. The mean weight of the biscuits in each packet is 300 grammes and standard deviation is 10 grammes. What proportion of packs will be:

(a) under 280 grammes; and
(b) over 310 grammes?

Answer (a)

280 grams is 2 standard deviations from the mean (i.e. 300 − 280 ÷ 10). 50 per cent of packets will be above the mean and 47 per cent will be within two standard deviations below the mean. In other words 97 per cent of packets will be heavier than 280 grammes leaving just 3 per cent under 280 grammes.

Answer (b)

310 grammes is 1 SD from the mean. Fifty per cent of packets will be above the mean although 34 per cent will weigh between 300 and 310 grammes. Hence, 16 per cent (50 per cent − 34 per cent) will be heavier than 310 grammes.

Normal distribution can also be applied to the testing of findings from a sample survey. This relates to area of statistical analysis known as binomial distribution which in a large sample size approximates to the normal curve.

EXAMPLE

1000 cat owners were asked if their cats preferred 'Georgie-Cat' biscuits to all similar products on the market. What confidence can we have in the result if 510 expressed a preference for 'Georgie-Cat'?

To answer this question we have to calculate the standard deviation. For a binomial distribution (e.g. a yes/no question) the formula is $\sqrt{npq}$ where

n   is the number in the sample
p   is the probability of one response
q   is the probability of the other response.

In a yes-no question it is to be expected that 50 per cent will answer yes and 50 per cent no.

Therefore, the standard deviation is
$$\sqrt{100 \times \tfrac{1}{2} \times \tfrac{1}{2}} = \sqrt{250} \text{ or approximately 16.}$$
510 is within 1 SD of the mean and we know that 68 per cent of responses will be within 1 SD of the mean. We would have to conclude that 510 is not sufficient to enable us to state with confidence that cats prefer 'Georgie-Cat'.

However, if 532 owners expressed a preference then confidence in the result would be enhanced: 2 SDs from the mean enables us to be 95 per cent confident of the finding. If 550 state a preference then the confidence level rises to 99 per cent. We can be 99 per cent confident that the opinions expressed in the sample reflect the preference of cats (and owners) as a whole.

Index numbers

Index numbers are designed to show average changes in a value (such as price or quantity) over time. The index number itself is a pure number which is given the value of 100 at the starting point (known as the **base year**). Any percentage rise (or fall) over the value at base year is shown by an equivalent movement above (or below) the base figure. This is illustrated in Table VII.

In this index, 1970 was chosen as the base year for both indices. The base year should be carefully chosen since the choice of an unusual year (such as a year of intense slump) will give a distorted figure. The 20 per cent rise in output to 1975 is shown by the index moving to 120. In 1980 the index stands at 150, i.e. 50 per cent over base and 25 per cent over the 1975 figure. We should not be puzzled by the labour index also having 100 as the starting point. This refers to the number of workers employed in the base year. One of the advantages of indices is that it is possible to compare trends in factors measured in unlike units. We can see relatively easily that, although output rose from 100 to 210 (110 per cent), it was achieved with only 50 per cent increase in labour employed. This represents an increase in productivity.

The most famous of all indices measures the trend in prices over time and is known as the

Table VII   Index of output and manpower

	Output (Tonnes)	Index of output	Labour	Index of labour
1970	500 000	100	1000	100
1975	600 000	120	900	90
1980	750 000	150	1280	128
1985	1 000 000	200	1300	130
1990	1 100 000	210	1500	150

Retail Price Index (RPI). Often known as the cost of living index, it shows the inflation rate experienced by the average family in the UK. To calculate the inflation rate it is first necessary to find out how the average family spends its income. The Family Expenditure Survey is a sample survey of the expenditure of 10 000 households and enables statisticians to attach weights to the various items of spending. The weights reflect their relative importance. Clearly a 10 per cent rise in the price of bread has a greater impact on the family finances than 100 per cent rise in the price of matches.

After attaching weights (out of 1000) to 11 categories of goods and services (food, alcohol, tobacco, housing, fuel and lighting, household durables, clothing, transport, services, meals out and miscellaneous goods) the statisticians then take samples to calculate the average price change in each category. We are now in a position to calculate the weighted average price change. In the Table below, the average household buys three categories of goods: food, housing and others. The items absorb different proportions of household spending and their prices rise at different rates. What is its average price rise?

Item	Price Relative	Weighting	Price Rise × Weighting
Food	4%	250	1000
Housing	20%	400	8000
Others	10%	350	3500
		1000	1000⎮12500
			12.5

The crude average of price rises is $4 + 20 + 10 \div 3 = 11.3\%$ but this has not taken relative importance into account. To calculate the weighted average, we multiply price relative (price in the year relative to the price in a previous year) by the weighting. The resulting figures are added together and divided by the total weighting to give a weighted average inflation rate of 12.5 per cent which is then expressed as an index number. The weighted average exceeds the crude average because of the high weighting given to the item that experienced the greatest price increase.

There are statistical problems with the RPI: for instance, it needs continual updating as spending patterns, the range of goods available and the quality of goods change. An index that updates the weights as spending patterns change is known as a **Paasche Index**. One that uses base period weights throughout is known as a **Laspeyre Index**. But the greatest limitation of the RPI is that it tells us only about inflation as it affects the average family. A household which does not conform to the average will experience inflation at different rates.

The RPI is only one price index. There are other indices covering building costs (used in index-linked house insurance), import prices and whole-sale prices (an indication of future inflation).

A note of caution

A great deal of statistical work in the business studies and social science fields attempts to:

1 identify relationships between variables (e.g. a rise in advertising and volume of sales; pay and productivity).
2 identify existing trends as a basis for extrapolation into the future. It is beyond the scope of this book to analyse the techniques involved but Business Studies students should beware of certain pitfalls.

First, consider correlation which is the relationship or association between two variables. There is a negative correlation if one variable rises and the other falls (e.g. price and quantity demanded). There is a positive correlation if both rise or fall (e.g. price and supply). As well as identifying relationships it is also important to discover the line of causation. There is a causal relationship if the rise in one variable causes the rise in the other.

Unfortunately, there are problems in identifying causal relationships. First, the apparent association between the variables may be coincidental: for example, if inward migration of storks is followed by a large number of human births we would be wrong to conclude that one causes the other. Second, causation in the social science field is similar to the 'chicken and the egg'. It is sometimes difficult to identify the cause and effect.

Extrapolation should also be looked at with caution. It is very tempting to believe that the graph showing steady upward trend will continue but it is important to remember the constantly changing environment.

Conclusion

There are some business decisions that are qualitative in nature (consideration of design, selection of a new marketing manager). However, many issues and problems can be expressed numerically. Data is, therefore, the raw material for rational decision-making. The business decision-maker needs a degree of competence in collecting, handling, interpreting and analysing data. We should be able to appreciate both the value and limitation of the data. The analysis will assist the decision-maker in drawing conclusions, making predictions and deciding upon the course of action.

EXERCISE ● ● ●

● 1   The *Financial Times* produces a number of indices of share prices:

- the ordinary index comprises the 30 largest UK manufacturing companies. Their relative sizes are not taken into account.
- the FT-Actuaries Index measures the performance of shares in 734 large UK companies. This is a weighted index which takes market capitalisation into account but is only calculated once a day.
- the FT-SE 100 Index (the 'Footsie') is based on the 100 largest UK companies, all weighted by market capitalisation. The Footsie is calculated every minute and although it contains only 100 companies' shares, experience shows that it closely mirrors the FT Actuaries Index. Consequently, it is seen as suitable for futures and options trading.

(Adapted from FT – SE 100 Stock Index Futures and Options, LIFFE).

(a) What do you understand by:
  (i) market capitalisation
  (ii) a weighted index
  (iii) futures and options trading

(b) Why is the FT Ordinary Index not considered representative?

(c) Why is a minute-by-minute calculation considered important by those trading in futures?

(d) What does 'closely mirrors the FT Actuaries Index' mean and why is it significant?

● 2 Calculate the average inflation rate from the following data based on 1986 weighting.

Item	Weighting	Price rise
Food	185	5%
Alcohol	82	4%
Tobacco	40	4%
Housing	153	8%
Fuel	62	8%
Durable goods	63	3%
Clothing	75	5%
Transport	157	10%
Miscellaneous	81	2%
Services	58	3%
Meals out	44	4%
	1000	

● 3 The data below comes from the Annual Report of British Telecom PLC (June 1987). Using the data:

(a) Construct a histogram showing the number of shareholders for each level of shareholding.

(b) Construct a pie chart to depict the major categories of shareholder.

(c) What conclusions can be drawn about the ownership of BT?

Size of shareholding

	Number of shareholders	Percentage of total	Number of shares held (millions)	Percentage of total
1–399	411 931	29.0	81	1.4
400 – 799	681 853	48.1	312	5.2
800 – 1 599	298 851	21.1	243	4.0
1 600 – 9 999	22 097	1.6	52	0.9
10 000 – 99 999	1 779	0.1	57	1.0
100 000 – 999 999	1 050	0.1	345	5.7
1 000 000 – 999 999 999	343		1 932	32.1
1 000 000 000 and above	1		2 988	49.7
	1 417 905	100.0	6 010	100.0

Classification

	Number of shareholders	Number of shares held (millions)	Percentage of total
HM Government	I	2 988	49.7
Trustees of Employee Share Ownership Scheme	I	57	0.9
Pension funds	1 504	973	16.2
Insurance companies	363	376	6.3
Banks	116	23	0.4
Unit and investment trusts	295	155	2.6
Charities	152	10	0.2
Nominees	2 307	460	7.6
Other corporate bodies	4 934	276	4.6
Individuals	1 408 232	692	11.5
	1 417 905	**6 010**	**100.0**

4 Study the statistics below and answer the questions.

	1	2	3	4
Year	No. of units sold (millions)	Sales value (£m)	Sales – real value (£m)	Profits as % of UK sales
1975	170	160	101	14
1976	159	172	94	13
1977	163	195	91	12
1978	196	250	108	8
1979	187	266	102	0
1980	170	252	82	−2
1981	170	262	75	−3
1982	168	272	72	1
1983	164	289	74	7
1984	177	329	80	4
1985	185	375	85	6
1986	198	425	94	6

(Adapted from J Day in *Business Studies* Magazine, November 1988).
Note units are singles, albums, cassettes and CDs.

(*a*) Calculate the percentage growth in: (*i*) units sold; and (*ii*) value of sales over the years 1975 to 1986.
(*b*) Offer two explanations for the divergence.
(*c*) Account for the changes in 'units sold' by referring to long-term trends and fluctuations around the trend.

(d) What does column three (real value of sales) tell us. How do you account for the rise in the value of sales but fall in real value?

(e) With suggested reasons, comment on the profitability of the record industry.

5 A windscreen replacement firm is trying to decide where to locate a new service centre to cover ten towns and villages in an area linked by a trunk road.

The chart below gives distances in miles from the town at one end of the territory. We are also told the number of call outs to each town per week over the last year during which time they occupied a depot on an industrial estate in Town B.

Town	A	B	C	D	E	F	G	H	I	J
Distance (miles)	0	10	20	30	40	44	48	51	55	60
No. of call outs.	30	10	30	15	15	5	5	6	5	2

(a) One director favours the town closest to the mean distance from Town A. A fellow director favours the town which is the median distance from A.

For each town chosen, calculate the mean distance from this town to all other towns involved.

(b) Taking frequency of calls into account, which town would you nominate as the location for the service centre?

(c) What additional factors should be taken into account?

6 The two pie charts shown below depict revenue received by a record store from the sales of singles, LP records, compact discs and cassettes. In 1989 total sales revenue was £300 000.

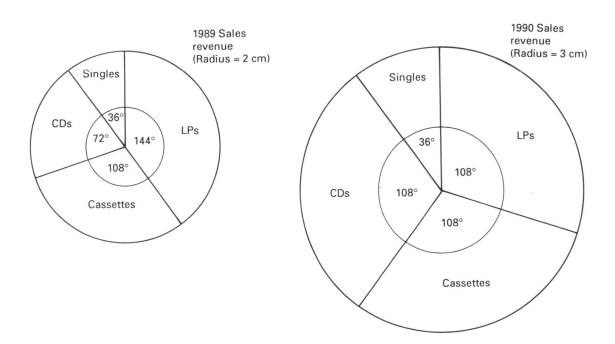

(a) Calculate sales revenue in 1990
    (*Note*: it is not £450 000).
(b) Calculate 1989 revenue from LP records. Did it decline in 1990?
(c) Calculate the percentage rise in revenue from compact discs.

7   A shop which holds 50 units of an item at the start of each week is concerned that this is too high a level of stock. Weekly sales of the item during the past two years have been as follows:

No. of items sold	No. of weeks
1 – 20	6
20 – 30	20
31 – 35	40
36 – 40	35
41 – 50	3
	104 weeks

(a) Identify the modal group and calculate the arithmetic mean and median value of the above distribution.
(b) Assess the appropriateness of the three measures of central tendency in the circumstances.
(c) Construct a histogram to depict the data.
(d) If each item makes a contribution (to fixed costs and profits) of £30, calculate the reduction in annual contribution that would result from maximum stock levels being set at 38 at the start of each week. State the assumptions you have made in arriving at your answer.

8   Four companies A, B, C and D have the same number of employees. From the information below sketch the distribution curves using the same axes for all four:
    ● the distributions of their salaries have the same modes
    ● the distribution for A and B are normal but that for A has half the standard deviation as that for B
    ● the distribution for C is negatively skewed
    ● the distribution for D is positively skewed.

The distribution of A's salaries is shown below:

Salary range (£)	No. of Employees
8 000 – 9 999	40
10 000 – 11 999	260
12 000 – 12 999	500
13 000 – 14 999	100
15 000 – 20 000	100

(a) Estimate the median salary.
(b) Construct a histogram to depict the data.
(c) The mean salary is currently £12 300. If this produces a wage bill 10 per cent higher than the previous year, calculate the mean salary in the earlier year.

9   The owner of a newly opened dry cleaning business commissioned some market research to discover the opinions of local people. They were asked to state the factor influencing their choice of dry cleaners. The results were as follows:

Factor determining choice of dry cleaner	Men	Women
Price	100	150
Opening hours	60	50
Speed of service	150	20
Quality of service	20	100
Range of service	20	50
Convenience of location	100	80
Friendliness of staff	50	50
	500	500

(a) Depict the data by use of an appropriate graphical technique. Justify your choice of graphical technique.

(b) People were then asked if they would use the new dry cleaner rather than rival dry cleaners if hours of opening were extended for the convenience of commuters: 535 out of the sample of 1 000 said they would use the dry cleaner if opening hours were extended. How confident can we be that this confirms with the opinion of the majority?

(c) What other factors should be considered before extending opening hours?

(d) The market research involved a random sample of 500 men and 500 women. Suggest reasons why this sampling technique might produce biased results.

FURTHER READING

QUANTITATIVE METHODS

E T MARTIN AND J R FIRTH *Statistics* (Mitchell Beazley/Northcote)
P HARRISON *Operational Research* (Mitchell Beazley/Northcote)
D GREGORY AND H WARD *Statistics for Business* (McGraw-Hill)
J HARRIS AND JOHN POWELL *Quantitative Decision-Making* (Longman)
B DAVIES AND J FOAD *Statistics for Economics* (Heinemann)
M BARROW *Statistics for Economics, Accounting and Business Studies* (Longman)
M TILLEY *Business Maths and Statistics* (Arnold)
H WRIGHT *Statistics for GCSE* (Pitman).

CHAPTER 6
Marketing

People involved in marketing would argue that it is the marketing function that provides the driving force for integration within the business organisation. If success comes from satisfying the customer then marketing must be the focal point of the whole organisation and all other departments exist to aid the marketing department. Therefore all decisions taken elsewhere are subservient to the marketing function. In this chapter we will look at marketing within the organisation and will discover that it is about serving rather than deceiving the public.

OBJECTIVES

1 To understand the function and the concept of a market-orientated firm.
2 To introduce important marketing concepts.
3 To investigate the life cycle of products and the marketing mix.
4 To understand the need for and methods of market research.
5 To investigate promotional activities.

To the cynic, marketing is an attempt to persuade people to buy goods and services they neither want nor need. This view is not only unfair on those people engaged in marketing, it is also contemptuous of the intelligence of human beings. It would be naive to deny that people are never deceived by marketing techniques, but the marketing philosophy is one of responsiveness to customer needs rather than deception. The fact is that most people can be deceived only once and the responsible and permanently successful business organisation seeks repeat orders by satisfying customers.

Marketing is defined as the management process responsible for identifying, anticipating and satisfying the requirements of customers profitably. This implies that the first task of marketing is to discover customers' current and future needs. Only by finding out the needs of customers can business organisations respond to these needs. The identified needs are satisfied by the provision of goods and services. These should be of the quantity and quality required and at a price and location satisfactory to customers. Consider two very different firms. One firm produces a product and then starts to consider how to sell it to customers. This can be called a product-orientated firm because it puts the product first and the customer last – this is not sound marketing. The other firm is market or customer-orientated. It discovers what customers want and develops products with the customer in mind. The customer, whose needs are always changing, is central to the firm's decision-making. The marketing department is not relegated to selling what the factory produces but is seen as the focal point of the firm's activities.

It is a fallacy to equate marketing with either advertising or selling. These activities are merely parts of the marketing function which can be broken down into the following components:

1 MARKET RESEARCH: identifying customer needs;
2 PRODUCT PLANNING AND DEVELOPMENT:

creating products to satisfy these needs;

3 PRICING: determining the value placed on the product by customers;

4 DISTRIBUTION: the movement of the product to customers;

5 PROMOTION: an exercise in communications which includes advertising and selling.

Before we look in more detail at these marketing activities, it is necessary to understand two basic concepts in marketing: the product life cycle and the marketing mix.

Product life cycle

A basic fact of business life is that all products (including services) pass through a number of phases from introduction, through growth and maturity, to decline and eventual elimination. We can draw the following analogy from the human life cycle:

Product	Human beings
Origination of an idea	Conception
Development	Gestation
Launch	Birth
Growth	Childhood and adolesence
Maturity	Mature adulthood
Saturation	Middle age
Decline	Old age
Elimination or product rationalisation	Death

The analogy can be carried further. In the development phase, success is far from certain. In fact, many products suffer a 'miscarriage' or abortion and, therefore, do not reach the launch phase. Even after lunch, the product, like the infant, is vulnerable and may suffer early elimination. There is no standard life (in years) of products. In the case of a 'pop' single record the cycle is usually complete within four months, whereas other products experience a long life. The

Mini car celebrated its thirtieth birthday in 1989 and products such as Coca Cola and Corn Flakes have also enjoyed a long life. There is another way in which products differ from the human life cycle: the elixir of life can be applied to products to extend their life. The rejuvenation process involves a change in the product, its packaging or the way in which it is promoted.

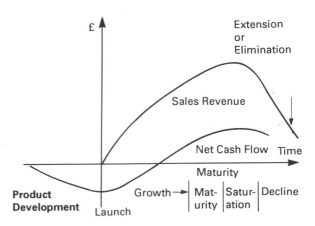

Fig 6.1   Phases of the product life cycle

The cycle is depicted in the Fig 6.1. Note that the sales revenue line (plotted on the assumption that price remains constant) shows growth from launch and only subsides in old age. The net cash flow line is initially negative, reflecting:

- heavy expenditure on developing and promoting the product;
- the absence of scale economics in production.

As sales grow, the product makes a net contribution to the firm. This is eroded in the decline phase, prompting the elimination of the product.

Product development

Innovation is necessary for the continued success of the firm. No matter how successful its products are at present, they will eventually enter a period of decline. New products are essential to replace declining products and, given the long period needed to develop products (five years for a new car, ten years or more for some pharmaceutical products) it is important to have new products in the pipeline.

Research is normally divided into **pure research**, motivated by curiosity, and **applied research**. Pure research sometimes results in commercial products, e.g. teflon saucepans as a by-product of space research, but this is not the main purpose. Business organisations are unlikely to put resources into pure research, preferring problem-orientated research with a view to commercial exploitation. Out of research comes ideas and inventions. But they have to be translated into useable and commercially viable products. This process is known as **development**.

A third stage in the creation of new products is **design**. Functional design is concerned with the structure and operation of the product (does it work? is it suitable for its purpose?). Formal design concerns the appearance of the product (is it appealing?). The designer's problem is to reconcile the functional requirements with formal requirements. Products which are attractive will not enjoy continuing success unless they serve the need for which they were intended. Similarly, a product which is functionally sound will fail if customers are repelled by its appearance. The relative importance of the two aspects of design varies from product to product. At the fashion end of the clothing market, formal design is crucially important (although the product must also be functionally sound). However, when designing machinery for factory use, appearance is far less important than the performance of the product. Motor cars are purchased partly on performance (speed, fuel consumption, reliability) and partly on appearance.

Customer requirements will be uppermost in the mind of product developers and designers. A judgement has to be made as to what is an unnecessary 'extra' facility and what is crucial in gaining customer acceptance. Many motorists regard a car radio as an essential feature of a car whereas the more economically minded motorist regards rear windscreen wipers or headlight wipers as an unimportant luxury with

which they could dispense. An analytical technique to aid decision-making in this respect is known as **value analysis**. The aim is to optimise the value of the product to the customer. The vital question to ask is whether the same result can be achieved more effectively or as effectively but at a lower cost. Consider a product assembled from a number of components. Suppose the finished product (e.g. a washing machine) has an expected life of 15 years but that one of its components will last for 50 years. We might be tempted to see this as evidence of good design and craftsmanship but it is not desirable commercially. The component is too good. If a less costly component with a shorter life is available it should be used. There is no point in producing components which outlive the overall product. Despite widespread criticisms of so-called 'built-in obsolescence' the fact is that many consumers will want to replace furniture or kitchen equipment after ten or twenty years. They do not always want goods that last forever and, consequently, the substitution of an expensive material by a cheaper (but less durable) alternative is not necessarily cynical exploitation of the consumer but can be sound marketing, responding to the needs of consumers.

In development and design there is a third criteria to satisfy. This concerns economy of manufacture and ease of storage and distribution. A product which is functionally sound and aesthetically pleasing but prohibitively expensive to manufacture will be of little use to a business organisation. In processes that involve cutting out shapes (e.g. in the clothing industry) design should take into account the production of scrap and waste materials. The greater the wastage and scrap element the greater the cost. Wine bottles are aesthetically pleasing and, unless dropped, functionally sound. However, they do pose distribution and storage problems. Waxed cartons are less attractive but easier to store and to transport, since there is no wastage of space.

In conclusion, the main factors taken into account in product development and design:

1 The PERFORMANCE of the product, which can be sub-divided into:

(a) efficiency
(b) reliability
(c) ease of operation
(d) safety in operation
(e) ease of maintenance

2 The APPEARANCE of the product;

3 ECONOMY OF MANUFACTURE, distribution and storage;

4 LEGAL REQUIREMENTS (e.g. there are controls over the paint used in children's toys or the materials used in teddy bears); and

5 ENVIRONMENTAL CONCERNS of the public. This is seen in the switch to unleaded petrol to which car manufacturers have had to respond.

Throughout the development phase, the product will be tested in terms of performance, ease of manufacture and customer acceptance. The stages involved in the development of a typical product is shown in Fig 6.2. Most products are eliminated before launch as a result of unsatisfactory performance, lack of customer appeal, change in the external environment or because of high manufacturing costs. In some cases a product which starts out as promising will be made obsolete by new technology before it reaches the market. A particular problem for the pharmaceutical industry is that new drugs may be functionally sound in treating the condition for which they were developed but produce

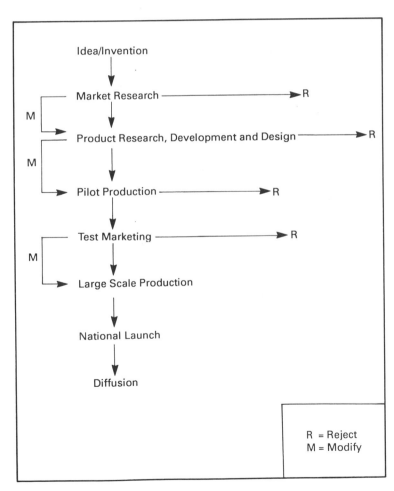

Fig 6.2   Product development

unacceptable, harmful side effects. Development is an expensive activity and clearly the earlier the elimination, the lower will be the losses. Development is a risky form of investment but unless it is undertaken new products will not be available to replace the mature products of today.

The main features of each subsequent stage in the product life cycle are as follows:

1   THE INTRODUCTION PHASE
   (a)   Low volume of sales
   (b)   High costs
   (c)   Heavy promotional spending
   (d)   High risks
   (e)   The aim of the promotional strategy is to create awareness
   (f)   The product is purchased by innovators.
2   THE GROWTH PHASE
   (a)   A higher volume of sales enables the firm to benefit from economies of scale.
   (b)   Profits grow as sales rise and costs fall.
   (c)   The product penetrates the market.
   (d)   The product is bought by early adopters who are 'trendy' rather than eccentric.
   (e)   The firm attempts to build up customer loyalty before the entry of competitors.
3   MATURITY
   (a)   Sales continue to rise but at a smaller rate.
   (b)   The product is now bought by the majority.
   (c)   Brand preference is a crucial factor in continuing success: therefore, packaging plays a significant part in the marketing effort.
   (d)   The firm aims to retain its share of the market by capturing sales from weaker rivals.
4   SATURATION
   The saturation phase sees a continuation of the trends of the mature phase. The major difference, however, is that sales level off rather than rise at a slower rate. As the name suggests, most people who are likely to buy the product have purchased it (if it is a product we only buy one of) or are purchasing it at a rate which is unlikely to rise.

5   THE DECLINE PHASE
   (a)   Sales and profits decline.
   (b)   Substitutes appear and the product becomes obsolete.
   (c)   The firm seeks to cut its losses by:
          (i)   cutting costs; or
          (ii) elimination of the product.

Elimination

When faced with a decline in sales for a particular product the firm has to decide whether the decline is:
   (a)   temporary;
   (b)   terminal and irreversible; or
   (c)   capable of being reversed by an adjustment in the marketing mix.

A product that is not making a contribution is, in effect, being propped up by others in the firm's product mix. This practice, known as **cross-subsidisation**, involves profits from some products covering losses on others. Cross-subsidisation is acceptable only if the firm is optimistic about an upturn in sales or where the availability of one product is necessary for the continuing success of another product in the firm's range. In other situations cross-subsidisation is undesirable. Economists criticise it as arbitrary redistribution of income since customers of profitable products are being asked to pay more to support products for which demand is inadequate. Marketers criticise the harm done to a firm's reputation by carrying weak lines which often take a disproportionate amount of time and effort. Low volume products also entail short production runs and therefore high costs. Elimination of the product is a harsh necessity even though it is likely to be resisted by customers and employees on grounds of sentiment or vested interest. When British Telecom ended the inland telegram service there were many complaints, despite the fact that few people were using a service that was clearly obsolete in an age of widespread access to telephones.

Extension strategies

Extension strategies aim to rejuvenate the product to prolong its life. This could involve a change in the product itself (e.g. new flavours of crisps), a change in packaging or a change in the way it is promoted. Oxo has enjoyed a number of extensions: in the 1950s the cube wrapped in foil rejuvenated the product. In the 1980s a further extension involved a change in the advertising theme away from the 'perfect' couple towards a more up-to-date image of a modern family with its typical problems. The Mini car has also enjoyed an extended life. When it was first introduced in 1959 it was intended as a small family car in a less affluent age. It enjoyed only modest success until it was marketed as a symbol of the 1960s driven by models and pop stars. Given the short life cycle of car models, it was likely to be phased out in the 1970s but was rescued by a new social phenomenon – the two-car family. The Mini was then marketed as the second car for short urban journeys. In the 1980s the Mini to acquire a 'cult' image especially among those who look back on the 1960s with affection. This theme was used by Rover in an advertisement featuring Twiggy looking back with affection to her Mini car of the 1960s.

A recognition of the product life cycle is crucial for production and marketing decisions. It illustrates the dangers of commitment to a single product. Ideally firms should produce a range of products selling in a diversity of markets and being located in different phases of the cycle. Profits from mature products should be ploughed back into research and development of new products. These profitable mature products become 'cash cows' to be milked. (This term is explained below.)

The Boston Matrix

The Boston Matrix is a classification of products according to (a) market share and (b) market growth.

Fig 6.3 The Boston Matrix

Four categories of products can be identified:

1 'STARS' enjoy both a high market share and high growth rate. Not only are they profitable but will continue to be so in the future.
2 'CASH COWS' have a high share of the market but a low growth rate. Cash Cows are 'milked' to supply finance for other products.
3 'QUESTION MARKS', as the name suggests, have an uncertain future. They have a high growth rate but only a small market share. To increase this share, further cash injections are necessary. Hopefully, they will become stars but, if not, they should be phased out.
4 'DOGS' have a low share and growth rate and, therefore, should be eliminated.

The well-run firm will be a multi-product firm with a portfolio of products across the Boston Matrix.

Market research

Marketing involves the identification of customer needs and the development of products and marketing strategies to satisfy those needs. If this is to be accomplished it is necessary to acquire information for sound decision-making. This is the role of market research which can be regarded as a risk reducing activity. Risks cannot be eliminated but they can be reduced by intelligence gathering and analysis. To use a military analogy, an army general will seek reconnaissance information before putting his battle plan into action. A careful investigation of the opposition and the environment will increase the chances of success.

Marketing managers will seek data on customer needs, the potential demand for the product, the type of people likely to buy the product and why they buy the product. By building up a consumer profile it is possible to identify distinct market segments which can be targeted. Understanding what motivates the customer to purchase can play a major role in developing the product and devising the advertising campaign. For instance, the revelation that the decision to purchase the goods is made at the point-of-sale will alter the promotional mix. Advertising will serve to present the product to the customer but resources will be switched to selling and sales promotion at the point of sale.

Market research is an essential complement to product research. It is important to discover the features of the product that the customer regards as essential. Do the bulk of potential customers want a video recorder which offers numerous recording opportunities within a 14-day period or merely a machine which enables them to view firms hired from the local video shop? If producers discover that the bulk of customers want a simple machine they will respond accordingly.

Holiday tour operators long ago discovered that the airport-to-hotel transfer was an essential part of a holiday package especially in the popular end of the market. The failure to include transfers in the package results in a substantial loss of bookings. Public transport organisations also need to clarify customer needs and the reasons customers buy the service. It would be tempting to state that people seek to be transported from A to B. However, in some cases (e.g. cruises, scenic railway journeys) the journey is more important than reaching the destination. Here people are buying an experience rather than a ticket which gives them access to their destination, and in such cases, the quality of the experience is more important than speed.

Market research is a continuing process and does not end with the launch of the product. As the business organisation exists within a dynamic environment, it must seek intelligence on the changes in the market and how best it can respond

Table VIII   The purpose of market research

Main areas	Specific issues investigated
1 The market	Size Segmentation Consumer behaviour Consumer profile
2 The product	Product development Identifying opportunities Testing the concept Identifying customer needs and preferences
3 Advertising and promotion	Formulating advertising themes Selection of media
4 Distribution	Identifying suitable outlets
5 Competition	Market shares Trends in sales Identifying unique selling points
6 Pricing	Consumer perception of value

to these trends. The main areas of market research are shown in Table VIII.

Market research takes many forms and it is a fallacy to equate it with questionnaires completed in the High Street. We should first make a distinction between **primary** research and **secondary** (or **desk**) research. The former involves the collection of raw data in the 'field'. Primary data refers to information which originates as a result of that particular investigation. Secondary research refers to the use and further analysis of data which has been collected for another purpose. Some of the material is available within the organisation (e.g. sales records, stock movements, accounts, earlier market research reports) while other material can be obtained from outside the organisation. The main sources include government publications (e.g. the annual *Social Trends*), research organisations, market intelligence organisations (e.g. the Economist Intelligence Unit), trade associations, the press and professional bodies. Desk research is obviously cheaper than primary research but the data may suffer from two serious defects. First, it could be dated, and second, it was collected for a different purpose. It should therefore be handled with care. By its nature, desk research is likely to be historical. Sales figures refer to past sales and may not reveal much about present and future trends.

Primary research is both costly and time-consuming. The accuracy of the findings is likely to rise the greater the resources employed and the greater the time allowed. However, there is no point in undertaking research if the costs exceed the benefits to the firms. Moreover, it is short-sighted to delay the decision in order to obtain more data if it allows rival firms to take advantage of the situation. A census (a survey of the entire 'population') is impractical and market researchers have to be content with a sample survey. This raises the question of how many people should be included, how should they be chosen and what credence can be put on the findings. For instance, if 60 per cent of the respondents expressed a preference, can we draw any conclusions? Clearly it depends on the number of people surveyed and the proportion of the 'population' they constituted. If 60 per cent of ten people out of a 'population' of one million expressed a preference, we cannot draw any conclusion. However, if 60 per cent represented 60 000 people out of 100 000 surveyed, we can place greater trust in conclusions drawn. Market research involves statistical analysis which requires some knowledge of sampling theory.

Primary research involves seeking people's opinions or making observations on how they behave. The main techniques are:

1 SAMPLE OPINION SURVEY involving the completion of a questionnaire. This can be undertaken by personal interview, by post or by telephone. The design of the questionnaire is crucial to the success of the exercise. Questions should be easily understood, they should not tax the respondent unduly and they should be framed in such a way that responses can be categorised. Each of the modes of delivery have problems. Personal interviews are time-consuming and unintentioned bias can affect the choice of respondents. Postal surveys suffer from a low response rate, and telephone surveys are expensive and could alienate the respondent disturbed while watching a favourite programme on the television. Both postal and telephone surveys suffer as a result of inability to control who answers the questions or the frame of mind in which they are answered.

2 CONSUMER PANELS involve a group of people who are questioned on their reactions to products or are asked to record details of their spending over time. From these panels it is possible to build up a picture over time. The major defect is that panels are not representative of the whole population. People with little time to spare will be reluctant to join the panel. Moreover, panels will be composed of gregarious people: those who prefer to maintain their privacy will be reluctant to join.

3 A USER TEST involves the consumer in using the product and recording views on performance.

4 TEST MARKETING constitutes a limited launch of a product to test reaction both to the product and to the way in which it is marketed. It has the advantage of reducing marketing costs and targetting a particular area before the firm is committed to a national launch. As Independent Television in Britain is regional, a test launch could be concentrated on, say, the North-East region which is served by Tyne-Tees Television. There are, however, two problems to note. First, the chosen region might not reflect the national trend. Second, it might not be possible to organise the effort nationally to reproduce the same result after a successful regional test launch.

5 A RETAIL AUDIT attempts to measure trends over time in a sample of outlets. Manufacturers commission such audits to investigate sales of rival products. The most well-known retail audit is the record charts. Audits measure past and present activity and are only useful for predictive purposes in as much as current trends can be projected into the future.

The marketing mix

The marketing mix refers to the factors which can be varied in order to increase customer appeal and, therefore, sales of the product. To economists the one way to increase sales volume is to reduce price. In marketing a change in price is just one way to achieve the desired result. The other methods are to change the product, the way in which it is promoted and the place from which it can be obtained. The popularity and sales of Oxo improved as a result of:

- changing the product from a powder to a cube wrapped in foil;
- changing the advertising strategy away from the 'perfect' couple (Philip and Katie) to the modern family where the mother escapes from the kitchen and the children were sometimes quarrelsome.

Record companies realised that to sell 'middle of the road' LP records it was necessary to move away from dependence upon the specialist record shop and towards supermarkets and large chains such as W H Smith. If the middle-aged, occasional record buyer, is discouraged from entering Virgin, HMV or Our Price shops it is necessary to choose a distribution outlet in which such a person feels comfortable.

Price, product, promotion and place are usually remembered as the 'Four Ps' of the marketing mix. Within each factor of the mix there is a number of separate elements that can be adjusted:

1 **Product**:	Quality
	Features, facilities offered
	Colour
	Guarantees and after sales service
	Size
	Packaging (sometimes treated as the fifth 'P')
	Name
2 **Price**:	Basic price
	Discount
	Credit facilities
3 **Place**:	Distribution outlets
	Availability of the product
4 **Promotion**:	Advertising
	Personal selling
	Sales promotion
	Direct mailing
	Publicity

The marketing department has to decide the right mixture of these elements for its particular product, bearing in mind the requirements of its customers. In the supermarket business, a firm such as Kwiksave places emphasis on low price, whereas Sainsburys has maintained reputation and market share through the range of products available in their shops. The Tesco chain has over the years moved 'upmarket', competing more on range and quality.

Airlines compete on price, frequency of service, range of destinations, in-flight facilities and promotional appeal. (They cannot compete on safety since this would suggest rivals are less than totally safe.) Virgin Atlantic, like Laker before, places low price as the key element in its mix. Conversely, British Airways, especially in appealing to the expense-account business traveller, emphasises the quality of service.

In the high fashion business, product is more important than price (perversely high price might, in fact, add to appeal). At the other end of the clothing trade, the stress is placed on price. In retail financial services (High Street banks and building societies) there are few differences in charges and types of product. What might give one institution the competitive edge is the availability of services (i.e. opening hours and number of cash dispensers).

In the search for differential advantage (or the unique selling point which sets it apart from rivals) firms will manipulate one or more of the 'Four Ps'. However, it is important to maintain consistency. Hence, people are suspicious if high quality is offered at low price. They are also suspicious if high quality furniture is advertised in a way reminiscent of a market trader.

Market segmentation

The market is not homogeneous but is divided up into a series of different segments. Each segment has a unity and a distinctiveness which separates it from other segments. The task for those in marketing is to identify the different segments and, if appropriate, devise marketing mixes to make the product appealing to particular segments.

A simple distinction is between consumers (households) and industrial customers (other firms). When the same product is sold in the consumer and industrial markets different promotional and pricing strategies are used. Industrial customers are less likely to be swayed by advertising and are more likely to make decisions on the basis of price and quality.

The consumer market can be segmented in terms of:

1   SOCIO-ECONOMIC CLASSES
A   Higher Managerial and Professional
B   Intermediate managerial and professional
C1   Supervisory or Clerical
C2   Skilled Manual
D   Semi or unskilled
E   Casual workers, those on benefit
2   AGE GROUPS.
3   GEOGRAPHY, e.g. regions of the UK may display distinct differences in purchasing behaviour.
4   INCOME GROUPS which are not necessarily the same as socio-economic class.
5   RELIGION OR ETHNIC ORIGIN.
6   HOUSING TYPE.
7   ATTITUDE TO LIFE.

One interesting classification is based on attitudes and motivation. Three distinct types can be identified:
(a) *Subsistence types*. These people choose on the basis of price and seek bargains.
(b) *Discriminators*. These people choose on the basis of quality rather than price.
(c) *Hedonists*. These people seek immediate gratification. This classification is independent of income so that the 'fun-loving' hedonist group includes both the very rich and also people of limited income who spend their money in the pub and at the dog track.

When faced with the existence of a heterogeneous market, the firm has to decide on its strategy with respect to the various distinct segments. Should it target a particular segment or attempt to sell to all categories of customer? If it adopts the latter policy should it offer the same mix of the 'Four Ps' to all segments or adopt different mixes for each segment. Three segmentation strategies can be identified (*see* Fig 6.4):

1   UNDIFFERENTIATED marketing can be compared to a shotgun. In effect, it ignores the existence of segments and offers a single mix to the heterogeneous market. This failure to target is likely to result in a disappointing level of sales.

2   In CONCENTRATED marketing a particular segment is targeted. The firm adopts a mix which it considers most effective and appropriate for that particular segment. If undifferentiated marketing can be compared to a shotgun, concentrated marketing is like a high-powered rifle. In some cases (e.g. retirement flats, Saga Holidays and 18-30 Holidays) the product is not available to people outside the target segment. In other cases, the product is available to all even though the firm expects only its target group to purchase the goods. For reasons of economy, small firms are likely to adopt a strategy of concentrated marketing rather than disperse their efforts far and wide.

Undifferentiated marketing

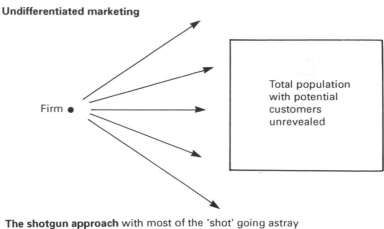

The shotgun approach with most of the 'shot' going astray

Concentrated marketing

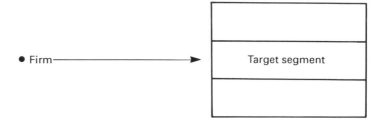

The rifle approach targets a particular segment

Differentiated marketing

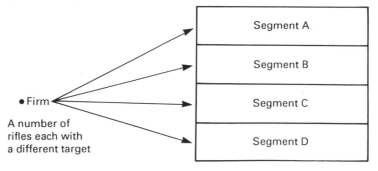

Fig 6.4   Three segmentation strategies

3 In DIFFERENTIATED marketing a separate mix is developed for each segment of the market. This strategy is very costly and is, therefore, only available to large firms. The major tour operators produce a general brochure for the majority of potential customers who like a family holiday with sun, sea and sand. They all produce separate mixes for specialist segments, e.g. those who like lakes and mountains or 'city break' holidays, skiers, those interested in activity holidays such as pony trekking, naturists, the young and the old. Banks and building societies have developed different accounts to suit the needs of different types of customer.

Firms may choose a particular type of household categorised in terms of the family life cycle, the phases of which are:

1 Bachelor – young, single.
2 Newly married – young, no children.
3 Full nest (1) – youngest child under 6.
4 Full nest (2) – youngest child over 6.
5 Full nest (3) – children still at home but working.
6 Empty nest (1) – children left home, one partner still working.
7 Empty nest (2) – both partners retired.
8 Solitary survivor (1) – still at work.
9 Solitary survivor (2) – retired.

Disposable income is an economic concept meaning take-home pay or income after compulsory deductions. More useful in marketing is the concept of discretionary income which is income after making allowances not just for tax and national insurance but also for regular commitments (mortgage, energy bills) and basic necessities like food. The income in the bachelor household may be lower than that in full nest (1) but discretionary income could be much higher. Discretionary income is income we can dispose of freely. It is likely to be high in full nest (3) and empty nest (1) as children enter the workforce and leave home, and when mortgage commitments come to an end. These groups with a high discretionary income represent useful targets especially by firms producing non-necessities.

The empty nest and solitary survivor households are likely to grow in importance:
(a) because with an ageing population there will be more pensioner households; and
(b) although many pensioners have low incomes and rely on the state pension, there is a growing number of people with an occupational pension and, moreover, a substantial asset (an owner-occupied house) which can be converted into cash. Business organisations are increasingly recognising the importance of this segment.

EXERCISE ● ● ●

● 1 Analyse the buying behaviour of a typical family as it moves through the family life cycle, taking into account its:
(a) income;
(b) discretionary income;
(c) likely commitments;
(d) needs;
(e) the purchase and replacement of consumer durables.

The promotional mix

Organisations engage in promotional activities to communicate with customers and thereby achieve organisational goals. There are four basic objectives:

1 To provide information about the availability of the product.
2 To position the product by targeting a particular segment of the market.
3 To increase sales.
4 To stabilise sales so as to facilitate planning.

The ultimate objective is to increase sales and profit but promotional activities might be designed to achieve the tactical objective of making people aware of the product. This recognises the fact that prior to purchase we move through a number of phases from unawareness through awareness, comprehension, preference, conviction to action. In the case of goods bought on impulse, these stages might be telescoped into a few minutes, whereas with other products the process may be spaced out over weeks or months. We start off unaware of the product and the task of marketing is simply to make us aware of its existence. There are many product of which we are vaguely aware but would find it difficult to recall without prompting. From this vague awareness we pass to a stage of knowledge and understanding of the product. In the next stage we begin to develop a preference for the product followed by a conviction that the product should be purchased. The final stage is the act of purchasing. Promotional activities attempt to move potential customers through this spectrum. Cynics would argue that the aim is to create demand where none currently exists. In fact, promotion merely converts latent demand into potential and actual demand.

So far advertising has not been mentioned and this is for one very good reason: advertising is only one of a number of promotional activities.

1 **Advertising** is non-personal, one-way communication to promote the sale of goods or services via paid-for advertisements in the media.
2 **Publicity** is promotion via press releases to the new media. They are made in the expectation that they will be given editorial mention at no charge.
3 **Direct mailing** is promotion via mailings through the post (known as mail shots) or by door-to-door distribution (known as mail drops).
4 **Packaging** is promotion through design and display. The intention is to create an impact at the point-of-sale.
5 The term **sales promotion** covers a range of activities such as competitions, gifts, point-of-sale displays, leaflets and sponsorship.
6 **Personal selling** is a promotional presentation made on a person-to-person basis. The significant feature of this activity is a two-way discussion between sales person and potential buyer.

Of the six activities listed above, advertising and personal selling are the two main ways in which products are promoted. The remaining four activities are used to back up one or both of the main promotional activities. As a general rule if products are inexpensive, simple and purchased by consumers they are advertised but there is little personal selling involved. When you buy a Mars Bar the sales assistant does not persuade you of its delicious taste or nutritional value. On the other hand, if you were purchasing complex and expensive machinery for a factory you would expect to engage in two-way conversation with the sales person. Advertising plays little or no part in the process. Between the two extremes, products such as cars or electrical goods (the consumer durable products) are purchased after the customer has experienced a combination of advertising and personal selling supported by other promotional activities.

EXERCISE ● ● ●

● 1   The term 'promotional mix' refers to the combination of promotional activities used to increase the sale of goods and services. The relative importance of these activities varies from product to product. Investigate and account for the promotional mix used for the following products:
(a) Everest Double Glazing.
(b) Wood treatment products such as Cuprinol.
(c) Houses on a new Barratt or Wimpey estate.

(*d*) Amstrad personal computers.
(*e*) Hotpoint washing machines.
(*f*) Fitted kitchens.
(*g*) School textbooks.

Advertising in the media

Advertisements seek to make people aware of the product, to inform, to persuade, to foster a favourable image and to remind people of the product. The exact nature and purpose of the advertisement changes as the product moves through its life cycle. In the initial stages the aim is to make people aware of the product and to provide information. In the case of innovatory products, it is necessary to inform people rather than stress the virtues of a particular brand or make. Hence, early advertising of Microwave ovens concentrated on the concept itself. People were in no position to evaluate different brands until they received basic information on the product.

Once initial demand is built up, the focus moves to persuasive advertising to improve the competitive status of the brand. The information content declines at this point. As the product moves into maturity it is still considered necessary to advertise the product. In a world where there is a constant stream of new products it is necessary to remind people of the existence of mature products. Kit Kat and Mars Bars have enjoyed a long life but their manufacturers consider it necessary to remind people. The information content of these advertisements is minimal since there is nothing new to say about these old favourites.

The advertiser should be clear about the objectives of an advertising campaign. These should be expressed in terms of sales volume, market share, market penetration or cash flow. After the objectives have been set, it is necessary to devise a message which enhances the appeal of the product. The medium (or media) should also be carefully chosen. The main media employed in advertising are newspapers, television, radio, magazines, cinema and outdoor posters. Although we frequently associate advertising with television,

it should be remembered that for the majority of firms in Britain, television advertising is not appropriate. The criteria by which the media should be judged are as follows:

1 The 'REACH' OF THE MEDIA or the proportion of the target audience that can be contacted. In the case of the printed media this refers to the readership of the publication (which incidentally is not the same as its circulation). In the case of television, the 'reach' should be revealed by the ratings figure. However, the fact that the television set was on does not prove that people were watching it or absorbing the message.

2 The SELECTIVITY OF THE MEDIA. Specialist magazines may have a small readership but these people may be the target audience. There is an old saying in advertising, '50 per cent of all advertising is wasted, unfortunately we don't know which 50 per cent'. Media that is highly selective will reduce the wastage in advertising.

3 The RELATIVE COST, e.g. cost per thousand of population. For firms that can afford television advertising rates, it is very cost-effective.

4 The IMPACT OF THE MEDIA. This refers to the extent to which the message is effectively taken in. Outdoor advertising is inexpensive and reaches large numbers of people but is the message absorbed?

5 The PRODUCT ITSELF. If it is necessary to demonstrate the product in action then television is the most appropriate media. If it is necessary to provide a vast quantity of information then the printed media is most appropriate.

6 The PERMANENCE OF THE ADVERTISEMENT. When advertising a service that people require infrequently, it is useful to advertise in a way that creates a permanent record. Firms that produce self-adhesive address

that creates a permanent record. Firms that produce self-adhesive address labels (e.g. Able-Labels) sold by mail order, advertise weekly in the national newspapers to ensure that information is available to potential customers whenever they need it. The local plumber similarly finds it useful to run a regular advertisement in the weekly free newspaper to ensure permanence of record – better still is a block advertisement in Yellow Pages.

EXERCISE ● ● ●

● 1 In terms of the criteria listed above, consider the merits of national newspapers, local newspapers, local free news sheets, radio, general interest magazines, specialist magazines, the cinema and outdoor posters for the advertising of:
(*a*) Fishing tackle
(*b*) A local designer-wear boutique
(*c*) A new soft drink
(*d*) Greenhouses
(*e*) A new car model
(*f*) Life assurance.

A common fallacy is the belief that advertising guarantees success. Advertising will only be successful if the chosen message and media are appropriate, if the product is able to satisfy a demand, if the economic climate is favourable and if other elements of the marketing mix are consistent. An inappropriate message will seriously harm the product. The famous Strand cigarette advertisements of the early 1960s led to the product being associated not with a Humphrey Bogart character, but a man in a dirty raincoat walking the darkened streets of London. The advertisement produced an effect opposite to that intended. Today's big budget television advertisements are aesthetically pleasing and can be minor masterpieces of cinematography. However, this is not the same as success and effectiveness from the advertiser's point of view. In the late 1980s, a major car manufacturer ran an advertisement which proclaimed that, as their car could run on unleaded petrol, it was, therefore, as 'ozone friendly' as it was economical. The manufacturers did not realise that there is no link between lead in petrol and the hole in the ozone layer, so after some embarassing publicity for the company concerned, the advertisement was withdrawn.

Sometimes an advertisement benefits rival products since the public remembers the jingle or visual image but may forget the name of the product.

The effectiveness of advertising is measured in terms of a change in sales revenue. Adapting the elasticity formulas encountered earlier we can measure promotional elasticity as:

Proportionate change in sales volume; and
Proportionate change in promotional expenditure.

However, this assumes that there is a causal relationship. The extra sales may have occurred quite independently of the advertising campaign.

In defence of advertising
1 Advertising informs.
2 It is part of the competitive process.
3 It allows the consumer to make a more informed choice.
4 It can act as a guarantee of quality.

5 It allows a reduction of expenditure on other forms of sales promotion, e.g. personal selling.
6 It acts as an aid to product identification.
7 By helping to reduce sales fluctuations, it assists in planning production.
8 An increase in the volume of sales leads to an increase in output and therefore economies of scale are passed on in lower prices.

Criticisms of advertising

1 Advertising raises costs and therefore prices.
2 Waste of resources.
3 It raises price 'without adding to the value' of the product.
4 It persuades people to consume unnecessary and unwanted goods and services (assuming that people are gullible).
5 It is often used as a way of maintaining monopoly power by preventing the entry of new rivals.
6 It can be misleading (but advertising is controlled by bodies such as the Advertising Standards Authority).
7 Advertising stimulates wants which cannot be satisfied.
8 The economies of scale are not passed on.

Personal selling

Personal selling takes the form of two-way communications of a persuasive kind and should be seen as a complement to advertising. Selling is directed at a specific target, presenting the product in an attractive way most suitable for the particular needs of the buyer. It is used when the product is expensive, complex and requires demonstration. Consequently, it is especially prevalent in the industrial goods market (as distinct from the consumer goods market) where the number of potential customers is limited.

There are a number of steps taken by salespeople to gain sales. **Prospecting** is the locating of potential customers (who are known as prospects). In the pre-approach phase, the salesperson gathers information on both the product and the prospect. During the approach the aim is to create a favourable impression. This is followed by a sales presentation in which the main features of the product are highlighted. The aim is to stress the differential advantage (or unique selling points) of the firm's product, and potential customers are invited to ask questions and articulate their worries. This should be seen as an opportunity to provide additional information. The next stage is 'closing the sale'. The seller will attempt to get a commitment from the buyer. Shop assistants will move towards the cash register to initiate the closing phase. In what is called the 'puppy dog close', the salesperson will give the prospect the opportunity of handing the goods so as to become attached to them. The final phase is the follow up, the purpose of which is to ensure customer satisfaction. Marketing, remember, is about responding to the needs of the customer and ensuring satisfaction. Hence, good sales staff channel information back to the firm about customer requirements.

Successful selling requires inter-personal skills, intelligence, a knowledge of and faith in the product and empathy with customers. The salesperson needs to be highly motivated especially if working long, irregular hours alone and far from base. A financial incentive in the form of commission on sales is therefore essential to secure commitment, although there is a strong argument against straight commission (with no basic salary) which might lead to a neglect of the business's long-term interests.

Branding

A brand is a product name which is designed to differentiate the product in the market place. Firms will seek to impress on customers the distinctiveness of their product. In some cases the differentiation is real while in others it is merely perceived by customers. Firms will hope to build up brand loyalty which gives it greater freedom of manoeuvre over price. With a loyal band of customers, prices can be raised without a total loss of the market. The choice of name is an important part of the marketing strategy. There will be a preference for short, distinctive names which reflect the characteristics of the product and the image the firm wishes to project. The makers of after-shave found that there was 'working class' resistance to the product. They overcame this resistance with names like 'Denim'. Traditionally the car makers chose names which implied aggression (Hunter, Avenger) but not only are such names criticised for encouraging the aggressive driver, they are also inappropriate for cars with a low engine size. Hence, 'fun names' are preferred at this end of the market (e.g. Samba, Fiesta, Panda, Cherry).

Related products are frequently sold under what is known as a family brand. The classic example is Heinz's 57 varieties. It is also a technique widely used by producers of perfumes and talcum powders. There are substantial economies in promotion and it is hoped that a favourable reaction to one product within the family will tempt the buyer to purchase related products. This is known as the '**halo effect**'. However, an unfavourable reaction to one member of the family will harm others.

Multiple branding refers to selling broadly similar products under a number of different brand names. It is a technique most clearly associated with soap powder manufacturers such as Unilever and Proctor and Gamble. It has the advantage of enabling the manufacturer to reach a number of market segments. The brand also serves to differentiate the product from others produced by the same firm. The Walt Disney organisation faced a major credibility problem whem producing films for a more adult market. Disney was too closely associated with Mickey Mouse and Snow White. It was, therefore, necessary to use the 'Touchstone' name for its adult films.

'House brands' or supermarket 'own brands' are of growing importance in modern retailing. In most cases they are a cheaper version of the famous name brand. The retailer uses the own brand to:

(a) create a store identity and loyalty
(b) protect profit margins
(c) assert control over the manufacturer.

The manufacturer is contracted to produce the goods and is able to leave the marketing to retailers. Manufacturers also see this as a useful way to utilise spare capacity. Although this apparently easy market is attractive to manufacturers, they should beware of being too closely tied to large retailers.

To sum up, the main functions of branding are:
1 to differentiate the product from rivals;
2 to aid identification;
3 to facilitate self-selection;
4 to segment the market;
5 to reduce the amount of persuasive selling effort; and
6 to create customer loyalty.

Packaging

Packaging is being considered under the heading of marketing because packaging performs more than the utilitarian function of containing and protecting the product. Packaging adds to the appeal of the product and often plays a key role in marketing. It can be regarded as the 'fifth P' in the marketing mix.

Packaging often becomes an integral part of the product: boxes of chocolates are often given as presents to mothers and girlfriends. If the chocolates were wrapped in a paper bag they would be less appealing and would not serve the function for which they were purchased. Packaging helps us to identify the product especially when the colours, logos and designs on the packaging are used as themes in advertising. Packaging therefore provides a unique promotional opportunity providing a constant reminder of the product. Firms will seek distinctive packaging so that the product is instantly recognisable (e.g. Toblerone and Biarritz chocolate, Mateus Rosé wine). Distinctiveness is very important when goods are competing with rivals on the shelves of supermarkets. If advertising informs customers, then packaging prompts their memory.

Packaging can be used to extend the life of the product either by revitalising interest in the product itself (e.g. a new cover design for a paperback novel) or to enable the product to penetrate new markets. The ring pull can, a device that some people deplore, has enabled soft drink and lager makers to expand their markets with the product being consumed by people 'on the move'. Similarly, the waxed carton has created new opportunities for the makers of orange juice and wine.

Channels of distribution

The channels of distribution are the paths that goods and services follow in moving from producer to customer. We are not so much concerned with the physical route which goods take but the institutions in the route of exchange. In industrial markets (where other firms are the customers) direct selling without intermediaries is common. The relatively small number of potential customers means that it is possible to maintain direct contact with the market. Direct selling also occurs in parts of the consumer goods market (e.g. mail order and manufacturer-owned retail outlets). Direct selling is an option if the manufacturer considers there to be a lack of suitable intermediaries or where existing intermediaries are considered insufficiently active in selling the goods. Manufacturers involved in direct selling face the expense and problems of maintaining direct communication with customers.

The traditional channel of exchange in the consumer goods market is:

manufacturer → wholesaler → retailer → consumer.

The use of intermediaries reduces the marketing risks and marketing effort required of the manufacturer who can instead concentrate more on production and product development. The wholesaler's traditional functions have been to break bulk, even out irregular flows, provide storage facilities and hasten the cash flow to manufacturers. The rise of the large retail chain has reduced the importance of the independent wholesaler. The large retail chains are able to undertake their own wholesaling.

There are important policy decisions to be made about distribution. One strategy is to secure as many retail outlets as possible for the product. Alternatively, they may prefer to concentrate on specific types of outlet (e.g. chemist shops). This is a form of **intensive** distribution. **Selective** distribution involves choosing outlets which are considered competent to offer the range of back-up services required by customers. When exclusive rights to sell the product in a particular area are conferred on a single firm it is known as **exclusive** distribution. Whatever strategy is chosen it is important not to be tied into a particular channel. Manufacturers who rely on a limited number or type of retail stores may suffer if the market moves against such stores.

Manufacturers who use intermediaries face the problem of only having indirect contact with consumers. They rely on intermediaries to be active and enthusiastic in selling their goods. When we remember that the intermediaries are also performing the same function for rival manufacturers we can appreciate the need to reinforce the enthusiasm of the intermediary. This is accomplished by a push-pull strategy. '**Pushing**' from behind requires the manufacturer to engage in personal selling (supported by sales promotion) to encourage the intermediary. **Pulling** is an attempt to appeal to customers over the heads of intermediaries. By advertising they hope to encourage customers to ask for the goods in the shop and so pull the goods through the channel.

Conclusion

Integration of the marketing effort is achieved by means of a marketing plan. This is a blue print for marketing action: objectives are clarified, options are identified and costed out. Like all plans, the marketing plan will conform to a format:

1 A review of the present situation highlighting strengths, weaknesses, opportunities and threats (SWOT analysis).

2 A statement of assumptions on which forecasts are based. These assumptions relate to the situations in the environment in the immediate future.

3 A statement of objectives to be achieved and the strategies to be used.

4 Detailed action programmes will be prepared (and costed) for the product mix, sales strategy, advertising strategy, sales promotion, distribution and market research.

5 Budgets will be prepared for each of the activities. Budgets, which are quantitative statements relating to expected receipts and expenditure, act as both a target and a control mechanism.

6 Procedure for evaluating performance against the stated objectives.

The external environment clearly acts as a constraint on the organisation in achieving the objectives. However, we should not neglect the internal factors: for instance the marketing people cannot achieve the required sales volume unless the production department delivers the goods. They cannot produce the goods unless they obtain the necessary inputs. The acquisition of inputs is a function of the availability of the inputs and the ability of the organisation to finance the purchase of them. Hence, the functional areas of the organisation have to work together if organisational objectives are to be achieved.

CASE STUDY 1
Californian wine

'Paul Masson Californian Carafes' is the most widely known brand of American wine sold in the UK. It was launched in Britain in 1980 by its producer, Seagram Distillers – a Canadian producer of spirits keen to extend its involvement in the wine market.

Seagram faced a number of problems:
- European resistance to wine grown outside the classic wine-growing areas of Europe.
- Lack of tied distribution.
- Brand loyalty of wine drinkers.
- The introduction of new brands (e.g. 'Le Piat' in 1981)

To acquire a share of the UK market, it was necessary to launch a major advertising campaign, both in order to create awareness of the product and to overcome the resistance to it. The advertising campaign was based around actor Ian Carmichael as a very aristocratic Englishman who proclaimed that 'They're really jolly good'. It was successful in building Paul Masson's market share and Paul Masson now ranks as the sixth leading brand, the leader in litre-size bottles and second (to Mateus) in rosés. As important as the sales, was the enhanced status that it gave to Seagram wines and Californian wines in general.

The Paul Masson success has contributed to the European acquisition of vineyards to the value of $1 billion in the Napa Valley, the main wine-producing area of the USA. Baron Philippe de Rothschild became involved in Californian wine production in 1980 and has since been followed by European multinationals such as Grand Metropolitan, Allied Lyons and Nestlé. The European involvement can be attributed to:

- the high and rising quality of Californian wines
- a weak US dollar
- a growing US market for wine
- political stability in the USA compared with the instability of alternative areas of investment in wine production such as Chile and Argentina.

This European involvement came at a time when US giants such as Coca-Cola and Pillsbury withdrew from Californian production. The differing US and European attitudes to investment in wine production can be attributed to American impatience to achieve rapid profit compared with European concern for the longer view.

(Sources of information: Cheryll Aimee Barron in *Business Magazine*, November 1989; L Buterfield in C Channon (ed) *20 Advertising Case Histories* (Cassell).

1 Explain the following:
 (a) tied distribution;
 (b) brand loyalty;
 (c) multinational.
2 Why does brand awareness matter?
3 Why were wine drinkers resistant to Californian wines?
4 What do you think was the reasoning behind the style of advertising for Paul Masson?
5 What was the significance of the weak US dollar?

6 Why would Europeans be interested in Californian wine production when there was an EC 'wine lake'?

7 Why is a long-term perspective important in the wine trade?

CASE STUDY 2
Hellman's Mayonnaise

CPC (UK) Ltd produces a range of grocery products such as Brown and Polson Cornflour, Knorr soups and Hellman's Mayonnaise. The last-named product was originally an American brand which was launched in Britain in the 1960s. It enjoyed a growing volume of sales in the 1960s and 1970s as distribution increased and also enjoyed a dominant 60 per cent share of the market in mayonnaise.

The question that confronted its producers in 1981 was whether the market for mayonnaise would grow sufficiently to justify continued heavy advertising expenditure. In terms of the Boston Matrix, Hellman's Mayonnaise was either a cash cow to be milked or a star which deserved increased promotional effort. Which category it deserved to be placed in depended upon the growth potential of the market, but a number of marketing problems were identified:

- In Britain, mayonnaise was associated almost exclusively with salad. This was partly the consequence of early advertising of mayonnaise, especially by Heinz Foods;
- It was seen as salad cream for 'special occasions';
- As a salad product it faced competition from other salad dressings;
- London and AB social classes accounted for a disproportionate amount of sales.

To overcome these problems it was considered necessary to 'reposition' the product by an advertising campaign.

(Source of information P Feldwick in C Channon (ed) 20 Advertising Case Histories, Cassell).

---

1 What is meant by 'repositioning' a product?

2 What particular marketing problems stem from the association of mayonnaise with salad?

3 Why do you think it was perceived as a 'special occasion' product?

4 Sales would grow if either;
   (a) more people bought the product; or
   (b) people used it more often.

Using the material in the case study suggest advertising strategies to achieve both objectives.

5 Can you think of other products and producers that have successfully broken out of the 'special occasion' category.

CASE STUDY 3
The toy market

The basic aim of all market research is to reduce the risks inherent in enterprise. By researching the wants and tastes of the customer the market researcher plays a major role in ensuring that firms produce goods for which there will be sufficient demand. Although risks can be reduced, they cannot be eliminated altogether. The fickleness of the market for toys presents major problems for toy manufacturers. Hence one year's favourite toy can soon suffer dramatic decline. The 'cabbage-patch doll' was a great success on both sides of the Atlantic in the mid-1980s. Production could not satisfy demand at one stage. However, the market rapidly turned against the product with the result that its manufacturer (Coleco) was forced into liquidation in 1988.

The large successful toy maker will launch a large number of new products in the hope that successes will outweigh the inevitable failures. Mattel is a good example of a company pursuing this strategy. It went through an unsuccessful period in 1986 and 1987 following the failure of a 'male action doll' known as Captain Powers, that it launched in America. Mattel's great winner is the Barbie doll which was first sold in the late 1950s. Barbie's continuing success is partly the result of extending the range of products associated with the basic doll (e.g. companion dolls, different outfits). Barbie represents Mattel's cash cow generating funds for further products and extension to new markets. It plans to develop production facilities in Japan (the world's second largest market for toys) and the USSR.

1 How can market research reduce the risks of business? Why can risks not be eliminated altogether?
2 Why is the toy market particularly fickle?
3 What is meant by a cash cow?
4 Do all toys have a short product life cycle?
5 What is meant by:
   (a) products extension; and
   (b) market development?
6 What parallels can be drawn between marketing in the toy industry and marketing records?

CASE STUDY 4
Commercial aspects of movie making – three basic rules

1 **'The sunk cost rule'** dictates that nearly all the cost of making entertainment software is fixed and up front. An average American film takes two years to complete from script to opening night. Its production cost is around $20 million, with a further $7 million to market it in America and $3 million of studio overheads. That $30 million cost is sunk – it will barely change whether the movie makes $10 million, $100 million or $1 billion.

2 **'The hit rule'** is that most profit comes from a tiny part of the output. Just three per cent of films released in 1988 accounted for close to a third of box office receipts. Because most of the cost is fixed, any revenue above that line is profit . . . only four out of ten films are ever profitable but they pay for a string of flops . . .

3 **'Nobody knows anything'**. Popular taste and creative talent being as fickle as they are, there is no surefire formula for making a hit . . .

(Adapted from the *Economist* 23rd December, 1989)

1 Analyse the marketing problems that arise from the three rules of movie making.
2 In the light of the three rules explore the advantages and disadvantages of producing sequels (e.g. 'Rocky V', 'Back to the Future II')
   (*a*) immediately after the original; and
   (*b*) after a time lag.
3 If most costs are 'sunk' what are the implications for the price charged by distributors for release to television networks?
4 'Batman' cost Warner $75 million but is expected to bring in around $1 billion. Suggest sources of revenue from 'Batman' other than box office takings.
5 Is there any point in undertaking market research?

EXERCISE ● ● ●

● 1 Study the article below on tourism and answer the following questions:

Lost resorts: The package falls apart

TOURISM

The Eighties have witnessed the rise and fall of the overseas package holiday. During the same decade its counterpart, the UK break, has pulled itself out of the doldrums and is enjoying an unprecedented boom.

Growth in the market for package holidays accelerated rapidly from 1980 to 1987 when the number of Britons hitting resorts in Spain, Greece and other Mediterranean spots rose from 5.3 million to 11.7 million (figures from Lunn Poly). This surge in demand for packaged sun, sea and sand was in part a result of the battle between tour operating multiples to gain market share, a battle notable for its severe price-cutting.

By 1988, however, volume plateaued and a steep slide began. Indeed, Lunn Poly estimates the market will have fallen back by five per cent this year and by ten per cent in 1990. Many observers claim these figures can be at least doubled since they believe that the era of the cheap'n'cheerful package is well and truly over. These are hard times: market leader Thomson Holidays has shed over 100 staff and Lunn Poly is cutting 60 as parent company Thomson Travel aims to save £5m.

The demise of the package in the late Eighties can be attributed to two main causes. As affluence increased at the top end of the market, many consumers began to trade up – seeking quality over price. Independent travel is consequently growing at the expense of the package resorts in the Mediter-

ranean, as are the cruise market and long-haul/exotic package trips. Furthermore, a thickening economic gloom comprising high interest rates and rising inflation has led many would-be holidaymakers to stay at home.

This second development gave a timely boost to the UK domestic holiday industry, which has spent unprecedented amounts throughout the decade on refurbishing amenities to compete with overseas resorts.

By 1990, for example, Butlins will have pumped £71m into its Holiday Worlds.

As economic pressures encourage Britons to test their own resorts again, many of them will be surprised by what they find – and be only too happy to return.
Franny Moyle

(Source: *Marketing Week*, 22 December 1989)

(*a*) What evidence is there that the current problems in the package tour industry are:
   (i) temporary; and
   (ii) permanent?

(*b*) Explain the state of the industry in terms of the product life cycle. What extension strategies can be pursued to prolong sales of the 'product'?

(*c*) Explain how holiday companies are affected by:
   (i) across-the-board changes in real incomes; and
   (ii) increases in the living standards of higher income earners but decline for the low income earner.

(*d*) What kind of refurbishment has occurred at British holiday resorts?

● 2 Read the article below on British Airways and answer the following questions.

David Churchill on the UK airline's latest marketing focus

The biggest and most elaborate television commercial on view in the UK over Christmas was undoubtedly British Airways' new global advertising campaign, made by the Saatchi and Saatchi agency and directed by Hugh Hudson of Chariots of Fire film fame. It features a cast of 4,000 extras set amidst the dramatic scenery of the American mid-west, and with appropriately stirring music from Delibes' opera, Lakmé.

With a total advertising spend of £14m budgeted for 1990, BA hopes to reach more than 600m people throughout the world with its message aimed (so Saatchi and Saatchi reveals) at "bringing more warmth and humanity to the airline's professional and efficient personality."

Such advertising jargon is well in keeping with British Airways' increasingly marketing-led approach over the past few years since its privatisation in 1987. Its marketing department, once seen virtually as little more than simply a sales and reservations office, is now regarded (both within the airline and outside) as one of the driving forces behind BA's projected growth in the 1990s.

To reinforce this approach, Sir Colin Marshall, BA's chief executive, has brought in a clutch of senior marketers from fast moving consumer goods (fmcg) companies such as Procter and Gamble, Unilever, Mars, and Whitbread. Heading the department is Liam Strong, a former senior marketing executive with Reckitt and Coleman, who joined BA last year.

Not surprisingly, the influx of external marketers (about half the marketing department were previously with fmcg companies) has prompted much talk within the BA hierarchy of concepts such as brand awareness, market segmentation, and product databases.

Strong believes this dovetails neatly with the "putting the customer first" corporate philosophy brought in by BA in the mid-1980s to counter it abysmal market image at the beginning of the decade. "Most airlines, and BA was once one, saw their business in terms of having aircraft which they then had to fill up with passengers," he says.

"Our approach now is the one that most fmcg companies would adopt: first you find out exactly what it is that the customer wants and then you create the product that best fits the bill."

Thus when BA re-launched its business class service last year – and its first class service earlier this year – it interviewed several thousand regular travellers to find out exactly what they wanted before bringing in the revamped operations.

At present, moreover, extensive market research is being carried out into what economy class passengers want from the airline before the planned relaunch of the economy service later next year.

"We are only really so far scratching the surface of the leisure travel market we expect to see in the 1990s," Strong points out.

Each separate category – first, business, and economy – is also now regarded as a separate brand within BA, with its own dedicated brand management team similar to that in a food or pharmaceutical company. Most airlines, in contrast, define their marketing operations geographically or according to aircraft type.

BA's move to brand marketing, however, has not developed without some internal resistance from non-marketing areas. "It's quite right that other people within the airline should look critically at our ideas," insists Strong.

"It would be alarming if there wasn't some creative conflict, especially in a business such as ours where marketing changes can lead to a large investment in new assets."

Strong, not surprisingly given his background in consumer goods marketing, is a firm believer in advertising support for brands. "But we have to find the right balance between support for our core brand of BA and for the subbrands of actual products," he says.

Strong and his colleagues decided that, six years after BA's last image-building compaign (a commercial with sc-fi overtones based on Manhattan flying through the air), it was time for a new corporate campaign. "We felt it time to put more emphasis on our 'umbrella' brand, not just in the UK but in many of our overseas markets," says Strong.

"We keep a careful check on how we are perceived, especially abroad, and this indicated we needed to soften our image." Hence the television commercial showing people rapturously greeting each other, interspersed with the creation of a smiling face when viewed from the air made up from thousands of people wearing different colours.

However extravagant the commercial may seem on first viewing, Strong insists that it offers good value. "Because it is so visual, it can be used in any market and means that we can undertake a global campaign for about half the cost of traditional advertising created for different markets."

(Source: *Financial Times*, 28 December 1989)

(*a*) Explain the following terms.
   (i)   fast moving consumer goods (Fmcg);
   (ii) brand awareness;
   (iii) market segmentation;
   (iv) brand manager.
(*b*) In the case of airlines, how is it possible to 'create the product that best fits the bill'.
(*c*) What does Mr Strong mean by finding 'the right balance between support for our core brand of BA and for the sub-brands of actual products'?
(*d*) Does it matter how BA is 'perceived'?
(*e*) How has BA's marketing department changed?
(*f*) Explain the role of advertising agencies like Saatchi and Saatchi.

3 Study the account of the alcohol market in the 1980s and answer the questions that follow:

The Eighties have been a watershed for the drinks industry. After years of sustained growth, the future health of the business is far from certain and the forecast is for tough times ahead.

Having successfully taken the tobacco industry to task, the Eighties' health lobby focused its attention on alcohol, often with Parliamentary support. The term "lager lout" became indelibly printed not only on the public's mind but also on the Government's and the image of the drinks business took a severe battering.

For an industry which prides itself on marketing expertise, the drinks business was ill-prepared for the onslaught. The formation this year of the Portman Group – an association created by the UK's leading drinks companies – is a measure of the industry's sensitivity to such criticism. Many believe too little has been done too late, however.

The industry is also worried about falling consumption of alcohol, a trend which began in the Eighties and looks set to continue despite the extension of licensing hours last year. Marketers have had to adapt to a more discerning drinking public: quality and not quantity has become the trend of the decade. Consumers wanted more choice of non-alcohol and low-alcohol brands, and they wanted lighter alternatives – hence the growth of wine at the expense of spirits. They rejected brands that didn't deliver, along with advertising which was tired and hackneyed.

Following the rise in disposable income and the birth of the yuppie, style in the drinks market became as important to some as flavour and price. What people drank said as much about them as what they wore. The industry responded with new badged brands, notably premium lager.

The industry has reacted to the changing market by consolidating; myriad small independents have been replaced by a handful of major players. Polarisation looks set to continue as the market rationalises, the single European market beckons and the first attack on the brewers' monopoly begins to take effect.

Companies will concentrate on their successful divisions, shedding those which under-perform.

The growth of leisure time has meant that an increasing number of people now drink at home. Multiple retailers have been quick to exploit the shift, forcing companies to improve their brand management and support, while creating successful own-label products.

The drinks industry is likely to be leaner and more polarised in ten years' time – and less visible than it is today.

Nicola Bungey

(Source: *Marketing Week*, 22 December 1989)

(*a*) Describe and account for the changes in the external environment mentioned in the article.
(*b*) What does the article tell us about the structure of the industry?
(*c*) Explain what is meant by:
   (i)   brand management;
   (ii) disposable income;
   (iii) consumption;
   (iv) marketing expertise.
(*d*) In your own words explain the sentence: 'Companies will concentrate on their successful divisions, shedding those which under-perform'.
(*e*) What do you understand by brand loyalty? Does it still exist in the drinks trade?

● 4   Study the article on Heineken and answer the following questions:

Heineken goes dry

The Japanese love the stuff; the Americans are beginning to develop a taste for it; and if Heineken, Europe's biggest brewer, has its way, Europeans will also soon be falling over themselves to sample the latest fad in alcoholic drinks – 'dry' beer.

In September Heineken became the first company in Europe to offer the product when it launched dry beer in the Netherlands. (Its Spanish associate El Aguila also began selling the product, albeit on a more modest scale, during the summer). If it catches on in these markets, Heineken plans to make it available elsewhere in Europe.

Among brewers, as with manufacturers of sherry and wine, 'dry' describes a taste that is produced by a process involving longer fermentation and fewer residual sugars and other extracts. In Japan, where the craze began three years ago with the introduction of a dry beer by the small Asahi brewery, dry beers tend to be more bitter and higher in alcohol content than others.

Not so Heineken's version. This is designed to be sweeter and to have less of an after-taste; in fact it is hardly like beer at all. Heineken describes the taste of its 'dry 100 mild beer' as more refreshing than Pilsener. It hopes that its target group – the occasional and unconverted beer drinker – will agree.

The launch of dry beer in the Netherlands is one response to three related and frustrating phenomena: stagnant beer consumption among the Dutch; a greater willingness to experiment with exotic drinks; and the company's own slight loss of market share. In 1988, the Dutch drank 83.3 litres of beer per caput, down slightly from 84.3 litres in 1987. And Heineken's commanding share of the beer market was reduced fractionally, to 52.5% from 53%.

To remedy the situation, Heineken has already has already introduced a virtually alcohol-free beer called Buckler, whose swift success has exceeded the company's wildest expectations. The brewer has also recently snapped up one of the few remaining independent brewers in the Netherlands.

The launch of dry beer is a sign of the increasing 'segmentation' of the beer market, not just in the Netherlands but also in much of northern Europe. Foreign premium brands are making headway on Heineken's hallowed turf; consumers are becoming less predictable, switching easily and frequently from one type of beer to another.

Heineken's market research has shown that the number of 'heavy users' (sic) of beer is dropping, while the number of casual beer drinkers is increasing. The trouble is that many of these casual drinkers are put off by the bitterness of most beers.

It is too early yet to say whether dry beer will create much of a following in the Netherlands. In Japan, it has captured 25% of the total beer market in just three years. In the US, the product's popularity has so far been encouraging but not earth-shattering.

What the effect of dry beer will be on Heineken's bottom line is equally difficult to forecast. While the Netherlands is important to the company, it represents only 13% of the group's worldwide beer sales; and dry beer will inevitably be only a tiny part of the overall market.

Nevertheless, the company – the world's third-biggest brewer after America's Anheuser-Busch and Miller – could do with a fillip. Its profits, at around Fl 290 million, have lately been as flat as beer consumption. The unspectacular performance is due partly to the company's heavy expenditure on refurbishing its old breweries and on buying new ones, particularly in southern Europe.

It is betting that it can persuade wine drinkers in such countries as France, Greece, Italy and Spain to switch to beer. The potential, if it is successful, is enormous. Italians, for example, still drink only one-sixth the amount of beer that West Germans do.

Ronald van de Krol

(Source: *Euro Business*, October 1989)

(*a*) Define and explain the following terms:
   (i) target group;
   (ii) market share;
   (iii) segmentation;
   (iv) foreign premium brands.
(*b*) Why do you think beer consumption is stagnant in the Netherlands?
(*c*) Why were 'occasional beer drinkers' targeted?
(*d*) Why did Heineken buy breweries in Southern Europe?
(*e*) Why is the 'effect . . . on Heineken's bottom line' difficult to forecast?

5   The diagram below illustrates sales revenue and profit for a product over its life cycle.

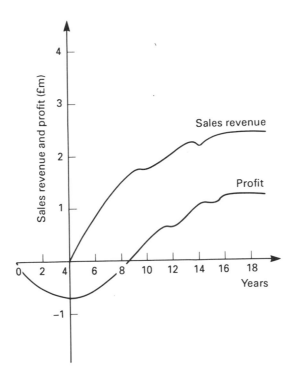

(a) Comment on the relationship between sales revenue and profits over the 18 years.
(b) In year 10 a design change was introduced to extend the life of the product. What was the impact on profits? A second extension strategy was pursued in year 14, but did not involve a design change. Suggest what it might have been.
(c) What evidence is there that the product had changed from being a star to a cash cow by year 16?
(d)   (i) What was the pre-launch R and D time for the product?
      (ii) Suggest, with explanations, **three** products for which R and D time is likely to be longer.
      (iii) Suggest **four** reasons why products are abandoned before launch.

6   Study the table on readership of selected magazines and answer the following questions.
(a) As an advertiser what additional information would you require before choosing *TV Times* and *Radio Times* to carry your advertisement?
(b) Suggest reasons for the variations in number of readers per copy.
(c) In addition to the 'readership' figure, advertisers need data on circulation figures (number of copies sold). Why should we treat both figures with caution?
(d) In what circumstances is *Exchange and Mart* the most appropriate media?
(e) Study the age structure of the readership of the listed womens' magazine. Suggest possible consequences for the type of advertisements carried in these magazines.
(f) In what way does the distribution of *Family Circle* differ from that of the other magazines?

Readership of Selected Magazines

	% of adults reading each maga- zine 1986	% of each age group reading each magazine				Reader- ship (M)	Readers per copy (Number)
		15/24	25/44	45/64	65+		
TV Times	21	25	23	19	17	9.5	3.1
Radio Times	20	22	22	19	18	9.1	2.9
Readers Digest	15	11	17	19	12	6.8	4.3
Smash Hits	4	20	3	1	–	2.3	4.8
Weekly News	4	3	4	5	6	2.0	2.4
Exchange and Mart	4	7	6	3	1	2.0	9.2
Woman's Own	11	13	13	10	8	5.0	4.1
Woman	8	10	10	7	5	3.8	3.3
Woman's Weekly	7	6	6	9	9	3.3	2.5
Family Circle	7	5	10	7	3	3.0	4.4
Good House- keeping	6	4	7	6	4	2.6	6.7
Woman's Realm	5	3	5	6	6	2.2	3.2

Note: Readership is defined as the average issue readership and represents the number of people who claim to have read or looked at one or more copies of a given publication during a period equal to the interval at which the publication appears.
(*Source: Social Trends 18*, 1988. Reproduced with the permission of the Controller of HMSO)

EXAMINATION QUESTIONS ■ ■ ■

■ 1   How might the manufacturer of a new chocolate bar decide to market the product?

(Cambridge, June 1987)

■ 2   A firm is about to extend its product range. Under what circumstances might the firm engage in market research and how might it be undertaken?

(AEB, November 1987)

■ 3   'A high quality product does not need marketing. It will sell itself. Marketing is only necessary to overcome consumer resistance to poor quality.' Do you agree with this statement? Explain your answer.

(AEB, June 1979)

■ 4   Review the constraints on a marketing director when formulating his marketing plan.

(AEB, June 1984)

5 What do you understand by the concept of the 'marketing mix', and what are the main elements of a typical 'mix'? Show, by reference to the marketing of a new video game produced by a firm new to the business, how the elements of a mix must be inter-related if a product is to be marketed successfully.

(Cambridge, June 1984)

6 The Emperor Garment Company is a medium-sized clothing manufacturer specialising in the production of a small range of high quality shirts and blouses, trousers, skirts and jackets, which sell at the upper end of the price range. It grew rapidly in the 1970s as the public chose these less common products in the High Street clothing shops and department stores through which Emperor marketed its output. However, between 1980 and 1983 sales began to level off and then decline. The Managing Director is considering the purchase of a small number of retail shops in prime sites. These shops would sell only 'Emperor' garments, supplemented by a range of ties, socks, knitwear and accessories bought in from other manufacturers.

As *Marketing Manager* you are required to prepare a report, using a suitable format, to help him in reaching a decision.

Your report should cover the following areas:

(*a*) Possible reasons for the decline in sales.

(*b*) Advantages and disadvantages to The Emperor Garment Company of having its own retail outlets.

(*c*) Alternative marketing strategies open to The Emperor Garment Company.

(AEB, June 1985)

7 Read the following extract on the marketing of the Cadbury Wispa and answer the questions which follow.

Marketing the Cadbury Wispa

The gigantic brands in the 'pure' chocolate market had, without exception, origins dating back to before the Second World War. Cadbury's Diary Milk was launched in 1905 and has sold prodigiously ever since. Some twenty years later Cadbury launched Flake, which was discovered as a by-product of manufacturing milk chocolate.

These two products set the pace in the market for eighty years. There have been many attempts to launch a product to stand alongside CDM and Flake. None succeeded until the late 1970s when Cadbury started a secret R & D project.

It was found that the latest technology applied to chocolate manufacturing could confer a different texture and new eating characteristics on the classic milk chocolate product.

All the pre-launch research suggested that the product was a winner. However, as years of bitter experience have taught many manufacturers in this market, having a product that the public likes is not always enough. The complete marketing package is just as critical.

Nothing new under the sun

This was the attitude of most consumers to chocolate products. They simply didn't believe you could produce anything new. Reversing this belief was the problem facing the Young and Rubicam advertising agency when Cadbury brought them the product now named 'Wispa', in 1980.

In October 1983 the product was launched . . . Cadbury spent heavily on Television Advertising . . . and on a massive poster campaign. Wispa is now the third largest brand in the total confectionary market and 11 weeks after launch spontaneous awareness among consumers reached 73%. Whichever way you look at it the product is a superb technical and marketing accomplishment, unique in a fiercely competitive market.

(Adapted from a Cadbury advertisement, *The Economist* March 1986.)

(*a*) Give *three* examples of what would be included in 'the complete marketing package'.

(*b*) The initial launch may well have been accompanied by special pricing deals. What factors might the company have taken into consideration when setting the long-term price?

(*c*) Cadbury now have three major confectionery products instead of two. What advantages does this give the company?

(*d*) Outline the factors that the company might take into consideration, before embarking upon a European launch of the product?

(AEB, November 1987)

FURTHER READING

MARKETING

P TINNISWOOD *Marketing Decisions* (Longman)

E T MARTIN *Marketing* (Mitchell Beazley/Northcote)

D LITTLER, *Marketing and Product Development* (Philip Allan)

B KENNY (WITH K DYSON) *Marketing in Small Businesses* (Routledge)

D FOSTER *Mastering Marketing* (Macmillan)

T CANNON *Basic Marketing: Principles and Practice* (Cassell)

M J BAKER *Marketing: An Introductory Text* (Macmillan)

M J BAKER *Macmillan Dictionary of Marketing and Advertising* (Macmillan)

D WATERWORTH *Marketing for the Small Business* (Macmillan)

G LANCASTER AND L MASSINGHAM *Essentials of Marketing* (McGraw-Hill)

T MCBURNIE AND D CLUTTERBUCK *The Marketing Edge* (Penguin).

G LANCASTER, R PEARSON, P L REYNOLDS *Marketing: A College Companion* (Letts)

N HILL *An Introduction to Marketing* (Business Education Publishers)

F JEFKINS *Modern Marketing* (Pitman)

CHAPTER 7

The International Dimension

Trading across national boundaries has unique features and problems, e.g. cultural differences, exchange rates. Whether we approach it in terms of economic or marketing theory, international trade deserves separate treatment.

OBJECTIVES

1 To understand the distinctive features and problems of international trade.
2 To investigate alternative ways of entering overseas markets.
3 To investigate multinational corporations.
4 To appreciate the significance of the EC Single Market.
5 To understand the effects of exchange rate movements.

Some economic concepts

Export markets provide new opportunities for British firms. If the domestic market is saturated it is tempting to look overseas for additional sales even though there are extra problems and complications associated with exporting. In those industries based on advanced technology there is need for large export sales to cover research and development costs. In turn the British market is open to foreign goods and services. Import penetration is frequently depicted as destroying jobs and undermining British industry. However, business is about satisfying customer demand. It is also important to remember that there are market opportunities for British service firms in supplying imported goods and services to British customers.

The **balance of payments** is a set of accounts recording Britain's transactions with the rest of the world, although it is useful to remember that 'Britain' neither imports nor exports. It is British firms that undertake the trade. It is usual to make a distinction between trade in goods (known as **visible trade**) and trade in financial and other services (known as **invisible trade**). The distinction between invisible exports and invisible imports sometimes causes confusion, but the easiest way to make the distinction is to consider the flow of money. If some activity (e.g. an American travelling by British Airways) leads to an inflow of money to Britain, then it is classed as an invisible export and it becomes a positive item on the balance of payments. If the activity (e.g. British goods being transported on a Greek ship) leads to an outflow, it is an invisible import and therefore a debit item on the balance of payments.

The difference between the value of exports and the value of imports is known as the **balance of trade** or **visible balance**. Similarly the difference between earnings from invisibles and payments for invisibles is known as the balance of **invisible trade**. Historically Britain has enjoyed a surplus on invisibles but has suffered a deficit on visibles. If the surplus on invisibles exceeds the visible deficit Britain has a surplus on the current account of the balance of payments.

The next part of the account concerns the movement of capital into and out of the country. If a Japanese company establishes production facilities in Britain, there is an inflow of capital which shows up as a positive item on the balance of payments. When the balance on the capital account is added to the balance on the current account, we have a figure for the overall balance of payments. The remainder of the account deals with how the deficit is financed (e.g. by running down foreign currency reserves) or how the surplus was disposed of (e.g. repayments to the International Monetary Fund).

When analysing overseas markets it is useful to group the economies of the world.

1 WESTERN INDUSTRIAL ECONOMIES. In this category are the countries of Western Europe (including non-EC countries such as Switzerland), North America, Australia and Japan. These are advanced, wealthy nations with open markets and convertible foreign currencies. A high proportion of world trade is between countries in this group.

2 COMMUNIST ECONOMIES OR EASTERN PLANNED ECONOMIES. Some of the eastern bloc countries are advanced and industrialised but trade with such countries remains relatively small. In part this is because trade, like other aspects of economic life in the planned economies, is subject to considerable control. Until now most Anglo-Soviet trade has been controlled by treaty on a barter basis. Barter trade eliminates the need for foreign currency as a medium of exchange. Perestroika in the eastern bloc could present British firms with new market opportunities.

3 OIL EXPORTING COUNTRIES. This group is separated out because possession of this natural resource has led to great wealth and prosperity. Some of the Gulf States such as Kuwait enjoy the world's highest income per head, suggesting that these countries are lucrative markets for British firms. However, the uneven distribution of income means that although such countries provide good markets for luxury goods and arms, there is less scope for British manufacturers of non-luxury consumer goods.

4 NEWLY INDUSTRIALISING COUNTRIES (NICS). Countries such as South Korea, Taiwan and Brazil are experiencing rapid growth and industrialisation. Ultimately they could provide British firms with substantial market opportunities but at present their use of trade barriers restricts British access to their markets. NICs currently occupy the same position in the world economy that Japan occupied in the 1950s – producers of inexpensive goods made with low cost labour.

5 DEVELOPING COUNTRIES. These range from middle-income countries with a large industrial base, such as India, to low income, agricultural economies (e.g. Ethiopia). Exports to these countries are limited because of low effective demand reflecting the poverty of these countries. In addition, import controls and foreign exchange controls limit the ability of people in these countries to purchase goods from British firms.

Trade barriers

As a major trading country, Britain has benefitted from access to overseas markets. Historically, economic growth in Britain has been closely linked with overseas trade. Not surprisingly British economists from Adam Smith onwards have been biased in favour of trade free from artificial controls. Free trade rewards the efficient, low-cost producer and results in countries specialising in those aspects of production for which they are most suited. Import controls on the other hand protect the inefficient, force consumers to pay more for goods and 'prop-up' those economic activities for which the country is ill-suited. Occasionally there are demands for protection based on social or political reasons (such as for the textile firms which are protected from imports from developing countries by the multi-fibre agreement) or to nurture the development of infant industries. There are also demands for protection against so-called 'unfair' competition, but generally British industry is willing to accept the cut and thrust of competition in the UK market to gain access to lucrative foreign markets.

Unfortunately, British export firms do face import barriers abroad:

1. TARIFFS. These taxes on imported goods do not stop imports but raise their price.
2. QUOTAS. By a quota we mean a maximum limit placed on imports.
3. NON-TARIFF OR TECHNICAL BARRIERS. Some countries exploit local product safety laws to prevent imports. Over the last few decades, non-tariff barriers have been used as a way of evading international agreements to maintain freedom of trade.
4. FINANCIAL SUBSIDIES to home producers to enable them to compete against foreign rivals.
5. EXCHANGE CONTROLS. Foreign governments control the access of their own citizens to foreign currencies. Without foreign currencies it will prove difficult, if not impossible, to pay for imports. In many Third World countries, shortage of foreign currency, together with tight controls over access to available supplies, reduces the volume of imports and therefore the ability of British firms to sell goods there.

Why the overseas market is different

The overseas market is a segment (or a series of segments) of the overall market for the products of UK firms. In the export market there are problems and risks which are not present in the 'soft' home market. The additional complications, which justify the separate treatment given to foreign trade, are as follows:

1. Foreign barriers to imported goods (e.g. tariffs).
2. Political risks (e.g. consequences of political instability abroad).
3. Legal difference (e.g. contract law, product safety).
4. Increased transport and distribution cost.
5. Longer supply chain and, therefore, remoteness from the customer.
6. Longer delay in receiving payment.

7. Cultural differences concerning:
   (a) the acceptability of the product;
   (b) the promotional mix;
   (c) choice of name;
   (d) the way in which business is conducted;
   (e) units of measurement;
   (f) packaging;
   (g) colour used in the product and packaging.
8. Economic stability abroad (e.g. firms dependent upon export markets are affected by the state of the local economy).
9. Exchange rates. We will look at exchange rates in more detail later, but the key point to remember is that a fall in the external value of sterling makes UK exports cheaper but imports dearer. The absence of a universal currency in overseas trade is perhaps the fundamental distinction between domestic and overseas trade.

Given the existence of this distinct market segment beyond our shores, the questions for British firms are whether and how they should enter foreign markets. Should they adopt a global strategy and attempt to sell the same goods in the same way abroad as they do in the UK? Alternatively, they may choose to modify the existing strategy to circumstances abroad (adaption strategy). Finally, a localised strategy involves devising individual products and/or marketing strategies for each separate market.

How to enter overseas markets

British manufacturing firms can exploit overseas markets in a number of ways. It is possible to profit from overseas markets without the export of goods produced in the UK. We can identify the following alternative ways of entering overseas markets:

1. EXPORTING. This involves the physical movement of goods produced in the UK. Within this broad category we can distinguish between a number of separate types of exporting based on the degree of activity or passivity of the UK firm. Passive exporting was a feature of mediaeval England when

French and Venetian merchants sailed up Southampton Water to trade with their less developed neighbours. Indirect exporting by a UK manufacturing firm is similarly a passive activity. The marketing and despatch of goods abroad is undertaken by import-export firms. Direct, active exporting involves a more positive commitment to overseas markets with the appointment of agents and sales people resident abroad. The UK firm is, therefore, actively involved in marketing the goods abroad.

2 LICENSING Under this system British goods are not shipped abroad but, for a licence fee, the UK company allows foreign manufacturers to use its brand names, designs, patents and expertise. Production under licence is widely used in the record and canned drink industries. This activity tends to be confined to areas of industry where technology is controlled and/or where patents and copyright apply. The foreign licensee is allowed to produce for specified overseas markets but not to be a direct rival to UK firms. It has the advantage of avoiding direct commitments in foreign markets.

3 CONTRACT PRODUCTION This is different from licensing in that manufacturing is undertaken by firms abroad, but on behalf of the British producer. Contract production might involve the local assembly of components exported from Britain and is especially attractive in situations where components are subject to lower tariffs than finished goods. The marketing of the assembled good remains with the UK firm.

4 DIRECT INVESTMENT ABROAD. To achieve greater control over all processes and to avoid the problems assciated with the physical movement of goods abroad, a UK company may decide to supply foreign markets by establishing production facilities abroad. In some cases it might be a joint venture with a local firm (especially where 100 per cent foreign ownership is forbidden) whereas in others it might be a wholly-owned manufacturing or assembly plant. The production facilities are acquired either by merger or take over or are built up from scratch. With production facilities abroad, the firm has become a multinational corporation (MNC).

5 MULTINATIONAL MARKETING involves international specialisation by plant with goods moving across international boundaries between subsidiaries of the same MNC. Car producers such as Ford concentrate production of different models in different locations from where the whole of Europe is supplied. A growing proportion of international trade is internal to MNCs.

Multinational corporations (MNCs)

To be classed as a MNC, a company has to do more than maintain sales outlets abroad. MNCs establish production facilities abroad. Although many MNCs (such as Exxon, General Motors, Texaco and Ford) originate in America, others originate elsewhere: hence, Sony, Cannon and Nissan are Japanese multinationals; Electrolux originated in Sweden and Ciba-Geigy in Switzerland. British multinationals include ICI and BP, whereas Unilever and Royal Dutch Shell are both Anglo-Dutch firms, although they both operate much further afield. Historically, MNCs were established to obtain raw materials, especially in the less developed parts of the world. British-owned firms operating plantations in the Americas or South African mines in the 19th Century were early examples of MNCs.

More recent MNCs have been established either:

(a) to obtain cost advantages from cheap labour or materials; or

(b) to reach markets protected by tariffs.

MNCs are the subject of great controversy along the lines of the social responsibility debate we encountered in Chapter 3. People's perception of MNCs is likely to reflect their political view. Supporters of the free enterprise system see multinational production as a rational division of labour producing mutually beneficial results. The MNC is able to take advantage of market opportunities and low cost production facilities. Consumers benefit from low cost, efficient production and countries that receive MNCs benefit from the transfer of technology, investment and production facilities. People in the political centre accept that MNCs are inevitable and a potentially beneficial part of the world economy, but are critical of some of the worse abuses associated with MNCs. These criticisms of MNCs are made more forcefully by radicals who see them as a malevolent force in the world economy.

The sheer size of MNCs leads people to be suspicious. Large MNCs control resources greater than medium-sized economies such as Belgium. It is argued that they owe allegiance to no one country. International management is willing and able to switch resources between countries to secure advantages in terms of cheap labour, preference treatment or low taxation. Trade unionists in western countries criticise MNCs for exporting jobs, and radicals in the developing world accuse MNCs of exploiting cheap local labour but remitting profits back to the rich world. The Green movement accuses MNCs of destroying precious natural resources such as the Amazonian rainforests.

Over one-eighth of world trade is now internal to MNCs. Those who accuse MNCs of not being 'good citizens' argue that transfer prices between subsidiaries of the same MNC are distorted to evade taxation. Adjustment of prices can result in high profits being declared in low tax countries and low profits in high tax countries.

The European Community

After the devastating experience of two world wars there emerged a growing desire for greater European cooperation, especially on economic and social policy. This led six Western European countries to sign the Treaty of Rome in 1957 which established the European Economic Community. Britain at first remained aloof partly because she clung to the outdated role of a leading world power with a large empire: however, postwar economic and military weakness led to a gradual (if somewhat reluctant) acceptance of Britain's changed position in the world. No longer a major world power, Britain saw her future in closer links with European neighbours. Even before Britain's entry into the EC in 1973, her European trade was of growing importance, whereas trade with the Commonwealth was declining in relative importance.

The EC now includes all countries in Western Europe with the exception of Norway (which elected in a referendum not to join because of her fishing industry) and a number of countries (e.g. Sweden, Switzerland) whose neutrality would be compromised by membership. The EC represents the largest market in the world: the combined population of member states exceeds that of the USA or Japan and the income of EC citizens is greater than that of the more densely populated countries such as India and China.

Regional groupings of economies are not uncommon in the world. The UK was a member of a regional group known as the European Free Trade Association (EFTA) before her EC membership. What makes the EC unusual (if not unique) is that cooperation extends further than a mutual agreement to abolish tariffs and other import controls. The creation of a free trade area was the first stage in European cooperation. It was followed by agreement on tariffs against non-EC goods. A common external tariff is a feature of a customs union. The next stage is the creation of a truly Common Market. It has always been the objective of the EC to create a situation where trade between member states was no different from trade within a member state (in which case we should eventually treat it as domestic trade).

Frustration at the slow progress led to renewed effort by governments to complete the process. In 1985 European heads of government committed themselves to the creation of a Single Market by the end of 1992.

The Single European Act defines the single market as 'an area without internal frontiers in which the free movement of goods, persons, services and capital is ensured'. Progress towards the Single Market will be enhanced by changes in decision-making within the EC. Under the SEA, majority voting (rather than unanimous agreement) is extended to most major areas of the Single Market programme.

The existing barriers to trade that will disappear can be classified as:

1 PHYSICAL BARRIERS – customs controls, documentation, border stoppages (although action to prevent movement of illicit drugs, terrorists and immigrants from Third World countries will still be permitted).

2 TECHNICAL BARRIERS – national product standards, technical regulations, conflicting business laws, public procurement policies.

3 FISCAL BARRIERS – especially differing rates of VAT and excise duties.

Like all open doors, the Single Market will facilitate the passage of goods in both directions. It will create both threats but also new opportunities. As the Cecchini Report (1988) puts it: 'For companies the challenge of success, but an end to national soft options'. The benefits to companies will come in the form of:

● New market opportunities
● Increased efficiency resulting from the incentive of competition
● Enlarged markets resulting in economies of scale
● Innovation in response to competition
● Access to lower cost inputs
● Access to new sources of finance.

The impact of 1992 on a particular firm (or industry) will depend upon two factors. First, the extent to which intra-EC trade is at present constrained by the non-tariff barriers that will be swept away. The Cecchini Report (produced for the Commission of the EC) sought to identify the relative importance of technical barriers to trade in various sectors of the European economy.

Those industries currently constrained by technical barriers will feel the greatest impact from the Single Market. British food and pharmaceutical companies are expected to benefit from the new

Table IX   Technical barriers to trade

High	Medium	Low
Electrical engineering	Automobile	Oil refining
Mechanical engineering	Office equipment	Footware, clothing
Pharmaceutical	Rubber products	Plastics
Food	Metals	Paper & printing

opportunities, but mechanical engineering could suffer from greater competition from European producers.

The second determinant of the impact of 1992 on firms is the extent to which they are ready (a) to take advantage of the new opportunities and (b) to face the challenge of greater competition from European firms. A failure to prepare for 1992 will not only result in lost opportunities but an increased threat to survival. The Department of Trade and Industry 'Action Checklist for Business' advises firms to consider the following questions:

1 How has the market changed for our business?

2 Should we become a European business, looking upon Europe as our primary market, rather than just the UK?

3 Would becoming a European business alter the scale of the targets in our plans?

4 In what ways will we be vulnerable to more competition in our present markets?

5 Should we form links, merge or acquire business to strengthen our market presence, broaden our range of products and services and spread our financial risk?

6 Is our management and structure appropriate to exploit new opportunities or defend our position?

7 What training, in languages and other skills, do we need to be ready for the Single Market?

8 Who in our firm is going to be responsible for

deciding how to make the most of the Single Market?

The Single Market will create a more competitive and dynamic economy. Cecchini estimates that savings from the integration of 12 national markets will amount to £140 billion per year. It will create millions of jobs throughout Europe and 'put Europe on an upward trajectory of economic growth lasting into the next century'. British firms will have to decide whether they will make the preparation to enjoy the benefits of 1992 or become one of the victims of 1992.

In this account of the EC no mention has been made of exchange rates, which remain the fundamental difference between domestic and international trade. It is now necessary to turn to this issue.

Exchange rates

The fundamental difference between international and domestic trade is the absence in the former of a universally accepted currency. The buyer of goods from abroad has to find a means of payment which is acceptable to the exporter. Hence, British firms engaged in importing might find that sterling is unacceptable to the foreign exporter who instead demands payment in dollars or yen. Problems in acquiring an acceptable medium of exchange can act as a constraint on trade, to the detriment of both buyer and seller.

The existence of national currencies inevitably means that there is an exchange rate between currencies. An exchange rate of £1 = $1.5 means that the price of one pound sterling is $1.5, whereas the price of $1 is £⅔. Countries operate a variety of exchange rate regimes ranging from fixed (such as the 19th Century gold standard), to freely floating. Between the two extremes there is a variety of forms of managed exchange rates. The western world operated on managed exchange rates from 1945 to 1971. National governments were required to take action (such as buying and selling their own currency and using fiscal and monetary policy) to keep the value of their currency within a narrow band relative to the US dollar which, in turn, was fixed in relation to gold. A revision of the exchange rate (known as **devaluation** or **upward revaluation**) was permitted if the country faced a fundamental problem but in ordinary circumstances governments had a duty to manage their exchange rates within the bands. In 1971 major currencies, including sterling, were allowed to float. In effect the exchange rate was treated as a price like any other and was not fixed by governments. Instead, sterling was allowed to find its own level in the market place. Sterling will fall in value (known as **depreciation**) if imports into Britain are excessive. British firms will sell sterling to buy foreign currencies in order to buy foreign goods. This will drive down the value of sterling. An export surplus will push up the sterling exchange rate as foreign buyers demand more sterling in order to buy British goods. This is known as **appreciation** of the currency.

The Exchange Rate Mechanism of the European Monetary System is a system of managed exchange rates between EC currencies. At the time of writing Britain is not part of the ERM and it is proving to be a major cause of political and economic controversy. Staunch supporters of European unity argue that stability of EC exchange rates is an essential feature of the 'Single Market'. While exchange rates fluctuate, intra-EC trade (i.e. between members) will not be the same as trade within each member state. ERM membership, however, reduces government freedom of manoeuvre in matters of economic policy since the Government would be committed to act to keep exchange rates within narrow bands.

Managed rates provide an element of stability and certainty in trading relationships whereas freely floating rates add an extra dimension of risk and uncertainty to international trade. A fall in the exchange rate of sterling (devaluation or depreciation, depending on its cause) makes Britain's imports dearer and British exports cheaper. This can be shown in a simple example (see Table X).

Table X   Fall in the exchange rate

Price of British goods	Exchange rate	Price in dollars
£100	£1 = $2	$200
£100	£1 = $1	$100

Price of US goods	Exchange rate	Price in sterling
$500	£1 = $2	£250
$500	£1 = $1	£500

Initially, more expensive imports appear beneficial to the country and to British firms. A simple application of demand theory leads to the conclusion that the volume of imports will fall, creating improved market opportunities for British firms. However, there are complications. First, British buyers' preference for foreign goods might be the result of the availability or quality of these goods. If demand is inelastic, buyers will continue to buy the goods, despite the rise in price. Second, many British firms are engaged in the import trade and they will suffer if the volume of imports falls. Third, many so-called 'British' goods have an import component. A fall in the exchange rate will raise the sterling price of the imported components or raw materials. The rise in costs will either be passed on to customers (with a possible fall in the volume of sales) or will be absorbed by British producers in reduced profit margins. As exports are now cheaper to foreigners the quantity could increase. However, this assumes that British firms are able to take advantage of the improved market opportunities and that price is a major factor in the decisions of foreign buyers.

A rise in the exchange rate (upward revaluation or appreciation, depending upon cause) makes British exports dearer to foreigners but imports cheaper. As exports are dearer, it is likely that the volume will fall unless British firms reduce the sterling price of their goods to maintain their competitive position. Consequently, a rise in the exchange rate might result in reduced profit margins rather than reduced volume of exports. Either way it is harmful to firms engaged in the export trade: cheaper imports are desirable from the consumers' point of view, but are harmful to British firms suffering from import penetration. To retain their domestic market shares British firms might be forced to reduce profit margins.

On the question of exchange rates, business people are like farmers who complain if it is too hot and dry and also when it is too cold and wet. Any movement in the exchange rate poses a problem for business (as well as creating new opportunities). Economists tend to concentrate on consequences for the volume of trade. We should take into account not just volume but also the consequences for the profit margins of specific British firms.

Conclusion

The international dimension warrants separate treatment because, despite MacDonalds and Coca Cola, 'it is different abroad'. Any venture into the international economy (whether as a buyer, seller or investor) involves problems and risks which are additional to those present in the domestic economy.

All the business concepts and decision-making techniques which are dealt with in the other chapters are applicable when the firm ventures abroad. What is different is the environment in which the firm operates. Overseas competitors are a constant threat to British firms but the overseas market provides opportunities that do not exist in this small island off the north-west coast of continental Europe. The challenge of overseas markets has inspired entrepreneurs for centuries and will continue to do so in the future.

CASE STUDY 1
Cross border acquisitions and investment

The late 20th Century has seen the internationalisation of capital on a scale hitherto unknown. Foreign acquisition of prestige British firms like Westland and Jaguar hit the headlines; less well publicised is British acquisition of substantial (and, in some cases, majority) holdings in overseas firms.

The 1992 M and A Monthly reported that in July 1989 UK companies targeted for cross border mergers and acquisitions constituted 40 per cent by value of all such targeted companies. This included Pepsi Cola's 100 per cent acquisition of Smiths and Walkers Crisps. At the same time UK firms were second only to the Americans in acquisition of companies beyond its border: for instance, Scottish and Newcastle Breweries acquired a 65 per cent share in a Dutch holding village operator called Center Parcs.

This two-way flow of capital is confirmed in figures from the US Commerce Department reported in the October 1989 issue of *Euro Business* magazine. Europeans increased their investments in the USA by 60 per cent to $64 billion at the end of 1988. The UK was the largest investor in the USA with Japan and the Netherlands following in second and third place. In terms of US investment in Europe, Britain was the preferred country: this is shown in the statistics below:

Country	European investments in the US ($ billion)	US investment in Europe ($ billion)	Net European investment ($ billion)
Belgium	4.0	7.2	− 3.2
France	11.4	12.5	− 1.1
Italy	0.7	9.1	− 8.4
Netherlands	49.0	15.4	+33.6
Sweden	5.3	1.1	+ 4.2
Switzerland	15.9	18.7	− 2.8
UK	101.9	48.0	+53.9
W Germany	23.8	21.7	+ 2.1
Other Europe	4.4	18.5	−14.1

1 Should we be alarmed at foreign take-over of British industry?
2 Is it 'unpatriotic' to invest overseas?
3 Why is there a two-way cross border flow of capital?
4 The absence of exchange controls in Britain has contributed to this process of internationalisation. Explain how.
5 'Synergy' is a much used word in discussions about mergers. What does it mean and to what extent is it evident in the two named acquisitions?

CASE STUDY 2
Why Barbados?

'Simply stated, Barbados is an ideal location to reduce costs, increase profits, gain exemptions and conveniently serve the United States, European, South American and Caribbean markets.

Because of its abundant supply of highly literate, enthusiastic, easily trainable and dexterous English-speaking workers and its co-operative government, manufacturing operations in Barbados are smooth and problems are minimal.

The basic infrastructure is excellent. Electric power, roads, telephone, telex, airport and seaport facilities (including container handling equipment) are, for all practical purposes, equivalent to those in the US and Europe.

Above all, Barbados provides economy of operation with savings of 30–50 per cent on US or European costs. Compared to Asian or African assembly, many products can be landed in the USA or Europe from Barbados at equal or lower total costs.

Under the Lome Convention, a wide range of manufactured products can be imported in the EC from Barbados free of tariffs and quotas ... US imports from Barbados benefit from tariff concessions'.

(Source: Barbados Industrial Development Corporation 1983)

---

1 Why is the Government of Barbados keen to attract multinational corporations to the island?
2 Explain what is meant by each of the following:
   (*a*) its co-operative government;
   (*b*) the basic infrastructure;
   (*c*) tariff concessions; and
   (*d*) the Lome Convention
Why are these important to firms contemplating establishing manufacturing facilities in Barbados?
3 Do low wages always mean low production costs?
4 Why are the stated attributes of the local labour force considered important when attracting multinational companies?

CASE STUDY 3
Public purchasing and 1992

Purchasing by governments and other public bodies accounts for as much as 15 per cent of the EC's gross domestic product.

EC directives are designed to open up the market by making sure that all companies in the Community have a fair chance when seeking public contracts. They lay down the requirement that public purchasing authorities buy from the sources which offer the best value for money. Nevertheless, the picture remains less than fair. All too often, suppliers trying to sell to public bodies in other member states comes up against barriers which discourage them from seeking business there. The barriers include:
- the tendency to 'buy national', leading to the refusal by public authorities in many areas even to consider bids from suppliers outside their own country;
- lack of information about contracts;
- discriminatory specifications;
- complex tendering procedures.

Completing the Single Market will mean that purchases by governments should reflect fair competition, not national identity. This will be achieved by:
- amendments to EC directives to make the application of rules more open (transparency principle).
- reduce the number of sectors excluded from single market provisions for public purchasing.
- compliance enforced by legal action against offending purchasers.

(Adapted from *The Single Market: the Facts*, DTI)

1 What is the ultimate objective of the Single Market Act and how will the establishment of a single market achieve that objective?
2 Explain the following terms used in the DTI statement:
   (*a*) discriminatory specifications;
   (*b*) tendering;
   (*c*) public bodies (other than Governments); and
   (*d*) EC directives
3 What legal institutions exist to enforce compliance?
4 Suggest types of enterprise likely to be affected by EC directives on public purchasing.
5 How will British firms be affected?

EXERCISE ● ● ●

● 1 Company X produces oil-based products. It buys raw materials priced in US dollars. Each tonne costs $2000 and is used to produce one tonne of saleable product which is sold in the European market at the price of 6000 D Marks. At present exchange rates £1 is equal to $1.50 and DM 3.0.

Calculate the impact on Company X if:

(a) sterling falls 10 per cent against the dollar; and

(b) sterling falls 10 per cent against both the D Mark and the dollar.

2   Euro Disneyland SCA is a company incorporated in France and was established to own a Magic Kingdom theme park and other attractions near Paris. In the autumn of 1989, the European public (including the British) was invited to subscribe to an issue of 10.7 million shares. The nominal value of each share was FF10 but were issued in the UK at the sterling price of 707 pence per share, payable in full on application. In all, just over 50 per cent of Euro Disneyland shares were on offer, the remainder were retained by the American Disney Corporation which also retained responsibility for managing the Magic Kingdom.

(Source: Mini Prospectus issued by S G Warburg)

(a) Why do you think Paris was chosen as the site of the first European Disneyland?

(b) What is the rationale for allowing an American company to run the Magic Kingdom?

(c) If the exchange rate is £=FF10.3, why were subscribers being asked to pay 707p? Why is 'payment in full on application' significant or unusual?

(d) What additional problems or risks are associated with investing in a foreign company?

(e) Why was the share offer made throughout Western Europe and advertised on television? What are the likely consequences for ownership of shares in Euro Disneyland?

3   Some important facts about three non-European countries are given below:-

	Country A	Country B	Country C
National income per head (US $)	17 000	430	2 300
Population (million)	17	100	100
Population growth (%)	1.2	3	2
Economic growth (%)	1.8	6	1
Inflation rate (%)	7.5	13	600

Country A is politically stable. There is a deteriorating trade balance which will force the government to adopt firm monetary and fiscal policies. Interest rates are expected to rise. Concern over environmental issues has led to the rise of a Green Party.

Country B has suffered from recent political turbulence. Ethnic tensions as well as the conflict between modernisation and traditional values are ever-present. IMF loans were conditional upon austere budget measures.

Country C. Stabilisation measures to deal with chronic inflation and debt will restrict government and private spending. Foreign assistance was conditional upon more market-orientated economic policies and the liberalisation of trade and foreign exchange. Potentially very rich, this country has suffered from inequality of income, corruption and political turbulence.

Assess each of the three countries as:

(a) a market for hi-tech goods from Britain;

(b) a market for engineering products;

(c) a market for British consumer goods; and

(d) a place for British investment overseas.

● 4   Study the statement from Paterson Zochonis and answer the questions that follow.

Paterson Zochonis plc – 1989

Summary of Results Year ended 31 May 1989

	£ 1989	£ 1988
Turnover	205.6m	190.4m
Profit before tax	23.4m	24.2m
Profit after tax	15.3m	14.9m
Earnings per share	30.14p	29.39p
Total dividends per share	8.60p	7.80p

West Africa. Profits of the Nigerian operations were 30% higher in local currency terms. However, the naira fell against sterling from 13.3p in May 1988 to 8.6p at 31st May 1989 and this was sufficient to reduce profits from Nigeria in sterling terms compared with those of last year.

Cussons. Cussons did well in the United Kingdom with Imperial Leather soap maintaining its market position and new shower gel and bathing foam products gaining increased sales.

In Australia the new factory is working well and recent product launches have increased turnover by 30%. During the year good progress was made in consolidating the position of the new operations in Thailand and Indonesia.

Current Year. In the current year further economic measures have been taken in Nigeria to tighten the credit squeeze and the naira remains at its May level of 8.6p. So far most group operations there are managing to maintain sales volumes though margins are lower. Elsewhere sales of Cussons' products continue to improve in most areas but the necessary support for expansion and new product launches is, for the time being, likely to more than absorb any increase in profits from these operations.

Present indications for the half year to 30th November 1989 are that group pre-tax profits will be broadly in line with those of the same period last year.

(a) Explain the following terms:
    (i) turnover;
    (ii) credit squeeze;
    (iii) new product launches; and
    (iv) margins.
(b) Why did Paterson Zochonis's profits from West Africa fall in sterling terms?
(c) Why did the Nigerian Government seek to halt the fall in the exchange rate of the naira?
(d) Explain the sentence: 'Elsewhere sales of Cussons' products continue to improve in most areas but the necessary support for expansion and new product launches is, for the time being, likely to more than absorb any increase in profits from these operations'.

● 5   Study the article on the European hosiery industry and answer the questions that follow:

Hosiery manufacturers try Europe on for size

Alice Rawsthorn on the industry's changing structure

For months the roads around Lake Garda in northern Italy have been clogged with lorries delivering new machinery to the hosiery factories in and around the region.

The Italian hosiery companies are preparing for battle. Traditionally the European market for stockings and tights has been fragmented between different companies concentrating on their own countries. But the market is changing.

The big European producers – such as Golden Lady and Omsa of Italy, Pretty Polly and Aristoc of the UK – are becoming increasingly internationalised. And Sara Lee, the Chicago-based consumer products group which dominates US hosiery, has entered the European market through a series of acquisitions.

It seems almost inevitable that the European market will become far less fragmented in the 1990s. A recent report by TMS Partnership, the London-based research consultancy, concluded that probably it would be shared between a small number of large companies. The fight is now on to see which companies these will be.

This picture of reshuffling and restructuring comes at the end of an extraordinarily buoyant period for hosiery in Europe. The most dramatic growth was in the southern countries, Spain and Italy, where hosiery sales almost doubled during the 1980s. The more mature markets of northern Europe benefited from a boost to sales as hosiery became much more responsive to fashion.

The industry is dominated by Italy, which accounts for almost half of production in Europe. The Italians – with Golden Lady and Omsa in the forefront – are also more export-oriented than their competitors. Half the industry's output is sold outside Italy.

By contrast, the other European companies have tended to concentrate on their own countries. France is dominated by Dim and Le Bourget; the UK by Pretty Polly, part of the BTR industrial group, and Aristoc, a subsidiary of Courtaulds; and West Germany by Fred Vatter and Kunert.

But Sara Lee has now arrived in Europe. The US company, which is better known by Europeans for chocolate cakes than tights, already towers over the US hosiery market. It is now intent on expanding into Europe.

It began in 1988 by buying Dim in France. In the following year it acquired a minority interest in Fred Vatter of West Germany. It then took control of Elbeo in the UK, one of Vatter's subsidiaries.

Sara Lee has since invested in extra capacity at Dim in France and has integrated Dim's operation in the UK with that of Elbeo. Mr Weldon Schenck, vice president, said it intended to increase sales to other countries. "But we are taking things day by day," he said.

Sara Lee's arrival poses a serious threat to the stability of the established European players. Golden Lady has already responded. It increased its capacity by 20 per cent last year and will do the same this year. Late last year it acquired Focus on Legs, a privately-owned company, as a marketing base in the UK.

Golden Lady has also changed its export strategy by emphasising branded products, rather than own-label. It is now Europe's biggest hosiery producer and exports half its output.

The other European producers are also becoming more active in other countries, albeit less aggressively than Golden Lady. The two largest UK manufacturers – Pretty Polly and Aristoc – presently export less than 5 per cent of output, but both intend to increase overseas sales, concentrating on value-added products.

Omsa of Italy is increasing its capacity. Le Bourget of France is becoming more active in other countries. Wolford, the leading Austrian producer, is strengthening its position in "designer" hosiery across Europe.

One catalyst for this activity is the conviction that the old differences in style between different countries are being eroded and that there is now an opportunity to operate as a hosiery producer across the continent.

But the new emphasis on exports is also fuelled by the fear that,

World Market 1988 (pairs)		
Europe	3.06bn	46%
US	2.06bn	31%
Japan	1.5bn	23%
TOTAL	6.5bn	

(Source: *The TMS Partnership*)

European production 1987 (pairs)		
Italy	1,295m	46%
UK	522m	19%
W. Germany	338m	12%
France	317m	11%
Spain	94m	3%
Ireland	88m	3%
Portugal	72m	3%
Greece	67m	2%
Others	27m	1%
TOTAL	2,820m	

(Source: *Maillewop*)

unless the established manufacturers increase sales to other countries, they could be very vulnerable if Sara Lee and Golden Lady were to make inroads into their own market.

It remains to be seen how successful Sara Lee and Golden Lady will be. In theory, hosiery looks like a market which is ready for a pan-European approach. In practice, things might not be so simple.

One problem is the fickle nature of hosiery sales which tend to wax and wane with the weather – the colder the better – and with fashion. The 1980s style of short skirts and shoulder-padded "power" dressing could scarcely have been better designed to boost sales of stockings and tights. The new trend towards sportswear is far less favourable.

Another problem is distribution. The large manufacturers have invested heavily in new technology to provide a faster, more flexible service. Retailers now expect hosiery to be delivered within a day or two of an order being dispatched.

This could favour local manufacturers, especially over a company like Golden Lady, which supplies its export customers from Italy. But such an advantage might be eroded after the introduction of the unified market in 1992, which should speed up the flow of goods across the continent.

Similarly, the differences between styles across Europe may have diminished but there are still significant differences between the type and even the size of hosiery preferred in different countries. "We talk about the European market, but it is still really a collection of national markets," said Mr Sandro Veronesi, vice president of Golden Lady. "But it is changing."

(Source: *Financial Times*, December 1989)

(*a*) Explain the following terms and expressions:
buoyant; mature market; capacity; pan European approach.
(*b*) Why is the European market expected to be less fragmented in the 1990s?
(*c*) What method is Sara Lee using to break into the European market?
(*d*) What is meant by the integration of Dim's operations with that of Elbeo?
(*e*) How is Golden Lady seeking to expand into the UK market?
(*f*) Why is the market fickle?
(*g*) Why are UK producers being forced into the export market?
(*h*) We are told that retailers expect deliveries within a day or two of an order being placed. What are the benefits to retailers and the consequences (beneficial or harmful) for manufacturers?

EXAMINATION QUESTIONS ■ ■ ■

■ 1 Examine the particular problems posed for a country by the existence of multinational firms.
(AEB, November 1987).

■ 2 The chairman of a large United Kingdom-based public company has given the strength of sterling in a particular year as a reason for the company's low level of profits. Other comparable United Kingdom companies attributed their high profit levels to the same cause.
Reconcile the apparent contradictions of this statement.
(AEB, June 1981).

■ 3 Most internationally traded products compete more on quality than on price. Exchange rate fluctuations are relevant only in that they alter individual importers' and exporters' profit margins.'
Comment on this statement and explain the relationship between exchange rates and profit margins.
(AEB, June 1987)

■ 4 (a) What do you understand by the phrases:
           'market share'; 'import penetration'; 'cross elasticity of demand'?
      (b) How might a UK-based firm attempt to counteract the problems of increasing foreign
           competition? (If you wish, you may choose to confine your answer to a specific industry.)

(Cambridge, June 1988).

■ 5 'Most bulk chemicals products are priced in US dollars' (*Financial Times*).
      Discuss the problems likely to be encountered by a British company involved in the chemical
markets at home and abroad.

(Cambridge, June 1987)

■ 6 'Without doubt, UK manufacturers are increasing their overseas involvement and shifting
      substantial parts of their operations overseas'. (P Dicken in Global Shift).
      Explain why and consider the consequences of such a shift.

■ 7 Explain the likely consequences for:
      (a) British firms;
      (b) West German firms; and
      (c) The EC;
      of a continuation of 'glasnost' (openness) and 'perestroika' (reform) in the Soviet Union and
      other parts of Eastern Europe.

FURTHER READING

THE INTERNATIONAL DIMENSION

F N BURTON *Contemporary Trade* (Philip Allan)

A NEALE AND C HASLAM *Economics in a Business Context* (Van Nostran Reinhold)

A LEAKE *International Trade* (Longman)

N WALL *The World Economy* (Collins)

P DICKEN *Global Shift : Industrial Change in a Turbulent World* (Paul Chapman Publishing)

P CECCHINI *The European Challenge: 1992* (Wildwood)

I BARNES WITH J PRESTON *The European Community* (Longman)

C TAYLOR, A PRESS AND G MARKS *1992: The Facts and Challenges* (The Industrial Society)

R OWEN AND M DYNES *The Times Guide to 1992* (Times Books)

J REDMOND *The EEC and the UK Economy* (Longman)

L PRACHT (ed) *Europe in Figures: Deadline 1992* (Macmillan/EC/HMSO).

CHAPTER 8
Production and Operations Management

If marketing is concerned with what is produced, production/operations management (POM) is concerned with how goods are produced (or services provided). POM is, therefore, concerned with the organisation and control of the production function. The aim throughout is to ensure that goods are made in the quantities and of the quality required, at the right time and at minimum cost.

OBJECTIVES

1 To survey the main areas of POM.
2 To understand the different production processes.
3 To introduce the concept of scheduling.
4 To investigate stock control techniques.
5 To investigate quality control techniques.
6 To integrate POM with other functional areas.
7 To introduce the principles of scientific management.

The role of the production/operations manager

If the marketing manager makes decisions relating to what is produced, the production manager has responsibilities in relation to how it is made. We use the term 'production management' for firms engaged in primary production (e.g. mining, oil drilling, forestry) and secondary production (e.g. manufacturing). However, for a firm in the tertiary or service sector, production management seems inappropriate and so 'operations management' is the preferred term. Whether the firm produces goods or provides services the principles of POM are equally applicable. In essence, POM seeks to ensure that goods (or services) are made in the required quantity, to the required standard, at the right time and in the most economically efficient manner.

There are both strategic and tactical decisions to be made by the production manager. Strategic decisions include:

1 LOCATION OF PLANT
2 PLANT LAYOUT. We can contrast layout by process (clustering of machinery performing similar tasks) with layout by product (combining in a logical sequence machinery used to produce particular goods). The choice of layout will in part reflect the process involved.
3 SELECTION OF PROCESSING METHODS, PLANT AND EQUIPMENT. The production manager will decide the most efficient way of carrying out each process.
4 PRODUCT DESIGN. Along with the R and D and marketing department, the production department will contribute to the design of the product. However, the interests of the production and marketing departments are likely to conflict over the question of varia-

tions of product style and the simplicity or sophistication of the product.

5 PRODUCTION PLANNING. The aim of production planning is to arrange the manufacturing in the most logical sequence, to produce goods in the most economic batch sizes, ensure maximum utilisation of machines and workers, and schedule work so that goods can be delivered at the time promised.

Tactical level decisions are necessary in relation to:

(a) *Stocks*. These must be sufficient to avoid stockout but, in view of the cost of stock-holding, must not be excessive.

(b) *Quality control*. Goods must conform to the specification and be of a consistent standard.

(c) *Control of labour engaged in production.*

(d) *Maintenance*. Preventive maintenance involves regular servicing. Consequently, machinery will be out of action from time to time, but this is planned rather than enforced by breakdown.

(e) *Production control*. This is a natural follow-up to production planning and is designed to ensure that production takes place in accordance with the plan.

Inadequate POM will result in:
- failure to deliver on time;
- short production run and therefore high set up costs;
- high production costs;
- excessive overtime;
- numerous rush orders;
- delays caused by shortage of materials;
- the 'robbing' of one order to fill another.

Production processes

Production involves the transformation of inputs into output by means of:
- extraction (e.g. mining);
- analytic techniques (breaking down substances);

- fabrication (joining together, e.g. welding);
- synthesis ('creating' new substances).

We can identify five types of production process, the choice of which is determined by the volume of output required and the extent to which the organisation seeks to produce differentiated (as opposed to homogeneous) products.

1 PROJECT PRODUCTION is used in large scale projects made to customer requirements (e.g. an oil tanker or a civil engineering project). The product is unique and is assembled on-site using skilled labour and flexible resources. Because of the size and complexity of the task, considerable planning is necessary. Quantitative techniques such as network analysis are essential to successful management of the project. Moreover, it is usually necessary to breakdown the overall project into manageable sub-tasks many of which are sub-contracted.

2 JOBBING PRODUCTION is also concerned with the production of unique, non-standard goods which are made to order. Unlike project production, the items are small-scale and made in a workshop (e.g. made-to-measure suits or sailing boats). The jobbing work shops is arranged by process. Hence, machines carrying out the same or similar operations are clustered together and the product moves from one work station to another. Multi-purpose machinery is combined with skilled, versatile labour. Job producers economise on stock holding since they do not carry stocks of finished goods but they do face other problems. Short production runs invariably raise unit production costs. Specialist equipment is likely to be under-utilised and delays between operating sequences will mean that total production time will be greater than processing time.

3 BATCH PRODUCTION. As the name suggests, this is the manufacture of different versions of the same basic product in batches (e.g. different colours or types of paint, different varieties of jam tart). Unlike the previous processes there is some repetition of produc-

tion which is for stock (rather than to order). However, production is not continuous. The relatively short production runs result in higher unit costs than would be the case if production was continuous. Change-over (and clean down) between batches mean that resources are at times idle. Consequently, production managers have to plan production schedules to minimise change-overs. The machinery employed will be more specialist than in the earlier processes but must retain some versatility to take account of the requirements of different batches.

4 LINE PRODUCTION is best understood by the example of assembly line manufacture of motor vehicles or electrical goods. Specialist (or dedicated) machinery will be used in the process and, because of the high capital investment required, it is essential to achieve a high level of use. This necessitates a high level of sales of a fairly standardised product made for stock (rather than to order). Line production links up with the strategy of undifferentiated marketing (whereas job and batch production suggests that the product is tailored to suit the needs of particular customers or market segments). The man-power required is specialist but low in skills and is performing repetitive work. The lay-out of the factory will be by process in a logical sequence to minimise the time and cost of movement. Line producers must invest heavily in stocks of raw materials to prevent stock-out (*see* p 126–8) but will keep stocks of work-in-progress to a low level. The great advantage of line production is that with long production runs, unit costs will be very low.

5 CONTINUOUS PROCESS takes line production to its ultimate limit. Dedicated plant is used to manufacture a single product on a continuous (24-hour) basis. It is best understood in terms of chemical manufacture or oil refining. Hence, whereas line production involves the manufacture of discrete objects, continuous or flow production is used for the production of fluids. Most of the characteris-

tics of line production are equally applicable but there is one vital difference: the main labour task in continuous production is that of monitoring the process and therefore skilled labour is required.

The scientific management school

The principles of scientific management were developed in America in the early decades of the 20th Century. The pioneers of scientific management were Frank and Lillian Gilbreth, Henry Gantt and, most important of all, Frederick Taylor. Taylor was critical of contemporary management and work practices. Management abdicated control over the work place and left manual workers to control the methods of operations. The piece-rate system in use did not provide an incentive for increased effort: instead, workers restricted output because they feared working themselves out of a job. Taylor's solution was the application of scientific principles to improve methods of operation to secure an increase in productivity.

The main principles of Taylorism are:
1 Greater division of labour with clearly defined tasks.
2 The application of logic to the management process.
3 Full managerial control over the workshop, especially in the selection and training of workers, and in devising the best way of working.
4 The measurement of work and the setting of appropriate piece rates.

Taylor believed in harmony between workers and management and thought this would emerge through their common interest in increased productivity. If scientific methods are adopted and work is accurately measured, there must be no artificial limit on the earnings of the efficient worker. In this way the practice of restricting output ('soldiering' as it was called) would be defeated.

Frank Gilbreth was a pioneer of **motion**

(method) study. By studying the work of brick-layers, he devised a method of working which cut the number of motions undertaken in laying a brick from 18 to 5. Without any increase in effort, the productivity of bricklayers doubled. Gilbreth's work was continued by his widow who was particularly interested in human aspects of work. Lillian Gilbreth concluded that worker dissatisfaction was caused not by the monotony of work but by management's lack of interest in workers.

Henry Gantt is primarily remembered for his graphical methods used in planning and scheduling work, facilitating greater managerial control. Unlike Taylor and the Gilbreths, Gantt did not believe in the single best method, but merely one that appeared best at the present.

Work study

Work study emerged from the scientific management school of Taylor and Gilbreth. As the name suggests, it involves an analysis of the human work task:

1 to determine the most effective and efficient way of carrying out the process; and
2 to measure the quantity of work.

These two components of work study are known as method study and work measurement respectively.

Method study requires accurate observation and recording of existing work methods. These records are then analysed to devise improvements in methods which might be seen in terms of:

(a) changes in the layout of the work place;
(b) improvements in the design of equipment;
(c) changes in product design;
(d) the elimination or combining of operations;
(e) changes in the sequence of operations; and
(f) economies in the amount of human effort necessary to perform the task.

Work measurement involves similar methods of observing, recording and analysing but the emphasis is quantitative rather than qualitative. By measuring the time taken to complete tasks (and, therefore, the quantity of work performed in a given time period), it makes a contribution to:

(a) costing;
(b) planning production;
(c) scheduling;
(d) determination of manpower needs; and
(e) motivating the workforce through incentive payment schemes.

In the case of a repetitive and existing job, a stop watch is used to measure the time taken to complete the task. The time taken for an experienced, competent operative to carry out the task can then be determined. Allowance will have to be made for different conditions of work, fatigue of workers or differences in materials and equipment. From the analysis, the standard time can be determined. More difficult for the purposes of work measurement are non-existing and non-repetitive jobs. There are various techniques (such as **Predetermined Motion Time Systems** or PMTS) whereby standard times can be calculated from a synthesis of times for carrying out the various motions within the overall task.

Standard times derived from a work measurement study can be used as the basis for a piece-rate system of payment. It is most applicable where conditions are standardised and the product is homogeneous. Under these circumstances, there is a direct relationship between effort and an output which can be objectively measured. It only succeeds if in addition workers are motivated to work harder by the prospect of increased financial reward.

A straightforward piece-rate system with a simple linear relationship between output and earnings may prove unsatisfactory. First, the employees may prefer the safety net of a basic minimum, irrespective of output. Second, management might wish to dissuade the workforce from producing more than can be sold. The logic of a linear relationship is that there is no limit on the earnings of individual workers, other than their own ability and energy. Third, workers might decide to reduce effort even though it involves a financial sacrifice. Man is not just an 'economic animal' motivated by money. Figure 8.1 illustrates a piece-rate system designed to encourage workers to reach the standard performance. A basic minimum wage is available as a safety net, and payments rise steeply with increased effort up to the standard performance. Thereafter, piece-rates are reduced to discourage over-exertion and to impose some degree of management control on overall production.

All systems of output-linked pay for employees require resources for administering the scheme.

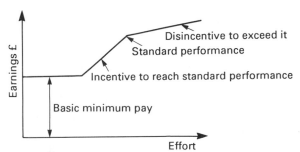

Fig 8.1 Piece-rate system designed to control effort

Management has to weigh the cost of administration against the additional productivity and/or control over the workforce. The administration of piece-rate payment is more difficult when we remove the assumption of standardised conditions and homogeneous output. A change in the layout of the work place might result in a rise in productivity (without any increase in effort of the workforce) and a substantial rise in earnings. The workforce is likely to resist any attempt to re-negotiate piece-rates downwards in the light of easier working conditions.

Job evaluation

Job evaluation is a systematic comparison of jobs designed to place jobs in a rank order based upon the demands the job places upon the worker. It is not the postholder that is evaluated but the job itself. Once a rank order is established, a rational pay structure can be introduced to replace arbitrary methods of pay determination.

Job evaluation methods can be classified as non-analytical and analytical. The former involves an impressionistic view of the job as a whole to produce either a ranking of jobs or an identification of jobs with predetermined grades. In the analytical methods, the job is broken down into components which are then used in the comparison with other jobs.

The **points rating system** is the most widely used of the analytical methods. Relevant job factors are agreed upon and given a weighting (or maximum score) for all jobs in the evaluation exercise. Job factors typically used in a points rating exercise are:

- Skill
- Responsibility/accountability
- Effort
- Working conditions.

Each job in the exercise is given a score for each of the factors which are then added together to produce a final rank order. The rationale for the points system is that it is claimed to be more objective than non-analytical ranking. Nevertheless, it is impossible to avoid an element of subjectivity in the process. Moreover, the exercise is only valid within a narrow range of comparable jobs inside the organisation. In view of the changing demands of work, it should not be allowed to fossilise pay difficulties. In practice, pay is determined not by how difficult or demanding the job is, but by the force of supply and demand in the market.

The scientific management school led to a systematic analysis of work and provided the means by which management and workers were able to achieve higher rates of productivity for mutual benefit. However, it reduced the role and the autonomy of the manual worker. Division of work led to boring repetitive jobs in which workers become alienated. Moreover, by treating workers as 'economic animals', it neglected the sociological and psychological aspects of work.

Purchasing

As production involves a conversion of inputs into outputs, it is necessary to acquire supplies of raw materials and/or components. The first decision that faces the organisation is whether to make the components itself or to buy them in from outside. The decision will be influenced by the availability and reliability of suppliers, delivery times, relative costs and the amount of specialist expertise and dedicated machinery required in the production of components.

If the decision is made to buy the inputs from supply firms, the purchasing department has to decide how and from whom to acquire the goods. **Vendor rating** is a technique to aid the selection of the supplier. Factors such as price, quality, delivery dates and reliability are weighted to enable purchasers to compare different suppliers. Centralised purchasing has the advantages of standardised procedures, utilisation of expertise in buying, reduced administrative costs and increased control over expenditure. On the other hand, it can lead to inflexibility, long lead times (delays in obtaining supplies) and a lack of awareness of needs at the local or plant level.

The terms on which inputs are purchased also have to be considered. The following policies are pursued:

1 PURCHASE ON CONTRACT. This is important where continuity of production is essential (e.g. flow production). Contracts commit each side to specific terms and might not be advantageous if there are substantial variations in price over time. Firms can reduce the risks involved by buying on a futures contract rather than buying at current or spot prices.

2 SPECULATIVE BUYING. This involves purchases in excess of immediate requirements to benefit from anticipated future price movements.

3 HAND-TO-MOUTH BUYING. Buying only when goods are required means less capital is tied up and there is less need for storage capacity. On the other hand, the purchase of small quantities raises unit costs and the purchaser may be forced to buy at high spot prices.

There are additional problems if inputs are purchased from abroad. Movements in exchange rates will change the sterling price of foreign inputs. The uncertainty can be reduced by holding bank accounts in different currencies or by buying 'currencies forward'. This means agreeing to buy currencies in the future at a price (exchange rate) determined today. Action to reduce uncertainty is called **hedging**.

Stock control

Stock represents an investment by the organisation. Money is tied up in goods for which the eventual payment may be delayed months and even years. Firms are willing to incur the expense of stock holding to ensure continuity of operations. Therefore, the aim of stock control is to maintain continuity while minimising the cost of stock holding.

First, we should investigate more fully why firms are willing to invest in stocks. Stocks of raw materials are held to allow for variations in supply and to take advantage of bulk-buying discounts and anticipated price rises. The main reason for holding stocks of work-in-progress is to 'decouple' the productive process allowing greater flexibility and improved machine utilisation. Finished goods are held in stock so that the firm can cope with variations in demand (e.g. seasonal goods) or an expected rise in demand. To cope with high demand, it may be necessary to build up stocks beforehand. Unplanned and unwanted stocks arise from an inability to sell goods, mistakes in planning, lack of satisfactory stock control procedures and poor communication between the various departments of a firm.

A stock control graph is depicted in Fig 8.2. Each vertical line represents a new delivery (either from an external source or produced internally within the organisation). Depletion of stocks through usage or sales is represented by the sloping lines. The rate of depletion can be gauged from the gradient: the steeper the gradient the faster the depletion. When stocks fall to the reorder level a new batch is ordered, but as there is a time gap between the order being made and the delivery of supplies, stocks continue to dwindle. This time gap is known as the **lead time**. In

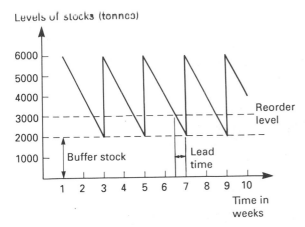

Fig 8.2   A stock control chart

conditions of certainty there is no need to hold stocks in reserve. Hence, stock levels can fall to zero in the knowledge that a new delivery will arrive in time to prevent stock-out. Japanese companies practise this technique in what is called the '**just-in-time**' method. Where depletion rates and lead time vary, it is important to carry a reserve which is known as the **buffer** stock.

To achieve the aim of minimising costs associated with stock while ensuring continuity, it is necessary to devise various techniques of analysis. First, an understanding of statistical analysis will enable the firm to identify the minimum level of stock to reduce and even eliminate the possibility of running out of stocks (known as **stock-out**). Second, the Pareto Rule enables the firm to identify which stock items deserve special attention. Third, the mathematics of Economic Order Quantity enables firms to decide on the optimum quantity in each delivery of supplies.

The probability of stock-out can be understood by the following example. Suppose a shop stocks an item for which demand is an average 30 per month, but fluctuates around this mean. We are told that demand is normally distributed with a standard deviation of five and that deliveries are at the start of each month. What is a safe level of stocks to avoid stock-out? If the firm had 30 in stock at the start of each month, there is a 50 per cent probability of stock-out before the end of the month. We know that 34 per cent of the area

under a normal curve is within one standard deviation of the mean. Hence, an opening stock of 35 would be sufficient in 50 per cent plus 34 per cent of months. This still leaves 16 per cent of months where stock-out will occur. If opening stocks were raised to 40, then stocks would be sufficient in 50 per cent plus 47.7 per cent of months. A firm might be prepared to work on the basis that stock-out will only occur in two per cent of months (i.e. once every four years).

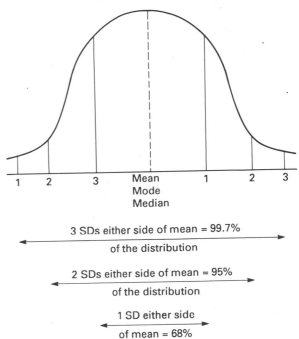

Fig 8.3   Normal distribution curve

Figure 8.3 illustrates the statistical analysis of normal distribution.

A problem for producers of complex, assembled goods such as cars is that thousands of separate items have to be kept in stock. Should the firm adopt the same elaborate stock control procedures for all items? A low-value component will not incur high stock holding costs but the consequences of stock-out could be substantial. The Pareto Rule divides stock items into three classes: Class A items form 20 per cent of all items, but 80 per cent of value. Class B items form 30 per cent of items, but 15 per cent of value; whereas Class C items are 50 per cent of the total, but only five per cent of value. An easy way to think of this classification is the stock held by a firm such as W H Smith where personal computers and electric typewriters are Class A items, whereas pencils and erasers are Class C. The logic of the Pareto Rule is that Class A items deserve closest attention since large amounts of finance will be tied up in them. Class C item such as nuts and bolts are inexpensive and can be kept at a high level in view of the low cost involved.

To understand optimum stock levels and optimum order quantities, it is necessary to identify the costs involved. First, there are costs associated with holding stock:

- Storage costs
- Insurance, security
- Deterioration, obsolescence, pilferage
- Interest on capital invested in stock.

These have to be balanced against the cost of obtaining new stock and the costs associated with stock-out. The cost of raising new stock can be itemised as:

- Clerical and administrative costs
- Transport costs
- The set-up and tooling cost associated with each production run (where stocks are obtained from internal sources).

Table XI

Benefits of frequent small orders	Benefits of infrequent large orders
Less risk of obsolescence and deterioration	Economies of purchasing and delivery
Economises on insurance	Profits from rise in price of stocks
Lower capital requirement	Security of supply
Economises on space	

The economies of bulk purchase and bulk delivery suggest that large orders made infrequently are more economic than small orders made frequently. The cases for infrequent large orders and frequent small orders are summarised in Table XI.

The cost of stock-out can be itemised as:

1 Lost production.
2 Extra costs associated with urgent, small batch replenishment purchase.
3 Lost contribution resulting from lost sales.
4 Loss of customer goodwill and therefore future sales.

The appropriate quantity to order each time will be that which minimises the sum of delivery and stock holding costs. In Fig 8.4 the larger the order size, the lower the ordering and delivery cost per unit. On the other hand, the larger and, therefore, less frequent the order, the greater the holding costs. Total costs are minimised at the intersection of the two curves.

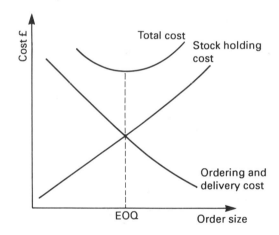

Fig 8.4   Economic order quantity

Quality control

The basic objectives of quality control are to maintain quality standards in order to ensure customer satisfaction and to reduce the costs associated with the scrapping of defective goods. Quality has two separate aspects:

1 QUALITY OF DESIGN relates to the suitability of the product for the customers' purpose. After establishing customer requirements (or the customers' perception of quality), it is embodied in product design and specification.

2 QUALITY OF CONFORMANCE relates to the extent to which the goods that are produced conform to the specifications laid down. This aspect of quality concerns consistency of product.

As with all business decisions, there is a trade-off between the costs associated with the maintenance of quality and the costs resulting from failures. Quality control involves the use of resources in the inspection process. To this has to be added the costs of prevention (special investigations into failure, training of personnel, additional maintenance, etc.) which have to be balanced against the cost of failure – scrap, reworking, sorting rejects, loss of sales, after-sales service, servicing complaints, additional operations. Figure 8.5 suggests that there is an optimum amount of quality control which minimises the total cost of achieving consistent quality.

Quality control costs can be reduced by the inspection of variables in the production process. These include the raw materials that go into the production process, work-in-progress and the machinery used. In an ideal world, efficient inspection of variables will obviate the need for inspection of finished products. Sample inspection of attributes (i.e. finished products) is employed because total inspection would be prohibitively expensive and in many cases testing involves destruction of the product.

Statistical quality control involves the use of mathematical analysis to define the likelihood of defects (defective goods) in the part of the batch not inspected. In the perfect case, all defects would be rejected and all goods which conform to the specification would be accepted. However, it is likely that some bad work will be passed (this is known as consumer's risk), whereas some satisfactory work will be thrown out (known as producer's risk).

The modern trend is to place more responsibility for quality control on the production workers themselves with inspectors being seen as 'long stops'. Greater involvement by the workforce in maintaining quality is also seen in the spread of quality control circles. These originated in Japan and take the form of volunteer groups of production workers meeting during company time to discuss issues relating to quality. The purpose is to raise 'quality consciousness' and to seek solutions to any deficiencies revealed.

Network analysis

Between waking up and setting off for school, college and work, the family has certain jobs to do: these include washing, dresing, preparing the breakfast, making the beds and feeding the cat. Some of these tasks are sequential (e.g. the breakfast has to be prepared before the family sits down to eat it) while others can occur concurrently (e.g. one person cleans the shoes while another completes the washing up). This distinction is the

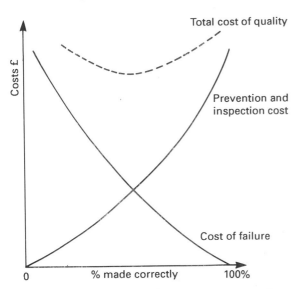

Fig 8.5   The trade-off between prevention and inspection and failure

basis behind network analysis which is a rational, systematic way of planning operations. By identifying critical activities (whose delay would retard overall progress), resources can be transferred to ensure completion at the earliest moment.

Figure 8.6 shows a network diagram. The lines represent activities which consume resources. The circles, known as nodes or events, symbolise the start of one activity and the finish of another. Where a line in the node is followed by a line out

again it means that the first task has to be completed before the second one is started. If two lines enter the node then both tasks have to be completed before the second is started. Where two lines leave the node it means neither task can be started until the first is completed. The dotted line is known as a **dummy** – an imaginary activity consuming neither time nor resources but introduced if there are two starting or finishing points.

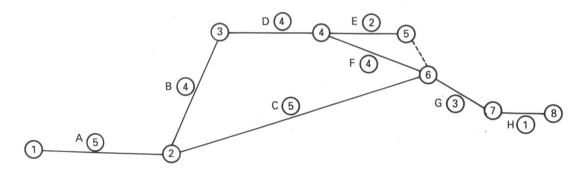

Fig 8.6   Network to identify the critical path
          Note: Letters refer to activities
                 Numbers in circles refer to duration of the task in days.

EXERCISE ● ● ●

●   1   Referring to Fig 8.6:
        (*a*) Identify the critical path;
        (*b*) What is the minimum time for completing the project?

We now add time duration of each task. This enables us to identify the **critical path** which is the shortest time in which the project as a whole can be completed. All activities on the critical path must be started as soon as the previous ones are finished if the project is to be completed on time.

You should notice that some of the activities not on the critical path are completed in a shorter time than is necessary to keep the project 'on target'. This spare time is known as **float**. There is no float on activities that are on the critical path: it

is only possible in the case of non-critical activities. Float can be calculated from the numbers in the circle: the left-hand side is the node number, and the top quantrant on the right-hand side gives earliest starting time which is defined as the earliest point at which a subsequent activity can be started (*see* Fig 8.7). The lower number is the latest finishing time of the preceding activity. A comparison of LFT and EST can be used to calculate float. Project managers should identify and quantify float to switch resources to activities on the critical path.

By careful planning it is also possible to reduce 'crash costs'. These are the costs associated with reducing the time to complete a task, e.g. the task can be speeded up by employing workers on overtime, but at higher pay rates.

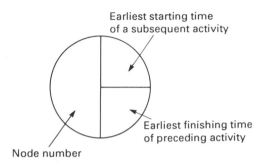

Fig 8.7   Information at the node

Conclusion: the marketing-production interface

The marketing department seeks to identify and then satisfy customer needs. However, to accomplish the second task it has to rely on other departments, most notably the production department. As the short-term interests and objectives of these departments are at times in conflict there is inevitably some tension. This is seen over the following issues:

1 NEW PRODUCTS. The marketing department, conscious of the product life cycle, will see new products as essential for the long-term success of the business. The production department will look critically at the costs of development, design and re-tooling.

2 PRODUCT-VARIATION. The marketing department is aware of the need to tailor products to suit the needs of different market segments. The production manager will point out the inevitable consequences: a broad product range will mean short, high-cost production runs.

3 QUALITY. Customers want high quality at a reasonable price and complain to the marketing department if this is not available. The production manager will point out the cost associated with improving the quality of the product.

4 PRICES. Marketing people want costs low enough for them to set competitive prices in the market place. However, satisfying the customer in terms of flexible response, high quality and variety raises production costs.

5 AFTER-SALES SERVICE. An after-sales service is part of the package bought by the customer in the case of complex products (moreover, the supplier has legal obligation in the immediate period after the goods were sold). To reduce the cost of the service it is necessary to ensure high quality and/or use components that are easily changeable. Both add to R and D and production costs.

6 PRODUCTION PLANNING AND SCHEDULING. To ensure that sufficient goods are available from stock to satisfy the customer, it is necessary to have accurate sales forecasts. These are the responsibility of the marketing department. Under-estimation of future sales will lead to inadequate stocks and, therefore, rush orders to rectify the mistake. Rush production always raises production costs (overtime pay, purchase of materials on unfavourable terms). In addition, there is the question of scheduling: a seasonal pattern of sales is not restricted to the obvious examples (e.g. Easter Eggs). Most products display some seasonality in sales (e.g. slipper sales are very seasonal despite their use throughout the year). The choice for the production department is either:

(a) to produce in excess for most of the year to build up stocks in time for the seasonal rush which is costly in terms of investment in stocks and storage space;

or

(b) to increase production immediately prior to the seasonal rush. This assumes that there is the capacity to step up output (in which case capacity is excessive at other times). The other problem that results is the high costs associated with rush production.

CASE STUDY
Production

The Davidson Pet Food Company produces a range of pet foods including 'Georgie Cat' biscuits and meat products. They sell the latter in sealed plastic containers that they purchase from Plastic Containers Ltd. The Davidson Company carries a stock of plastic containers which are essential for the continued production of 'Georgie Cat'. Diagram A depicts the stocks of plastic containers during 1989.

In 1989 Davidson launched a new product in the 'Georgie Cat' family brand. Although they had undertaken extensive market research they soon discovered that customer orders were substantially greater than expected. Diagram B depicts actual and projected orders for the new product. Unfortunately, Davidson has little spare capacity and consequently cannot step up output of the new product without switching resources from established products.

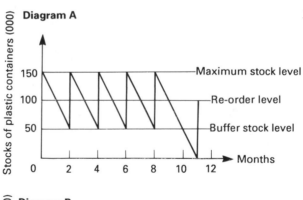

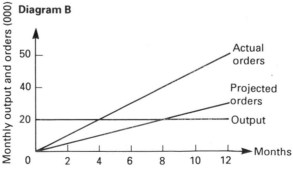

Fig 8.8

1   Calculate the lead-time for plastic containers.
2   How many containers are delivered each time?
3   Why do you think the buffer stock level was set at 50 000 and the maximum stock level set at 150 000?
4   Suggest explanations for what happened in the eleventh month.
5   Why does the Davidson Pet Food Company 'buy in' its plastic containers?
6   What is meant by a family brand (give real life examples)?
7   At the end of which month did the shortage of new product become real?
8   What factors should Davidson consider when switching resources from one product to another?
9   One solution for Davidson is to subcontract production of some of its products to the rival Jones and Green Pet Food Company. Under what circumstances might Jones and Green be willing to produce 'Georgie Cat'?
10   Why did Davidson's market research prove to be inaccurate?

EXERCISE ● ● ●

●   1   The completion of a project involves a number of different operations some of which occur concurrently and other sequentially.

     The various operations, their sequence, time duration and labour requirements are set out below.

Operation	Sequence of activities: the activity is only possible after:	Time (days)	Labour required
A		5	10
B	A is completed	1	5
C	A is completed	1	5
D	C is completed	2	5
E	Both B and D are completed	20	12
F	E is completed	1	5
G	C is completed	3	3
H	F is completed	6	2
I	A is completed	5	3
J	G, H and I are completed	6	10

(a) Draw a network diagram to illustrate the sequence of events.

(b) Identify the critical path. Assuming the absence of labour constraints calculate the minimum time needed to complete the project.

(c) A hold up in supplies results in a delay in the commencement of
     (i) activity B by 4 days
     (ii) activity I by 5 days
     (iii) activity G by 10 days

In each case state, with reasons, whether the delay leads to a failure to complete the project in the minimum time.

(*d*) Ignore the delays in the previous question. Unfortunately only 12 workers are available at any one time. Is it possible to complete the project in the minimum time period? Explain your answer, making clear the assumptions you have made.

2   The Cosy Slipper Company concentrates on producing a range of slippers. Fifty per cent of its output is sold under its own 'Cosy' brand. The remainder are produced under contract for a large retail chain for sale under the store's 'own brand'.

   The graphs depict the volume of sales and output over the year.

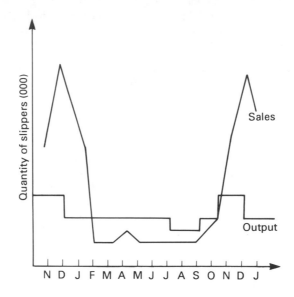

(*a*) Why do retail chains market 'own brand' goods? What are the advantages and disadvantages to manufacturers of producing retailers' 'own brands' under contract?

(*b*) Suggest reasons for fluctuations in the volume of (i) sales and (ii) output.

(*c*) Analyse the production, personnel and financial problems associated with such fluctuations.

(*d*) Suggest marketing techniques to reduce the seasonal fluctuations in sales.

(*e*) Analyse the implications for the production department of diversifying into new products such as trainer shoes.

3   A large manufacturing firm producing a standardised product currently employs manual workers at a wage rate of £4.00 per hour on a 40-hour week. The firm is considering the adoption of a piece rate system of payment. Before adopting a piece rate system, it is necessary to find out the average output per worker. Rather than producing data on the whole workforce, a sample is taken.

(*a*) Advise on:
   (i) the most appropriate type of sample to use;
   (ii) the most appropriate measure of central tendency; and
   (iii) factors to be taken into consideration in deciding the sample size.

(*b*) It is discovered that the mean output per worker is 10 units per manhour and that piece rates be set at £40 per 100 units produced. This would give the average worker the same earnings as before. Assuming that the standard deviation around the arithmetic mean was

16 and that the piece rate does not lead to increased exertion by workers, what percentage of workers would receive:

   (i) less than £144 per week; and
   (ii) more than £192 per week?

(c) The piece rate system of payment does in fact lead to an increase in productivity.
   (i) What is meant by productivity?
   (ii) If productivity rises by 10 per cent and 1000 people are employed on a 40-hour week, what is the increase in the weekly wage bill for the firm?

4 Harry was the Production Manager for a medium-sized firm producing paints. After a meeting with other departmental managers, he called Brenda, his deputy, in for a crisis meeting.

'I have had to endure two hours of complaints from the other departmental managers. Robinson (Marketing Manager) went on and on about our failure to deliver on time. I said that 95 per cent of our deliveries were on time but that it was only that large special order for the DIY Superstore Chain that caused the problem. Robinson's promise on delivery time was unreasonable and given without consultation. He is obsessed about pandering to these large customers and their never-ending search for new colours and new types of paint. Don't they realise that as batch producers we lose valuable production time every time we change to a new batch. Poor planning and control said Robinson. I would like to see him do better!

After Robinson, I had an 'earbashing' from Smith-Jones (Finance Manager). He said we were over budget because stock levels were too high and too much overtime was being worked. I pointed out we carry large stocks because of the policy of extending the product range. The overtime was necessary to satisfy promised delivery and because of the problems of recruiting labour'.

At this point Brenda, a recent graduate in production management, reminded Harry of her ideas on production planning and control . . .

(a) What is meant by batch production and what special problems does it cause?
(b) Should the firm 'pander to large customers and their never-ending search for new colours'?
(c) Why does a large product range necessitate higher stock levels?
(d) Explain the impact on the wage bill of using overtime labour rather than recruiting new employees.
(e) 'Crash' production raises costs and reduces profit margins. Explain.
(f) What is meant by production planning and control and how could it reduce Harry's problems?

EXAMINATION QUESTIONS ■ ■ ■

1 How far do the marketing and production functions have to compromise their objectives in order to accommodate each other?

(AEB, June 1986)

2 (a) What are the principal types of production system?
   (b) How would the management of a catering establishment choose between them?
   (c) What problems might arise in moving from one system of production to another?

(Cambridge, June 1985)

■ 3 (*a*) What are the objectives of stock management?

(*b*) How might each of these objectives be achieved?

(Cambridge, June 1985)

■ 4 (*a*) Differentiate between job and batch production systems.

(*b*) How might a biscuit manufacturer benefit from changing production processes from batch to flow?

(*c*) Discuss the potential problems that might arise from such a change.

(Cambridge, June 1989)

■ 5 (*a*) What do you understand by the term 'critical path analysis'?

(*b*) As a management consultant, write a report to a client in the house-building industry recommending the adoption of this system as an aid to project control.

(Cambridge, June 1987)

■ 6 'Taylor's major concern . . . was that of increasing efficiency in production, not only to lower costs and raise profits but also to make possible increased pay for workers through their higher productivity'. (Koontz and Weihrich).

(*a*) Explain the distinction between production and productivity;

(*b*) Explain how Taylor's principles can be employed to raise efficiency;

(*c*) Under what circumstances are piece rates appropriate?

FURTHER READING

PRODUCTION

J POWELL *Production Decisions* (Longman)

G CLEWS AND R LEONARD *Technology and Production* (Philip Allan)

T HILL *Production/Operations Management* (Prentice/Hall)

R MARTIN AND B MOORES *Management Structures and Techniques* (Philip Allan)

R HUNTER *Production* (Mitchell Beazley/Northcote)

T HILL *Small Business: Production/Operations Management* (Macmillan)

CHAPTER 9
Accounting

Accounting is a technique for collecting, analysing, summarising and presenting financial data relating to a particular organisation so as to describe the present financial position and to aid the process of decision-making. In Business Studies students are not required to construct a set of accounts but instead they are required to demonstrate an ability to interpret and analyse them.

OBJECTIVES

1 To understand some major principles used in accounting.
2 To interpret and analyse the financial accounts of business.
3 To investigate stock evaluation and depreciation.
4 To introduce budgeting and management accounting.
5 To become familiar with the major accounting ratios, their uses and limitations.

Financial accounting

The financial accountant produces the annual accounts of the firm which are made available for external use. Accounts are essential for ensuring that directors and managers are accountable to the shareholders and that they act honestly and efficiently in the interests of shareholders. The controllers of the company are, in effect, stewards entrusted with the resources of the firm. Under company legislation they are required to make decisions in the interest of shareholders.

Financial accounts are also produced for the benefit of creditors, prospective creditors and prospective investors. In addition, the accounts of businesses are required by the tax authorities to assess tax liability. Customers, suppliers, the community at large and employees may also be interested in company accounts. UK and EC legislation require companies, especially public limited companies, to make extensive disclosure of accounts and other information relating to the firm.

There are a number of fundamental accounting concepts of which we should be aware:

1 GOING CONCERN. In accounting it is assumed that the business is a going concern and will continue.
2 CONSISTENCY OF METHOD. Accounts have to employ consistent methods if they are to be useful in making comparisons over time or between firms.
3 EXTERNALLY IMPOSED REQUIREMENTS. Accounts have to conform to the Statement of Standard Accounting Practice (SSAPs) drawn up by representatives of the professional bodies in accounting. Moreover, under company and tax law, there are regulations about the form of published accounts and the method employed in their construction.
4 DOUBLE ENTRY. All transactions are looked at from two angles (e.g. expenditure of money and the acquisition of an asset) and are recorded in two ways.
5 VERIFICATION. In final accounts all statements must be capable of being verified.

6 PRUDENCE. Final accounts record the least favourable position. Revenues are only included when they are realised (the chickens are only counted when they are hatched) but known expenses are provided for.

7 SPECIFIC TIME PERIOD. Accounts refer to a specific period of time (usually a year). Financial accounts are historic in that they record what has happened in the past. Their usefulness in decision-making for the future is limited.

Management accounting

Management accountants seek to support management decision-making by the provision of information and the analysis of financial performance. Whereas financial accounts provide data for external use, management accountants provide data for internal decision-making. The main functions of this form of accounting are:

1 To classify and calculate costs of production. This is known as **cost accounting**;
2 To provide estimates of future expenses and revenues. This is known as **budgeting**;
3 To provide data on which investment decisions can be based;
4 To identify inefficiencies within the organisation;
5 To control costs and manage the flow of cash;
6 To seek opportunities, e.g. to identify 'tax breaks', possible cost savings and movements in the foreign exchange rates which could be exploited by the firm.

The balance sheet

A balance sheet is a statement of the firm's assets, its liabilities and owners' equity at a specific date. The Profit/Loss Account concerns a period of time (usually a year) but the balance sheet is a 'snapshot' at a particular moment in time. It summarises the financial state of the business at that date but, for reasons that will be made clear later, it is a fallacy to believe that the balance sheet shows what a business is 'worth'.

Traditionally, balance sheets depicted assets on one side and owners' capital and liabilities on the other. Assets refer to property, goods and money owned by the business (or owed to it). Liabilities on the other hand refer to money owed by the business to outside bodies. Shareholders' capital or owners' equity refers to finance raised from the owners of the business. When added together the liabilities and owners' equity represent the sources of capital, whereas the asset side of the account tells us how the money was spent. The two sides of the account must balance since every penny raised as capital must have been used for some purpose and must therefore be accounted for. Any cash held in reserve would show up as an asset to balance the two sides.

Using elementary algebra, we can draw an important conclusion about the relationship between the items.

If Assets = Liabilities + Equity
Then Equity = Assets − Liabilities

The owners of the business own the assets of the business minus what the business owes to the others.

The traditional balance sheet has been superseded by the modern form which is shown in Table XII. This is known as the **vertical**, the **narrative** or the **net asset form**. The Account starts with various types of asset with the least liquid at the top and the most liquid at the bottom. **Liquidity** refers to the ease (or otherwise) of conversion of the asset into cash. Hence, it is more difficult and time-consuming to sell the firm's premises, if forced to, than it would be to dispose of stock. **Fixed assets** take the form of premises, plant and machinery used in the production process. The firm acquires such assets to use rather than to sell (although they may be sold off when the firm no longer requires them).

Premises, unlike other fixed assets, are likely to rise in value. Therefore, if the balance sheet records the value of premises in terms of historic

Table XII Balance Sheet at 31/3/1990

	(£000)	
Fixed assets		
Premises		500
Plant/equipment	200	
Less accumulated depreciation	100	100
Total Fixed Assets		600
Current assets		
Stock	70	
Debtors	50	
Cash in bank	50	
	170	
Less current liabilities		
Creditors	50	
Provision for tax	20	
Overdraft	30	
	100	
Working capital		70
Net assets		670
Financed by		
share capital		
Shares issued	400	
Reserves	50	
Share premium	50	500
Long-term liabilities		
Loans/debentures		170
Total capital employed		670

purchase price it will considerably understate the current value of business assets. In the case of a public limited company, this could make the business a target for take-over especially by people more interested in acquiring assets (e.g. a prime site) than acquiring the business as a going concern (asset stripping). When a business is about to be sold it will be necessary to revalue premises. Obviously if there is a change on the asset side there must be an equivalent charge on owners' equity since assets always equal the combined total of liabilities and equity. Machinery, plant and vehicles used in the business are also fixed assets but are likely to lose value over

time. Eventually they will need to be replaced. Depreciation refers to the decline in value of fixed assets through use or over time. It also represents finance set aside for replacement. It is not a production cost but it is a 'provision' of money earmarked for the future. You should notice that the value of fixed assets is shown net of accumulated depreciation. By adding the value of premises to the value of equipment less depreciation, we arrive at the total value of fixed assets.

The term **current assets** covers three items. Stock refers to goods that the firm possesses and expects to sell in the normal course of business. It is usual to distinguish three forms of stock: raw materials, work in progress and finished goods. The importance of each category varies with the nature of the business. Hence, bespoke tailors are unlikely to hold large quantities of finished goods, whereas retailers are unlikely to hold stocks of raw materials. There are problems about how such stock should be valued and this is a topic to which we will return later.

The debtors item in the current assets concerns goods and services sold but not yet paid for. A small proportion of this money may become 'bad debt' with little likelihood of receiving payment, but for the bulk of the money categorised as 'debtors' it is only a matter of time before it is received. Cash in the bank is self-explanatory. All firms should hold some money in reserve to meet forthcoming payments. As payments and receipts are not synchronised, some reserve is essential. However, excessive holdings of cash are undesirable. Businesses profit by putting money to good use. Cash is liquid but not profitable to hold, especially in an inflationary period.

Listed after the assets are the liabilities of the business starting with current liabilities. These are defined as obligations or debts of the business with settlement due within a year. Creditors refers to money owed to, say, supply firms. Expected tax payments are also treated as a current liability. The business is making provision to discharge its tax obligations. Similarly, dividends to shareholders which have been declared (but not yet paid) are treated as a current liability for which provision is being made. Finally, overdrafts are regarded as a current liability since banks can demand repayment without notice.

The sum of fixed assets and current assets less current liabilities is known as the net assets of the business. It is the net worth of the business in terms of the balance sheet but it should not be regarded as the real value of the business unless account is taken of:

(a) the current value of premises, referred to earlier; and

(b) the value of intangible assets such as goodwill, brands, patents and copyright. When a business is sold as a going concern it should be valued at assets net of liabilities plus goodwill and other intangible assets. The value of goodwill is based on a number of factors such as reputation, contacts and skills of the workforce.

The final section of the balance sheet concerns sources of permanent capital or, more simply, where the permanent finance originates. Share capital is money subscribed by shareholders who are, of course, members and owners of the company. The balance sheet records the nominal (face) value of shares that have been issued (together with a statement of the authorised capital). Share premium is money subscribed in a share issue over and above the nominal value. Retained profits are ploughed back into the business rather than distributed as a dividend. It can be regarded as money that would otherwise have gone to shareholders but was withheld from them: in that sense, it is money they contributed. Revaluation reserves arise from the revaluation of fixed assets such as property. As the asset side has shown a rise it is necessary to account for that rise, and logically, as there has been no rise in liabilities, owners' equity must increase.

The other source of permanent capital is long-term loans or debt capital. Creditors are not owners of the business and, therefore, have no right to participate in decision-making or share of profits. They do have a right to repayment of capital and interest and they are entitled to sue if payments are not forthcoming. The balance between shareholders' equity and debt finance has important implications for dividends, cost of finance and the vulnerability of the business. We will return to the balance (known as **gearing**) in the next chapter.

The Profit/Loss Account

The Profit/Loss Account is a statement showing profits over a period of time (e.g. a year) and the uses to which the profits have been put (or how the loss was financed). Once again, the vertical format has superseded the traditional format and this is depicted in Table XIII.

Table XIII   Profit/Loss Account 1/4/89 – 31/3/90.

Sales revenue		1000
Less cost of goods sold		
Materials	300	
Direct labour	200	
Production overheads	100	600
Gross profit		400
Less selling expenses	100	
Administrative expenses	100	200
Trading (operating) profit		200
Add: Non-operating income		10
Profit before interest and tax		210
Less interest expense		50
Profit before tax		160
Less taxation		60
Profit after tax		100
Less dividends		20
Retained profit for the period		80

The first line gives the firm's revenue from selling its goods and services. From this we deduct the costs directly associated with the production of the goods and services. Cost of sales includes cost of materials used, labour charges associated with the production and production overheads. Sales revenue less operating costs is equal to gross profits. However, we have not yet accounted for administrative and distribution expenses. When these are deducted, the result is called **trading (or operating) profits**. These refer to profits from normal trading activities.

In the published version of the Profit/Loss Account, the various costs are not itemised: in fact, the first line (sales revenue) is immediately followed by trading profit, omitting the items in the box. The next two adjustments are to add on any income from other activities (such as renting out premises) but to deduct a figure for interest charges. The resulting figure is known as **profit before tax**.

The final part of the account is known as the **Appropriation Account**. It provides information on the way in which the profit is dispersed. Part is taken in tax payments and some is drawn from the business as dividend distributed to shareholders (or profits distributed to partners). The remainder is retained within the business for reinvestment.

From this brief survey, there are clearly some problems associated with the notion of profit. First, we have identified three definitions of profit:

1 Gross profit = Turnover less cost of sales.
2 Trading profit = Gross profit less overhead costs.
3 Profit before tax = Gross profit less interest charges.

There is a further problem. The size of profit is affected by the method chosen to calculate (*a*) the value of stock, and (*b*) depreciation of fixed assets. It is to these problems that we now turn.

Stock valuation

Valuation of stocks is necessary for the final accounts of the business and for pricing issues of materials from store. The principle of prudence dictates that the value attached to stock must be the lower of the purchase price or **net realisable value**. In an inflationary period it is likely that the current realisable value will be greater than the purchase price but the problem is which purchase price should be chosen for valuation purposes. It is likely that materials in store were received at different times, perhaps from different sources and probably at different prices. It would be impractical to value each issue from store at the price paid for that particular delivery of materials. Instead one of five methods will be chosen.

1 FIRST IN, FIRST OUT (FIFO). FIFO assumes that the oldest stock is issued first. Therefore, the price paid for the first batch of materials to the business is used for all issues until that particular batch is used up. Thereafter, the issue price is based on the price paid for the next batch until that in turn is depleted. The method is shown in Table XIV. It is a

Table XIV First In, First Out

Date	Receipts into stores			Issues to production
	Quantity	Price £	Value £	
1.6.1990	100	10	1000	
10.6.1990	150	12	1800	
12.6.1990				125
20.6.1990	50	15	750	
31.6.1990				150

complex method requiring considerable record keeping. FIFO is acceptable to the Inland Revenue for tax purposes since costs are related to those actually incurred and the value of closing stock is close to current market value. When used for costing pur-

poses it has the disadvantage that the issue price lags behind current prices. There will be a delay before prices paid for materials are passed on to production. In a period of rising prices FIFO undervalues issues, whereas it overvalues issues when prices fall.

EXERCISE ● ● ●

● 1   Using Table XIV, calculate (*a*) Issue price at which goods will be charged to production; and (*b*) Value of closing stock.

Answer

(*a*) Date of issue	Calculation	£
1.6.1990	100 × 10	1000
	25 × 12	300
		1300
31.6.1990	125 × 12	1500
	25 × 15	375
		1875

(*b*)   Closing stock 25 × 15 = £375
Check   Total receipts: £1000 + £1800 + £750 = £3550
        Total issues: £1300 + £1875 = £3175
        Closing stock = £375

2 LAST IN, FIRST OUT (LIFO). The LIFO method prices issues from stock at that of the most recently purchased batch. When that batch has been used up, the price of the previous batch is used. The effect of LIFO is that production is charged with costs that are close to current market values. Consequently, LIFO understates the profitability of the firm and is, therefore, not acceptable to the Inland Revenue for tax purposes. This does not prevent the firm using LIFO for its own internal use. One major advantage of

LIFO is that the price of the latest items quickly passed on to production. LIFO is illustrated in Table XV.

3 REPLACEMENT PRICE METHOD. Using this method, materials are valued at the replacement price on the day of issue from stores. Consequently, production is charged at current prices. Once again it is a method that is unacceptable to the Inland Revenue. Since it does not use costs incurred it produces a fictitious figure for profit or loss.

Table XV Last in, First Out

Date	Quantity	Price £	Value £	Issues to production
1.6.1990	100	10	1000	
10.6.1990	150	12	1800	
12.6.1990				125
20.6.1990	50	15	750	
31.6.1990				150

EXERCISE ● ● ●

● 1 Calculate (*a*) Issue prices at which goods will be charged to production; and
(*b*) Value of closing stock at 31.1.1990.

Answer

(*a*) | Date of issue | Calculation | £ |
|---|---|---|
| 12.6.1990 | 125 × £12 = | 1500 |
| 31.1.1990 | 50 × £15 = | 750 |
| | 25 × £12 = | 300 |
| | 75 × £10 = | 750 |
| | | 1800 |

(*b*) Closing stock £25 × 10 = £250
Check Total receipts: £1000 + £1800 + £750 = £3550
　　　　Total issues: £1500 + £1800 = £3300
　　　　Closing stock = £250

4 WEIGHTED AVERAGE COST (AVCO). This is a comparatively simple method and is acceptable to the Inland Revenue. All stock is valued at a single representative average cost, calculated by dividing total stock by the number of items. All issues are valued at this single price which is between those produced by the FIFO and LIFO methods. It has the advantage of smoothing out price fluctuations, but on the other hand, issue price does not reflect actual buying-in price.

5 STANDARD PRICE METHOD. This is a predetermined price for all issues. It eliminates price fluctuations and establishes a measure of control over purchasing operations. The major problems are that it does not use

actual costs and it is difficult to determine the standard to be adopted.

Depreciation

A motor car purchased for £6000 in 1990 might have a trade-in value three years later of £3000. Over the three years the car has depreciated in value by £3000. The principle of depreciation is, therefore, well known to the motorist. Not only has a prized possession fallen in value, but when the owner comes to replace it he or she will need a further £3000, and this assumes that car prices remain static over the three years.

For a firm with a variety of vehicles, machines and equipment it is important to make some allowance for depreciation. The objectives of the exercise are:

(*a*) to account for loss in value;
(*b*) to allocate the cost of an asset over time;
(*c*) to provide a fund for replacement.

A common mistake is to regard depreciation as an expense against the business: this is derived from the fact that it is treated as a negative item in the profit/loss account, but an expense suggests that the money has left the business. Instead, depreciation should be treated as a provision – money set aside for replacement of the asset at some time in the future.

How much an asset depreciates each year depends upon:

(*a*) the original value of the asset;
(*b*) its life in years; and
(*c*) the residual value of the asset.

The first item is known but the other two can only be estimated from past experience. A change in the external environment (e.g. change in customer demand or in technology) will affect both the commercial life of the asset and its residual value. It is worth pointing out that residual value does not necessarily mean scrap value but value when the owner disposes of it. Aircraft are bought new by the flag-carrying national airline. After a

time they might sell them to charter airlines who, in turn, sell them to Third World airlines. The residual value to the national airline is the price it obtains from the charter airline.

If we know the original purchase price and can estimate the life and residual value of the asset then we can calculate expected depreciation per year. The simplest method is known as **straight-line depreciation**. If an airline owns an aircraft for five years before disposing of it, then the aircraft will have an annual depreciation of 20 per cent of the difference between original price and the residual value.

Annual Depreciation
= Original Price – Expected Residual Value
  Time in years the business expects to own the asset.

This uncomplicated method has one sure disadvantage – it is unrealistic to assume that an asset will depreciate by an even amount each year. New cars decline dramatically in value during the first day on the road. Conversely, an old car bought for £250 will retain its value while it remains in running order.

The reducing balance method takes this phenomenon into account. Depreciation is greatest in the early years but slower later. By this method the asset depreciates by a fixed percentage of value at the start of the year.

EXAMPLE

	£
Original price	100 000
Depreciation year 1 (50%)	50 000
Balance at start of year 2	50 000
Depreciation year 2 (50%)	25 000
Balance at start of year 3	25 000
Depreciation year 3 (50%)	12 500
Balance at start of year 4	12 500
Depreciation year 4 (50%)	6 250

The asset declines in value by 50 per cent per year but it is 50 per cent of the value at the start of the year. The difference between the two methods is illustrated in Fig 9.1.

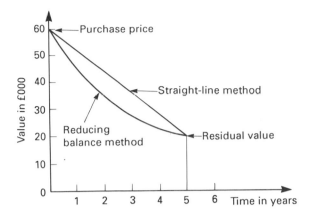

Fig 9.1 Depreciation of fixed assets

Ratio analysis

A statistic has little value in isolation. Hence a figure of £100 million profit is meaningless unless it is related to either the firm's turnover (sales revenue) or the value of its assets. Accounting ratios attempt to highlight relationships between significant items in the accounts of a firm. By calculating ratios we can assess the profitability, efficiency and solvency of the firms. Areas of concern can be highlighted and decision-making can be improved.

The accounting ratios can be grouped into five categories:

1 PROFITABILITY RATIOS relate profits to sales and assets.
2 LIQUIDITY RATIOS show the extent to which the firm can meet its financial obligations.
3 EFFICIENCY RATIOS indicate how active the firm has been.
4 GEARING RATIOS show the balance between equity and loan finance.
5 SHAREHOLDER'S (OR INVESTMENT) RATIOS are a measure of the return on investment.

The last two categories are more appropriately dealt with in the next chapter so we will now concentrate on the first three categories.

Profitability ratios

1 The gross profit margin $= \dfrac{\text{Gross profit}}{\text{Sales revenue}} \times 100.$

This shows the % gross profit from sales which is available to pay for overheads. Most businesses require a gross profit of at least 20 per cent if overheads are to be covered. If the ratio is falling over time it could be because of failure or inability to pass on cost increases to customers, stock losses, fraud, a change in the mix of sales in favour of lower margin goods or an attempt to increase market share by keeping prices down.

2 Gross profit mark-up $= \dfrac{\text{Gross profit}}{\text{Cost of sales}} \times 100.$

Mark-up is the amount of profit added to the cost of goods sold. A low mark-up might reflect an attempt to increase gross profit by gaining a larger volume of sales.

3 Net profit margin
$$= \dfrac{\text{Net profit (or earnings before interest and tax)}}{\text{Sales revenue}} \times 100$$

The EBIT ratio indicates the percentage of operating profit generated from the sales effort. As interest is excluded, it shows the operational efficiency of the business without reference to the method by which it was financed.

4 Return on capital employed (ROCE)

$$= \dfrac{\text{EBIT}}{\text{Capital employed}} \times 100$$

Once again this is a measure of the operational efficiency of the business. Capital employed is equal to owners' equity plus long term debt and is equal to the net asset figure in the balance sheet. If ROCE is lower than interest rates in the market, it is very unsatisfactory since it indicates the business would have prospered better by depositing the money in a bank.

Liquidity ratio

To understand liquidity ratios it is necessary to look at **working capital**. This is the 'life blood' of any business since without it the business will not survive. When the business commences it is necessary to invest in stocks of materials. These may be held for a long period before they are sold to the customer. Moreover, receipt of money from the customer may be delayed and the business then has the problem of financing the purchase of further stocks. Working capital is equal to current assets (stocks, cash and debtors) minus current liability (debts due for repayment within a year). If current liabilities exceed current assets the business will be unable to meet its debts. It is, therefore, important to control working capital to ensure that cash flows in sufficient amount and at appropriate times to meet the liabilities of the company.

The two liquidity ratios measure the extent to which the business can meet its immediate obligations.

1   Current asset ratio $= \dfrac{\text{Current asset}}{\text{Current liabilities}}$

As a general rule it should be between 1.5 and 2. If the ratio is too low the business may face difficulties in repaying debts. If the ratio is greater than two, it suggests that money is tied up unprofitably in excess current assets. This could either be money remaining idle in bank accounts or excessive stock levels. Although 1.5 to 2 is generally regarded as an ideal ratio, it should be seen as merely a rough guide.

If a high proportion of current assets take the form of stock, the business might be faced with a difficult dilemma. To meet current liabilities it might be necessary to sell off stock quickly and, therefore, at a discount. Hence, a second ratio is devised to give a better indication of liquidity.

2   Acid test (or quick) ratio
$= \dfrac{\text{Cash} + \text{debtors}}{\text{Current liabilities}}$

As a general rule the ratio should be 1. If a combination of cash held by the business and cash it expects to receive when customers eventually pay is equal to current liabilities, the business should have little difficulty in meeting its obligations. Furthermore, it can do this without selling off stock at a discount. However, we should be flexible in the interpretation of a business's quick asset ratio:

for instance, a toy shop in early December may have invested heavily in stock and have a high expectation of a substantial cash inflow before the end of the year. A low quick asset ratio should not always be interpreted as a sign of imminent business failure.

Efficiency ratios

1   Stock turnover
$= \dfrac{\text{Cost of sales for a period}}{\text{Average stockholding}}$

In general, a high stock turnover suggests that the business is active and efficient in selling goods quickly to customers. A stock turnover of 10 suggests that stock is turned over every 36 days. It will vary from business to business but firms supplying high value goods will generally turn over stock slowly, whereas suppliers of low value goods will turn over stock more rapidly.

2   Fixed asset turnover ratio
$= \dfrac{\text{Total sales revenue}}{\text{Fixed assets at net book value}}$

This is a measure of the productivity of assets. An investment in fixed assets should pay-off in terms of an increase in sales.

3   Average trade debtor collection period ratio (or debtor days)
$= \dfrac{\text{Average trade debtors}}{\text{Total credit sales} \div 365}$

$= \dfrac{\text{Average trade debtors}}{\text{Total credit sales}} \times 365$

This shows the average time taken to collect trade debts. If debtors are taking a long time to pay the business could be in trouble in paying its own debts. There is no typical figure to use as a yardstick since it will vary according to the type of business.

4   Average trade creditor payment period (creditors days)
$= \dfrac{\text{Average trade creditors}}{\text{Total credit purchase}} \times 365$

This shows the average length of time taken by the business to pay its own debts. If this is rising, it could indicate difficulties in finding sufficient cash to meet its obligations.

5 Other efficiency ratios include:

(a) $\dfrac{\text{Sales revenue}}{\text{No. of employees}}$

(b) $\dfrac{\text{Selling expenses}}{\text{Sales revenue}} \times 100$

This shows the percentage of sales revenue absorbed by the cost of selling the goods.

(c) $\dfrac{\text{Administration expenses}}{\text{Sales revenue}} \times 100$

This shows how much sales revenue is absorbed by administration costs.

Limitations of ratio analysis

Ratios are a useful tool of analysis but should always be used with caution. First, we should always remember the accounting conventions and procedures by which various values were arrived at. The fact is that most accounting information lacks precision. Second, although ratios are useful in making comparisons over time, we should bear in mind the effects of inflation and changes in both conditions and methods of calculation. Third, when ratios are used for inter-firm comparisons we must bear in mind differences between the product mixes of firms and accounting methods used. Fourth, ratios highlight problems, but other non-quantitative information should also be taken into account. Ratios are more useful in depicting trends over time than in isolation. These comments are also applicable to the ratios we will encounter in the next chapter.

Statement of sources and application of funds

The short-title for this third set of accounts is the **funds flow statement**. In effect, it provides a bridge between the profit and loss account and the balance sheet informing us of:
1 the source of funds during the financial year.
2 the uses to which such funds were put.
3 the effect on the balance sheet.
4 the effect on the financial health of the business.

A funds flow statement is depicted in Table XVI. The upper part deals with the inflow of funds to the business. It should be noted that the first item is net profit rather than sales revenue. This enables us to dispense with operating costs which are an immediate outflow and are not retained. The profit figure is 'before tax and interest' for the simple reason that these two items show up as outflows in the second part of the account. Depreciation is added back onto the profit figure because, although depreciation is often seen as a cost, it is not an outflow from the business. We should think of it as money set aside within the business: consequently, the figure for profit understates the amount of money flowing in. Net profit plus depreciation represent internal sources of funds which are generated from normal trading operations. We should add to these proceeds from the sale of fixed assets and external funds in the form of new share capital and additional long-term liabilities.

Table XVI Statement of sources and application of funds, year ending 31st March, 1990

Sources of funds

Profit before interest and tax	500	
Depreciation (add)	100	
Disposal of Fixed Assets	50	
Increase in Share Capital	300	
Increase in Loan Capital	100	
Total sources of funds		1050

Application of funds

Interest payments	200	
Tax payments	100	
Dividends paid	300	
Loan repayments	50	
Purchase of fixed assets	300	
Total applications		950

Increase/decrease in working capital

Stocks (Increase)	100	
Debtors (Increase)	20	
Cash in bank (Increase)	20	
Creditors (Increase)	(40)	
		100

The lower part of the account provides information on how the funds were used. The first claims on the funds are interest payments, taxation, repayment of loans and distribution of profits in the form of dividend. Funds are additionally used to purchase new fixed assets. This gives a total figure for application of funds which, if we deduct it from the total sources, enables us to see the changes in working capital: for instance, if sources exceed applications by £1 million, then one (or a combination) of the following happened:

1 the money was retained as a liquid reserve in the bank.
2 the business invested in stocks.
3 goods were sold on credit with a consequent rise in the creditor figure in the balance sheet.
4 current liabilities were reduced.

Budgets

The Institute of Cost and Management Accountants defines a budget as: 'A financial and/or quantitative statement, prepared and approved prior to a defined period of time, of the policy to be pursued during that period for the purpose of attaining a given objective'.

In essence, it is a financial plan setting out expected income and expenditure over a future period. A budget is more than a forecast, which is merely a prediction of what is likely to happen. In budgeting, management uses the forecasts to produce an operational plan of action.

Business organisations will produce budgets for the major functional areas: marketing, production, purchasing, administrative, research and development, capital expenditure and finance. In addition, a cash budget will be prepared. This is a schedule of cash inflows and outflows expected as a result of activities contained in the functional budgets. The **master** budget is a statement of the future profit/loss account and balance sheet resulting from the operation of the plans. We should distinguish between a **fixed** budget (relating to a single level of activity) and the more complicated **flexible** budget. These project figures for varying levels of operations to suit differing business conditions. A zero-based budget is preceded by a critical review of each activity before it is budgeted for, which is designed to overcome the tendency to accept the status quo with a percentage added on for inflation.

The objectives of budgeting are:
1 To force each functional area to **forecast** and plan the future.
2 To **coordinate** the activities of the organisation by integrating the functional budgets into the master budget. The objectives contained in the marketing budget are only attainable if they are consistent with the objectives and plans of other functional areas such as production.
3 To control.

Budgetary control involves a comparison of actual financial performance against that contained in the budget for the particular activity. The difference between the forecasted and the actual figure is known as a **variance**. If actual costs are less than budgeted costs it is a positive or favourable variance. If they exceed budgeted costs, it is called **negative** or **adverse** variance. An acceptable level of variance will be agreed in advance but any excessive variance (both positive or negative) will be investigated. In some cases, the variance is unavoidable and relates to matters outside the organisation's control. Where the variance is avoidable it needs to be investigated and those responsible held accountable.

An integral part of the process is the acceptance that performance can be traced back to the person or department concerned. These responsibility centres take three forms: the sales department is a revenue centre responsible for generating income; a cost centre is a functional department or unit of activity for which costs are accumulated. The centre has responsibility for spending and is accountable for that spending; and a profit centre is a department or division of the organisation responsible for controlling both its expenditure and revenue and is assessed by the profitability. In effect, a profit centre is expected to operate as an independent business. In budgetary control, responsibility for spending or revenue generation or both is assigned to a responsibility centre.

There are problems associated with budgetary control:

- it uses resources.
- its value depends upon the quality of information.
- it may be adopted inflexibly.
- it may obscure inefficiencies not included in the budget.
- management may become over-dependent upon the budget and neglect the process of management.

Against these problems there are substantial advantages:

- responsibilities are clarified.
- performance can be measured against a quantitative target.
- co-ordination is achieved.
- expenditure is controlled.
- scarce resources are used in the most efficient and profitable manner.
- problems can be anticipated in advance.
- it is a form of management by exception with deviations (variances) being reported and investigated.

Standard costs

The calculation of standard costs is an essential pre-requisite of budgeting. These are pre-determined estimates of what costs are likely to be.

To establish standard costs it is first necessary to obtain data on standard quantities of inputs for both labour and materials. This refers to the physical relationship between inputs and outputs. In the case of labour, this is scientifically determined by means of work study. Once standard quantities are calculated, the cost accountant requires information on standard prices for inputs. To these direct costs will be added a share of indirect or overhead costs. These are less easy to determine partly because unit overhead costs are dependent upon the level of activity. It is therefore common to produce separate calculations for:

1 IDEAL ACTIVITY (what could theoretically be achieved with perfect efficiency).

2 EXPECTED CAPACITY (the level of activity necessary to meet expected demand).

3 ATTAINABLE CAPACITY (the volume of production which is attainable given the likelihood of breakdowns etc).

By adding a share of overhead costs to expected direct costs, it is possible to estimate standard costs.

Actual costs can be compared with standard costs and variances can then be analysed. There are six types of variance:

1 MATERIAL USAGE VARIANCE. The use of excess quantities of material reflects inefficiency, incorrect machine setting, theft, or defective materials.

2 MATERIAL PRICE VARIANCE. This reflects unanticipated price changes or errors in purchasing.

3 LABOUR EFFICIENCY VARIANCE. Actual labour hours will exceed standard labour hours if untrained workers are used, or if employee morale is low.

4 LABOUR RATE VARIANCE. This is caused by a rise in wage rates above standard, the use of higher grade labour than that specified or the use of labour on overtime rates.

5 OVERHEAD CAPACITY (VOLUME) VARIANCE. This arises from a difference between budgeted overheads and the overheads absorbed. Where absorption is related to production time, any unexpected increase in production time will result in variance.

6 OVERHEAD BUDGET VARIANCE. This arises from a difference between actual overheads and budgeted overheads. If, for any reason, overheads are different from expected, variance will result.

In some cases variances are linked. Hence, the use of inferior materials will result in a favourable material price variance but if it results in excessive wastage of material, the material usage variance will be adverse.

Standard costs are a yardstick by which deviations from the expected can be investigated. Expenditure can be controlled and areas of inefficiency can be highlighted. Once again it provides for management by exception. Management's attention is directed only to those items which are not proceeding to plan.

Conclusion

There is an old saying that accountants are never out of work. In the good times they count the profits; in the bad times they dispose of insolvent companies. This somewhat jaundiced view only tells part of the story. It is true that the accountant is both the official historian of a business, documenting and analysing what did happen, and the undertaker disposing of the corpse. However, the accountant should also be seen as a doctor in preventive medicine monitoring the patient to detect early symptoms of problems. A lengthening of creditor and debtor periods, a rising burden of interest and a decline in liquidity are all symptoms which, if not treated, could cause major problems in the future. Early detection of problems will obviate the need for drastic surgery (or worse still the undertaker) in the future.

Accountants are also employed as 'miners' extracting the raw material for decision-making, in particular, data for investment and pricing decisions. It is to these two areas to which we turn in the next two chapters.

EXERCISE ● ● ●

● 1 Using (a) LIFO, and (b) FIFO, calculate the price of issues from stock and the value of the closing stock on 1.6.90.

Date	Purchases	Issues
1.1.90	100 at 50p	
1.2.90	100 at 60p	
1.3.90	100 at 70p	
1.4.90		250
1.5.90	100 at 80p	
1.6.90		100

● 2 Davidson Pet Foods has recently acquired new machinery to be used in the making of 'Georgie Cat'. The purchase price of the machinery was £100 000 and it is expected to have a useful life of 10 years after which it will be sold for scrap at an estimated value of £10 000.
(a) Explain the term depreciation. Why is it treated as a provision rather than an expense?
(b) What is meant by the useful life of a machine? What might happen to foreshorten it?
(c) Explain the difference between straight line and reducing balance depreciation.
(d) Calculate the annual depreciation on the machinery when using the straight-line method.
(e) Using the historic cost of £100 000 and 20% annual depreciation with the reducing balance method, calculate the net book value of the asset after 6 years (show your working in full).

● 3 After studying the following two sets of accounts, undertake a full ratio analysis of this firm.

Profit/Loss Account (1989/90)		£m
Sales revenue		800
Less Cost of goods sold		
Materials	200	
Direct labour	200	
Production overheads	50	450
Gross profit		350
Less selling expenses		50
Administrative expenses		50
Trading (operating) profit		250
Add: Non-operating income		50
Profit before interest and tax		300
Less interest expense		100
Profit before tax		200
Less taxation		50
Profit after tax		150
Less dividends		50
Retained profit for the period		100

Balance sheet at 31/3/1990

		£m
Fixed Assets		
Premises		1500
Plant/equipment	750	
Less accumulated depreciation	250	500
Total Fixed Assets		2000
Current Assets		
Stock	50	
Debtors	50	
Cash in bank	50	
	150	
Less Current Liabilities		
Creditors	70	
Provision for tax	30	
Overdraft	30	
Working Capital	130	20
Net Assets		2200
Financed by		
Share Capital		
Shares issued	1000	
Reserves	500	
Share premium	200	1700
Long-Term Liabilities		
Loans debentures		500
Total capital employed		2200

4 Smith and Jones Ltd produce one product for which a standard costing system is used. The following standards were calculated for one unit of the company's products:
   - standard price of direct material 50p per kilo
   - standard quantity of direct materials 10 kilos per unit
   - standard direct labour £3 per hour
   - standard number of direct labour hours 10 per unit.

The company budgeted to produce 10 000 during October 1989 but in fact produced 7000 units with the following results:

Direct material bought and used (65 000 kilos)	£30 000
Direct labour used (80 000 hours)	£250 000

(a) Calculate:
   (i) the standard cost of producing each unit of output;
   (ii) the standard cost of producing the 7000 units of output;
   (iii) the actual cost of producing this level of output;
   (iv) total cost variance;
   (v) labour variance; and
   (vi) materials variance.

(b) Suggest reasons for both the labour and materials variance.

(c) Why produce standard cost figures if they prove so inaccurate?

5 Arrange the following data into a vertical balance sheet, filling in the missing information:

	(£000)
Long-term liabilities	5 000
Fixed assets at historic cost	40 000
Stock	11 000
Debtors	8 000
Capital: ordinary shares fully paid	25 000
Reserves	?
Current liabilities	?
Working capital	6 000
Balance at bank	3 000
Current assets	?
Depreciation	10 000

6 Arrange the following information in the form of a Profit and Loss Account.

	(£000)
Dividend paid	50
Sales revenue	500
Retained profit	?
Operating profit	90
Tax paid	20
Interest expense	10

7 Study the abridged Profit and Loss Account below and answer the questions that follow:

(£m)	1989	1988
Turnover	1500	1450
Cost of sales	1000	1050
Gross profit	500	400
Distribution costs	200	150
Administration costs	100	100
Trading profit	200	150
Interest	20	20
Profit before sharing	180	130
Tax	40	35
Profits available for distribution	140	95
Dividends	70	45

(a) Calculate retained profits for each of the two years.
(b) What factors determine the size of dividend declared by the company?
(c) In 1989 earnings per share were 50p. Calculate:
    (i) the number of shares issued; and
    (ii) the dividend per share.
(d) Suggesting reasons for the differences, comment on costs in the two years.
(e) The company has loan capital on which interest is payable at 12 per cent. Calculate the loan capital.

8 The following data from the Bank of England Quarterly Bulletin (November 1989) refers to the Return on Capital Employed (%) for an average of UK companies.

Study the data and answer the questions that follow:

Table A

Date	Industrial Companies	Oil and Gas
1975	15.7	29.4
1976	17.9	29.0
1977	17.6	29.4
1978	16.8	22.9
1979	16.5	34.3
1980	13.8	27.5
1981	14.1	20.1
1982	14.0	17.7
1983	15.6	18.9
1984	16.7	20.0
1985	17.1	22.6
1986	17.7	13.0
1987	19.8	16.1
1988	19.8	14.6

Table B

Consumer Goods Companies 1988	
Brewers and distillers	14.7
Food manufacturers	20.9
Food retailers	21.2
Health and household products	32.6
Leisure	12.9
Packaging and paper	23.0
Printing publishing	16.4
Stores	19.2
Textiles	19.2

(a) What is meant by the Return on Capital Employed? How is it calculated?

(b) Describe the trend in ROCE for industrial companies. Offer explanations for the trends you perceive.

(c) Account for the greater fluctuation in ROCE for oil and gas companies.

(d) Explain the value, and limitations, of ROCE statistics.

(e) What factors affect the ROCE for a particular company?

9 The following figures relate to two similar businesses.

	A	B
Average stock carried at selling price	30 000	40 000
Rate of stock turnover	10	6
Gross profit as a % of sales	15%	10%
Net profit as a percentage of sales	5%	5%
Capital employed	£250 000	£100 000

(a) For each business, calculate:
   (i) sales revenue
   (ii) net profit
   (iii) return on capital employed
   (iv) total expenses as a percentage of sales
(b) Comment on the expenses involved in running the two businesses.
(c) Assuming that 10 per cent is the general level of interest rates, what can we conclude about the profitability of the two businesses.

EXAMINATION QUESTIONS ■ ■ ■

■ 1 What are the limitations on the use of ratios to determine a company's liquidity position from its final accounts? How might these limitations be overcome and what other sources are available?

(AEB, November 1985)

■ 2 Briefly describe the reasons why an accounting profit is important to a private sector enterprise. Comment on the problems encountered in measuring and evaluating profit from an accounting standpoint.

(AEB, June 1982)

■ 3 (a) What does an accountant understand by the term 'liquidity'?
   (b) Outline a method by which a firm might predict future liquidity problems and explain how these may be averted.
   (c) Does the method of depreciation of fixed assets have any bearing on a firm's cash position, and if so, why?

(Cambridge, June 1988)

4 The following are details of the movements in the stock level of a product which is purchased for resale:

Date	Purchases (Units)	Purchase Price per unit £	Issues (Units)	Balance (Units)
1986				
1st June B/Forward	—	—	—	300
8th August	200	8.00	—	500
15th September	—	—	500	—
17th September	500	8.25	—	500
1987				
5th January	—	—	100	400
8th January	—	—	200	200
16th March	200	8.75	—	400
31st May	—	—	200	200

(a) Explain the meaning of the following terms:
  (i) FIFO
  (ii) LIFO
(b) Using the available information, calculate the value of the closing stock on 31st May 1987:
  (i) If the method of valuation is FIFO
  (ii) If the method of valuation is LIFO
(c) The budget for the current year contained a figure for the purchase price of £8.35 per unit. Calculate the average price actually paid.
(d) Actual results usually exceed or fall short of budgeted targets. Why then do firms bother to budget?

(AEB, June 1987)

5 The balance sheet is a statement of a company's financial position but it does not tell us how much a company is 'worth'.
  Explain and discuss.
6 Companies are forced into liquidation not through lack of profit but through lack of cash.
  Discuss.
7 Business failure is seldom sudden and is seldom the result of a single factor.
  Analyse the causes of business failure and identify symptoms of impending failure.
8 What is the function of cost and management accountants within an organisation? Explain how this form of accounting differs from financial accounting.

FURTHER READING

ACCOUNTING

A ROBB AND R WALLIS *Accounting Terms Dictionary* (Pitman)

D R MYDDELTON AND P CORBETT *Accounting and Decision-Making* (Longman)

G TAYLOR & C HAWKINS *Accounting for Business Organisations* (Macmillan)

J R DYSON *Accounting for Non-Accounting Students* (Pitman)

A P ROBSON *Essential Accounting for Managers* (Cassell)

R HUSSEY *Cost and Management Accounting* (Macmillan)

P BIRD AND B RUTHERFORD *Understanding Company Accounts* (Pitman)

R H PARKER *Macmillan Dictionary of Accounting* (Macmillan)

D A HARVEY AND M NETTLETON *Management Accounting* (Mitchell Beazley/Northcote)

R OLDCORN *Company Accounts* (Macmillan)

J DICKINSON *Management Accounting: An Introduction* (Longman)

CHAPTER 10
Business Finance

When establishing a business it is necessary to acquire various resources, for instance machinery, stocks of goods, premises and labour. These resources usually have to be purchased and so finance is needed to launch, expand or even just to sustain a business. In this chapter we will be looking at the sources of finance and how it is deployed.

OBJECTIVES

1 To investigate the sources of finance available to business organisations.
2 To investigate shares and dividends.
3 To understand the effect of gearing.
4 To understand and be able to employ the major techniques of investment appraisal.

Type of finance

Finance needed to launch a business is known as **venture capital** and clearly the notion of risk-taking emerges from the use of the word venture. **Investment capital** is finance to acquire new fixed assets, e.g. machinery. These assets will either replace existing assets or be added to the stock of assets of an expanding firm. Continuation finance for the day-to-day running of the enterprise and to pay costs as they become due to known as **working capital**. In an ideal world this will be financed out of the proceeds of the sale of goods and services but because the purchase of inputs will precede the sale of output – often by months and even years – there is a need for finance to fill the gap.

We can categorise finance in alternative ways. First we should distinguish between **debt** finance (which must be repaid with interest) and **equity** finance (provided by the risk-taking owners of the business). A distinction which overlaps this one is between external finance (provided by outsiders) and internally generated finance. Internally generated finance consists of (*a*) retained profits (profits less dividends paid) and (*b*) accumulated depreciation funds. As we saw in the previous chapter, this refers to funds set aside for replacement of equipment. Internally generated funds have the advantage that no repayment or interest payment is necessary. However, it is only available as a source of finance to businesses that are (*a*) already established, and (*b*) generating a positive cash flow. Moreover, although shareholders, being risk takers, have no legal right to a dividend, it is still necessary to satisfy them with distribution of profits. Even though a shareholders' revolt at the Annual General Meeting is a rare occurrence, the dissatisfied shareholder in a public limited company will be tempted to sell shares, making the company vulnerable to takeover.

Finance can be raised by the issue of shares. Companies are permitted to issue shares up to the authorised capital which reflects the value of real assets owned by the company. The major methods of issuing shares are summarised in Table XVII. It is, however, an error to regard share issue as the major form of finance for expansion. Shareholders in a private company are reluctant to

Table XVII Methods of share issue

Public issue by prospectus	1	An offer for sale Shares are sold at a price fixed in advance.
	2	Offer for sale by tender Shares sold to the highest bidder
	3	Placing The issue is 'placed' privately with financial institutions.
	4	Rights issue Existing shareholders are given the option to buy at a discount.
	5	Bonus issue Shares issued free to existing shareholders.

accept new shareholders since that will dilute ownership. In any case, under the Companies Act 1985 there is a limit of 50 on the number of shareholders in a private company and an appeal to the public to subscribe to the issue is not permitted. In the case of a public company, a share issue is a possibility but the process is expensive and not worthwhile unless large sums of money are involved.

A comparatively inexpensive way of issuing shares is known as a **rights issue** in which existing shareholders are given preferential treatment to buy shares at a discount. It is worthwhile remembering that a successful share issue of any kind requires confidence in the business and optimism about the future.

Internally generated funds and share capital together constitute a firm's equity finance. This is money provided by the risk-taking owners, either explicitly in the form of subscribing to a share issue or implicitly, in accepting a sacrifice of distributed profits. Loan finance can be categorised in terms of duration.

Long-term loan finance may take the form of a bond or a debenture. Despite being a marketable security like a share, bonds and debentures confer no rights of ownership. Bond and debenture holders have a priority claim on the business, both in terms of payment of regular interest and in terms of the distribution of the proceeds from the sale of assets at dissolution. There are also tax implications to consider: whereas profit available for distribution to shareholders is calculated after tax, interest payments on loans are a business expense acceptable against tax. Where a debenture is secured against a specific asset it is known as a **mortgage debenture**, where this is not the case it is known as a **floating charge debenture**.

Medium-term finance usually takes the form of a loan from a financial institution such as a bank, although until recently Britain's High Street banks did not have a reputation for providing funds for industry and commerce on anything other than a short-term basis.

Medium-term loans have the advantage of flexibility, with the possibility of early redemption, but against this the business organisation must make provision for repayment in a comparatively short time span.

Hire purchase is a method of paying for assets by instalment. The financier remains the legal owner of the asset until the hirer exercises his/her option to purchase at the end of the repayment period. The major advantage of hire purchase is that payment is phased over a period. **Lease purchase** is similar to hire purchase but does not involve the payment of a deposit.

Leasing involves the acquisition of an asset but ownership does not pass to the user. Hence, a lease is a means of financing the use of an asset rather than its purchase. The advantages of leasing are:

- it minimises initial outlay;
- maintenance is provided with the package;
- the equipment can be updated to avoid obsolescence;
- the user can claim tax relief against lease payments;
- it is a form of 'pay as you use'.

However, there are disadvantages to consider:
- all payments are outgoings;
- payment is greater in the long run;

Table XVIII   Sources of finance

Internally Generated

	Depreciation	Owners'
	Retained profits	Equity
		(Permanent)

Externally Generated

Long term liabilities (10+ years)	Share issue Debentures Mortgage	
Medium Term (3-10 years)	Hire Purchase Bank Loan Lease Sale & Lease back	Loan Capital
Short Term (Up to 3 years)	Overdraft Trade Credit Factoring Bill Discounting	

- the lease might place limitations on use or compel the use of specified complementary goods;
- leased assets (and assets still being paid for on a hire purchase basis) cannot act as security for future loans;
- the user does not benefit from residual value when the equipment is upgraded.

Sale and leaseback involves the sale by the business of an asset (e.g. a building) to a finance company which then makes the asset available for the use of the business on a leased basis. It releases capital for use in the business and it is a useful way of raising finance for other purposes. It means, however, that the business no longer owns the asset and rent must be paid.

Short-term finance to provide working capital is necessary because of the gap in time between purchase of inputs and sale of assets. Ideally, once a business is established, the flow of cash will finance purchases of inputs and will, therefore, act

like a fountain of water. Where the flow of cash is delayed or inadequate a further injection may be needed. The process is depicted in Fig 10.1.

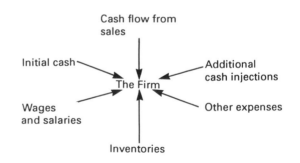

Fig 10.1

A major form of short-term finance is an **overdraft** from a bank. This is a flexible form of finance, is unsecured, is renewable and interest is charged only on the negative balance outstanding each day. In the case of a business account which fluctuates considerably this works out cheaper than interest on other loans. Against these advantages it should be remembered that technically overdrafts are repayable on demand and interest rates reflect current market rates rather than being fixed in advance.

Table XIX   Share capital v loan capital

Share capital	Loan capital
1 Represents ownership	1 Represents debts
2 Confers membership	2 Creditor not member
3 Voting rights	3 No rights of participation
4 Dividends are part of the earnings of the firm	4 Interest is an expense
5 Dividend is paid at the board's discretion	5 Priority over dividends
6 No power to force liquidation	6 Interest must be paid to avoid legal action
7 No maturity date – cannot be repaid	7 Power to force liquidation
	8 Must be repaid

Delayed payment for materials is known as **trade credit**. Unlike most other forms of finance it is provided by suppliers rather than financial institutions. Ostensibly an interest-free loan, the supplier encourages prompt payment by means of a discount. In effect, the loss of discount constitutes the interest payment.

Businesses experiencing problems as a result of their own customers delaying payments may use the services of a **factor**. The factor is prepared to purchase debts at a discount. Even though the business seeking repayment does not receive all money owed to it, there are advantages in early receipt of the money.

Table XX   Factors affecting choice of finance

1 Availability of different sources of finance.
2 Relative cost of different methods.
3 Consequences for control of the business.
4 The implications for shareholders dividend.
5 Tax implications.
6 The risk element involved: risky ventures should be financed by equity capital.
7 Terms and repayment period for loans.

Shares and dividends

A shareholder is a part-owner and, therefore, a risk-taker in the business organisation. Ordinary or equity shareholders have last claim on profits and a share out following liquidation, but in return for risk-taking they receive a dividend out of the profits or earnings of the company. Preference shareholders receive a fixed percentage dividend and have a prior claim on earnings. In view of unfavourable tax treatment and the effects of inflation, preference shares are now very unpopular and uncommon. Consequently, we will concentrate on ordinary or equity shares.

Each share bears a nominal (or face) value which is an arbitrary amount established in the company charter, and is printed on the share certificate. Shares can be issued up to the authorised capital of a company which reflects the value of the company's real assets. The company may choose to issue fewer shares than its authorised amount and, as a consequence, both values are noted in the balance sheet. Where the share issue is less than that authorised, a further issue can be arranged without further authorisation. Moreover, as not all the finance is required immediately it is common to allow purchasers of shares to pay by instalments. When additional capital is required, further calls will be made on shareholders up to the point where shares are fully paid. If the company is forced into liquidation, shareholders who have not fully paid for shares will be required to make a contribution up to the full nominal value of shares. When shares are fully paid up, no further claim can be made on the shareholder.

In the case of private companies, share issues are made privately and no appeal to the public is permitted. Public companies can appeal to the public to purchase shares, usually by means of issuing a prospectus. This is a lengthy account of the company, its structure, voting rights, performance and expectations for the future. The detailed work involved in the share issue is undertaken by a merchant bank or issuing house. To avoid the risk of under-subscription it is necessary to have the issue under-written by a financial institution. For a commission the institution guarantees to buy up any unsold shares. This cost, together with advertising costs and the commission paid to the issue house, makes a public share issue very expensive and feasible only when very large sums are required. An alternative method of issuing shares is an offer for sale by tender, which means that the investing public is invited to submit bids with the shares sold to the highest bidder. Market forces will ensure that all shares will be sold although the price is uncertain. In favourable market conditions the shares will be sold at a premium, thus bringing additional funds to the company (recorded as share premium in the balance sheet).

If the issue is relatively small the company and its advisors may decide to 'place' shares privately with selected institutional investors, such as an insurance company. This is an inexpensive method but may be resented by those not invited to subscribe to the issue. In a rights issue, existing shareholders are given the option to buy additional shares at favourable prices (or to sell the option to a third party). This is seen as an inexpensive way of raising finance, but the company is foregoing higher premiums that would have been available in the open market.

Bonus shares are issued free to shareholders. Obviously this does not raise additional finance for the company, but it is a capitalisation of accumulated reserves. Remember a problem for public companies is that when the value of real assets is substantially in excess of the share value of the

company, it is vulnerable to takeover. A new share issue wards off the danger of takeover and also rewards shareholders with marketable securities which might be preferable to an increased dividend.

In the 20th Century, individual shareholders have declined in importance relative to institutional investors. These are the financial institutions (pension funds, insurance companies) that collect surplus funds from the public and invest them in marketable securities such as Government bonds and company shares. One consequence of the rise of the institutional investor is a preference for safe rather than profitable investments. Economists see this as a market imperfection which favours the large 'dinosaurs' and discriminates against the smaller dynamic and innovative company. The Thatcher Government has attempted to reverse the decline of the small, private investor. The privatisation issues have discriminated in favour of those who apply for small allocations of shares. However, the policy of spreading share ownership will be undermined if the new small investor, seeking quick profit rather than a long-term investment, sells out to the big investor. The conversion of the Abbey National from a building society (owned by its savers and borrowers) to a joint stock company (owned by shareholders) was permitted under a change in the law on building societies. It doubled the number of private shareholders in the UK. The return of the private investor is seen as beneficial to the functioning of the market and has led to more people owning a stake in business enterprises. Greater involvement in the company in which people work (i.e. the worker-shareholder) is seen as a way of securing greater industrial harmony. The creation of a 'share-owning democracy' could have profound economic, social and political consequences.

Shareholders profit from owning shares in two ways. First, they can enjoy a capital gain from a rise in share prices: the market value of shares reflects the recent and expected performance of the company and of the economy as a whole. Second, shareholders receive a dividend which is a share of company profits expressed as a percentage of the nominal value of shares. The size of the dividend depends upon (*a*) the size of profits, and (*b*) decisions by directors on how much should be retained and how much should be declared as dividend. Legally, shareholders are only entitled to the dividend declared by directors. In practice, however, directors have to satisfy shareholders if they are to avoid the risk of a shareholders' revolt or a takeover. Consequently, it is incorrect to see share capital as zero-cost capital: the organisation must work to produce a satisfactory dividend.

The dividend is expressed as a percentage of nominal value, but this is not very meaningful if the current market value was substantially different from nominal value. For instance, a 10 per cent dividend on a £1 share means a pay out of 10p per share. If the share has a current market value of £2 then effectively the dividend is only

$$\frac{10}{200} \times 100 = 5 \text{ per cent.}$$

This is known as the **dividend yield** and is calculated by

$$\frac{\text{Declared dividend per share} \times 100}{\text{Market price of the share}}$$

There are other shareholder ratios to which we should refer:

1 DIVIDEND COVER measures the number of times the dividend is covered by earnings.

Dividend cover
$$= \frac{\text{Post tax profit available for distribution}}{\text{Dividend to be paid}}$$

A dividend cover of two means that half the earnings available for distribution were, in fact, distributed to shareholders.

2 EARNINGS PER SHARE is the relationship between earnings and the number of shares issued.

$$\text{EPS} = \frac{\text{Net Profit available to shareholders}}{\text{No of shares issued}}$$

This expresses in money terms the earnings made on each share. It should be remembered that earnings refer to post-tax profit not all of which is actually distributed as dividends.

3 THE PRICE/EARNINGS RATIO (P/E RATIO) is the ratio of a company's share price to its earnings per share.

$$\text{P/E Ratio} = \frac{\text{Market price per share}}{\text{Earnings per share}}$$

A P/E ratio of 10 would mean that at present earnings (and assuming that all earnings were distributed) it would take 10 years to retrieve the capital outlay required to buy the share.

Gearing

As we saw earlier, external finance can be either through loans or by a share issue. Creditors have no rights of participation in the company but are legally entitled to receive interest payments. Shareholders, as members of the company, are considered to be risk-takers. They have participation rights but no legal entitlement to a dividend unless directors choose to declare a dividend. Gearing relates to the balance between loan and equity or share capital in a particular business.

Gearing is measured in a number of different ways depending on the purpose of our investigation. If we are concerned with the vulnerability of the company to legal action culminating in involuntary liquidation then we would use the formula

$$\frac{\text{Loan Capital}}{\text{Capital Employed}} \times 100$$

If the resulting figure is high, the company is said to be highly geared since a high proportion of finance comes from loans. The company will be committed to high interest payments which are a charge on the company irrespective of its profitability. Moreover, there is increased risk of company failure through inability to satisfy creditors. Many of the assets of the company will have been pledged as collateral for loans making it unattractive for others to lend to the company in the future.

Gearing has implications for shareholders' dividends. The higher the gearing, the greater the dividend fluctuation and therefore the risk element for equity shareholders. We should now amend our gearing ratio to

Fixed Interest Capital (Preference

$$\frac{\text{Shares + long term loans)}}{\text{Capital employed (Shareholders'}} \times 100$$

Funds + long term loans)

The reason for this amendment is that as far as the dividend on equity shares is concerned, it is irrelevant whether the remaining capital is loan or preference share capital. Both have priority and receive a fixed percentage annually. The equity shareholder only receives a dividend after interest and preference shareholders have been satisfied. If profits available for distribution are high, dividends can be high. If profits are only sufficient to cover priority charges then no dividend will be paid on equity shares. To fully understand the way in which dividends fluctuate more dramatically in the highly geared company it is necessary to work through the following exercise.

EXERCISE ● ● ●

● Two companies (High Gee and Lo Gee) are identical in most respects. They are charged the same rate of interest, the capital employed is the same and they achieve the same level of operating profits. The only significant difference is their gearing ratio: High Gee has borrowed £7 million at 10 per cent per year and has issued 3 million £1 equity shares, but Lo Gee, on the other hand, has financed the bulk of its capital by share issue. Hence, its debts are only £2.5 million at 10 per cent and it has issued 7.5 million equity shares at £1.

(a) Calculate the gearing ratios for High Gee and Lo Gee using the formula

$$\frac{\text{Preference shares + long term loans}}{\text{Shareholders fund + long term loans}} \times 100$$

(b) Complete the tables to calculate percentage dividend on the assumption that all profits are distributed and none are retained.

	Years			
High Gee Company	*1*	*2*	*3*	*4*
Operating profit (£m)	1.2	1	.8	.7
− Interest paid (£m)	.7			
= Dividend (£m)	.5			
% Dividend	16⅔%			
(Dividend ÷ Equity Shares) × 100				

	Years			
Lo Gee Company	*1*	*2*	*3*	*4*
Operating Profit (£m)	1.2	1	.8	.7
− Interest paid (£m)	.25			
= Dividend (£m)	.95			
% Dividend	12.6%			

You should have discovered that in years of high profit, High Gee paid a higher dividend but as profits fell so did dividend payments but the fall was more pronounced in the case of High Gee.

The advantages of high gearing can be summarised as:
- Increased opportunities for equity shareholders
- The company has increased capital without diluting equity
- Interest on loans is an expense for tax purposes whereas dividend is declared after tax has been calculated.

Against the advantages there are the following disadvantages:
- Increased risk of company failure
- Increased risks for shareholders
- Assets will be pledged
- Dividends fluctuate dramatically
- Reduces prospective creditors' willingness to grant further loans.

Investment appraisal

All businesses require capital equipment such as machinery, premises and vehicles. The acquisition of such assets is known as investment and is undertaken for the following reasons:
- to replace equipment
- to expand productive capacity to meet demand
- to reduce production costs
- to provide new facilities in order to produce new products.

Investment, like all other business activities, involves an element of uncertainty since expenditure is incurred today to produce some benefit in the future. For the moment we will assume that the future can be predicted with total certainty. Investment appraisal techniques are designed to aid decision-making regarding investment projects.

Economists analyse the determinants of private sector investment in terms of the microeconomic and macroeconomic factors which affect the decisions of business. The major factors are:

1 Government policy in respect of:
   (a) interest rates;
   (b) taxation (e.g. rates of taxation and rules on depreciation);
   (c) the availability of government grants to subsidise investment;
   (d) government spending. Keynesians see government spending as boosting private sector investment whereas the monetarists perceive it as 'crowding out' the private sector;
2 the cost and availability of finance;
3 the liquidity position of the firm;
4 the degree of confidence in the future;
5 the rate of change of demand for goods produced with the machinery (this is known as the **accelerator principle**);
6 the amount of technological change;
7 the expected yield from the investment relative to cost.

This was left to the last because it is the key factor. All previous factors affect the investment decision via their impact on either the expected yield (or benefit) or on the cost to the firm.

The yield (or benefit) from investment can come in one of two ways. In the case of an expansion project, the benefit takes the form of increased production and, hopefully, sales revenue and profits. There are, however, problems with the concepts of profits and sales revenue. In the case of profit, much depends on how it is defined and calculated. In the case of sales revenue, new machinery does not benefit the firm if additional revenue is achieved at the expense of increased costs of complementary inputs. The way to avoid these problematic concepts is by analysing additional cash flow net of operating costs incurred in working the new equipment. Expansion projects are analysed by comparing expected additional net cash flow with the cost of the asset.

The other type of project does not add to output or sales but reduces costs (e.g. the acquisition of labour-saving equipment). Hence, the benefit takes the form of lower costs but the principle is the same. The expected annual reduction in costs is compared with the cost of the equipment.

A manufacturing company is considering investing £500 000 in new equipment. The equipment is expected to last seven years and to increase the firm's cash flow (net of operating costs) by £150 000 per year over its life. Is the investment worthwhile? Initially you will be surprised that this question is asked at all. The total yield from the investment is £150 000 × 7 which equals £1 050 000 compared with a cost of £500 000. However, we have failed to take into account the delay in receiving the yield. It is only in the fourth year of operation that the machinery has paid for itself. When investment projects are appraised it is necessary to take into account not only the size of the yield but also its timing.

Payback

Payback is the simplest method of investment appraisal and is usually preferred by small businesses because of its simplicity. Large businessess may use it as a screening process before embarking on one of the more complicated techniques. The payback period is the time taken for the equipment to generate sufficient net cash flow to pay for itself. In the above example the payback period was 3.3 years.

Firms can use this technique in one of two ways. First, a firm could set an upper limit on the time allowed for payback. Any project which is not expected to payback within the period is rejected. Second, when faced with a choice of projects, the payback method can be used to rank projects according to the speed with which they payback.

The payback method ignores the total return on investment, the earning after payback and the timing of the return prior to payback. It discriminates against projects which produce a slow but, in the long run, substantial return (for example the Channel Tunnel would be rejected if it was required to payback within five years). The payback method favours those projects which produce a rapid return. Where the external environment is uncertain, where rivals are likely to catch up quickly or where the firm is short of liquid assets, a quick return is very important. Nevertheless, there is a danger that profitable projects will be rejected because of the delay in producing a return.

Average Rate of Return

The Average Rate of Return takes the total yield

EXERCISE ● ● ●

● Each of the projects involves a cost of £1m but produces a net cash flow as shown:

Project	Year				
	1	2	3	4	5
A	0	½	½	½	½
B	½	½	½	0	0
C	0	0	½	1	1

(All figures in £m)

(a) Using a payback rule of (i) 2 years, and (ii) 3 years which projects are worthwhile?
(b) Rank the projects in terms of payback period.
(c) Comment on the suitability of the payback method.

over the whole life of the asset into account so, therefore, overcomes one of the defects of the payback method. To understand the arithmetic, consider a capital item costing £1m. It is expected to last five years and to produce an annual net cash flow of £½m. The total yield net of both operating costs and initial capital cost is $(5 \times £½m) - £1m = £2½m - £1m = £1½m$. Annually this works out at £1½m divided by $5 = £0.3m$.

As a percentage of the initial investment it is

$$\frac{£0.3m}{£1m} \times 100 = 30\%$$

To recap, the steps to be taken are:

1 aggregate the forecast net cash flow;
2 deduct the capital cost,
3 divide the resulting figure (known as the surplus) by the expected life of the equipment; and
4 express this annual figure as a percentage of the capital cost.

As with payback we can use the ARR in two ways. First, the firm might set a predetermined level (e.g. 25 per cent) and reject any project whose expected ARR was less than this percentage. Second, when faced with a choice of competing alternatives, projects can be ranked by ARR.

EXERCISE ● ● ●

● A firm is considering four projects. The maximum life of each asset is three years and the capital cost is £100 000 in each case. The table below depicts net cash flow (in £000) in each of the three years.

Project	Year 1	Year 2	Year 3
A	50	50	50
B	100	20	—
C	0	50	140
D	90	60	—

(a) Rank these projects by payback
(b) Calculate the Average Rate of Return for each project but bear in mind that projects B and D have lives of two years, not three.
(c) Rank the projects by ARR.

The great defect of this method of investment appraisal is that it attaches no importance to the timing of the cash flow. ARR treats all money as of equal value irrespective of when it is received. Hence, a project might be favoured even though it only produced a return over a long period of time.

The more sophisticated methods of investment appraisal take timing as well as the size of return into account. Suppose your grandmother offered you a choice of a £100 money gift today in anticipation of your success in the 'A' Level examination or £100 after the results are announced. Which would you prefer? Quite sensibly, you will prefer the money today but let us analyse why.

First, you will prefer the money today because of the greater certainty involved. Your grandmother might make the gift conditional on success at 'A' Level. Second, aware of inflation in postwar Britain, you would prefer to have the money today because its purchasing power will be greater today than it will be in the future. Both these points are valid but should not obscure the essential point. Even when the money is guaranteed in the future and when inflation is non-existent, it is still preferable to have the money today. After all, with £100 today you can buy 15 LP records and enjoy them in the immediate future. If you are prudent you will deposit money in a building society account and gain interest. It is always better to have the money today rather than waiting for it. This is known as the **time value** of money. £100 today is more valuable than £100 guaranteed in a year's time. We can rewrite this statement as £100 guaranteed in a year's time is worth less than £100 today. It has a lower present value because of the inconvenience of having to wait.

Present value

The return on an investment comes in the form of a stream of earnings in the future. The **Discounted Cash Flow** method of investment appraisal takes into account the size of the return over the life of the equipment but makes adjustment for the timing. A greater weighting is given to the return in the early years. The weighting can be calculated from a formula which is derived from the formula for compound interest

$$PV = \frac{A}{(1+r)^n}$$

where PV is the present value of a net return in the future

A is the sum concerned
r is the rate of discount
n is the number of years.

This enables us to calculate the present value of money **net of operating costs** to be received in n years. Hence, £100 in two years at a 10 per cent rate of discount has a present value of

$$\frac{£100}{(1+1\frac{1}{10})^2} = \frac{£100}{(\frac{110}{100})^2} = \frac{100}{(1.1)^2} = \frac{100}{1.21} = £82.6$$

The stream over the years is

$$\frac{A}{(1+r)} + \frac{A}{(1+r)^2} + \frac{A}{(1+r)^3} \cdots\cdots$$

If the mathematics looks rather daunting do not worry. Accountants use present value tables to obtain the weighting or discount factor. In examinations you will be given the discount factor so you do not have to work it out.

The sum of present value is then compared with the initial capital cost of the project. If the sum of present values minus the capital cost is positive it is worthwhile proceeding. If the resulting figure is negative then the project should not be undertaken. To extend your comprehension of the technique you should complete the following exercise.

EXERCISE ● ● ●

● 1   In appraising a £300 000 investment project a firm uses a discount rate of 10 per cent. The equipment will produce a return (net of operating costs) of £100 000 per year over a five-year period. At the end of the five years the firm expects to sell the equipment for £10 000.

Calculate the net present value by completing the table:

Year	Cash Flow (£000)	×	Discount Factor	=	Present Value (£000)
0	−300		1		−300
1	100	×	0.909		90.9
2	100	×	0.826		
3	100	×	0.751		
4	100	×	0.683		
5	100	×	0.621		
Residual Value	10	×	0.621		____
		Net Present Value			
					____

Two points should be noticed. First, the capital cost is included as a negative item since it is an outgoing. As it is incurred today it has a discount factor of 1.0 (i.e. it is not discounted). The residual value is a positive item since it is a cash inflow that the business expects to receive in the future. However, as it received at the end of five years, the £10 000 is considerably discounted.

● 2 After completing the project appraisal at the 10% rate, recalculate the net present values using a discount rate of (a) 20%, and (b) 8%
The relevant discount factors are:

Year	@20%	@8%
1	0.83	0.93
2	0.69	0.86
3	0.57	0.79
4	0.48	0.74
5	0.40	0.68

What conclusions can you draw?

An important question to ask is why a specific rate of discount is chosen. This is significant since the profitability of the proposed project depends on the chosen rate of discount. The selected rate reflects interest rates in the market. This is important if the firm has to borrow money to finance the investment. It is also important if the investment is to be financed out of retained profits. The firm should consider what else it could do with the money: in other words, the opportunity cost of the investment in capital equipment is the sacrifice of interest in a financial investment the firm might otherwise have undertaken.

INTERNAL RATE OF RETURN

So far we have used a predetermined discount rate to assess whether the sum of present values minus the initial cost was positive or negative. An alternative method involves the determination, by trial and error, of the discount rate which produces a net PV of zero. This is where the sum of the present values is exactly equal to the capital cost of the project. The discount rate which equates the two is known as the **internal rate of return**. If the IRR exceeds the market rate of interest (which has to be paid to secure the funds) then the project is worthwhile. If the IRR is less than the interest rate charged then the project should be rejected. This is shown in Fig 10.2.

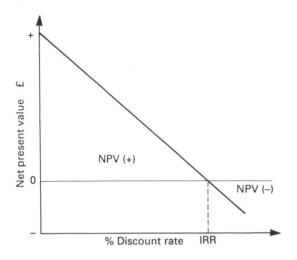

Fig 10.2   NPV of returns from a project at various discount rates to illustrate Internal Rate of Return

So far we have assumed that money will retain its value and that the discounting technique was necessary only because of the inconvenience of waiting for the return. As inflation has been a constant feature of the post-1945 era, we should make adjustments for the declining value of money received in the future. Provided we can accurately predict future inflation, it is possible to calculate NPV in **real** terms (i.e. at constant prices). The PV of a sum (s) received after n years using a discount rate (r) and assuming an inflation rate of f is given by the equation

$$PV = \frac{S}{(1 + r + f)^n}$$

Hence, if the discount rate is 10 per cent and inflation is 12 per cent the revised discount rate is 22 per cent. The PV of £100 in four years in **real** terms is

$$\frac{100}{(1.22)^4} = £45.2.$$

Obviously, the defect here is the difficulty of accurately predicting inflation even one year ahead.

The other complication concerns the uncertainty about the future. No matter how sophisticated the technique, the whole appraisal process is based on assumptions, expectations and guesses about an uncertain future. There is uncertainty about:

- the technical life of the asset
- the commercial life of the asset
- operating costs
- the demand for and therefore price of goods produced by the asset.

All these uncertainties may lead businessmen to prefer projects with an early return.

Decision trees

Decision trees are a pictorial method of showing a sequence of inter-related decisions with their various outcomes. A significant feature of the technique is that the subjective probability of the outcome being achieved is taken into consideration as well as the magnitude of the outcome itself. The purpose is to clarify the options available when management engages in decision-making.

Figure 10.3 shows the basic structure of a simple decision tree. The squares, known as **decision nodes**, are points where management decisions have to be made. The circle, known as **outcome nodes**, represent the outcome of a particular decision. The figure at the right-hand side of each branch is the pay-off expected as a result of certain action. In the figure net cash flow will rise by £2 million if the new product is successful. However, the probability of success is (subjectively) calculated at ¼. When we multiply the pay off by probability, the resulting figure, known as the **expected value**, is £2m × ¼ = £0.5m. Successful adaptation of the existing product will not produce such a large increase in net cash flow but the probability of success is greater.

After calculating expected values (outcome × probability) for each branch we work leftwards. At the outcome node in the case of branch (a) the expected values are £0.8 (2/3 × £1.2M) if successful and £0.2m (1/3 × £0.6m) if unsuccessful. These are added together to give a figure for the expected value of modifying the existing product. The expected value of the net cash flow from modification of existing products is therefore £1 million from which we have to deduct cost of development of £0.1m. Branch (a) has an expected value of £0.9m.

For branch (b) the expected values are ¼ × £2m = £0.5m (successful) plus 3/4 × £0.8m = £0.6m (failure). From the aggregate of £1.1 million we must deduct development costs of £0.3m. The decision tree leads us to conclude that modification of existing products is more worth-while than developing new ones. This is represented on the tree by hatching on the rejected branch (b).

This was a simple tree in that choice was restricted to two alternatives and there were also only two outcomes in each case. Other trees have multiple branches and other complications. However we should always remember a few simple rules:

1 In the calculation start on the right and work backwards.
2 Multiply outcomes by probability to get expected values.
3 Add expected values at each node but deduct any costs incurred.
4 Use hatching to show branches not taken. This is very important if we have a multiple branching tree.

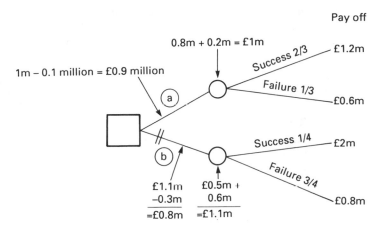

Fig 10.3   Decision trees

Decision: (a) Modify existing product. Cost £0.1m.
(b) Develop new product. Cost £0.3m.

Conclusion

The entrepreneur is a risk-taker who risks funds to enjoy a financial return in the future. This chapter has concentrated on specific issues relating to the raising of funds and the use of these funds in investment.

The manner in which finance is raised has important implications for the control of the business, the return of owners' equity, the vulnerability of the business and, therefore, its very existence.

Decisions about whether to invest or what to invest in are made difficult by the uncertainty about the future and the problem of linking the present and the future. The investment appraisal techniques discussed in this chapter provide the tools by which the problem can be analysed and the decision made. But no matter how sophisti-cated the quantitative analysis, much will depend upon the hunch and the mood of business people (or what Keynes called 'animal spirits').

CASE STUDY 1
An acquisition

TVS holds the ITV franchise for south-east England, apart from London. An agreement between the big five ITV Companies (LWT, Thames, Central, Yorkshire and Granada) results in a national network dominated by programmes of the big five with other com-panies (such as TVS) relegated to screening the programmes of other companies and producing regional and specialist programmes. Although TVS has one of the most lucrative ITV franchises its limited role is a source of frustra-tion. Moreover, with ITV franchises up for renewal in 1992 there is uncertainty about its future.

In 1988 TVS bought MTM, the American company which produced successful television series such as 'Hill Street Blues' and 'St Elsewhere'. TVS was attracted to MTM by the prospect of (a) ownership of a back catalogue of programmes on which it could hope for earnings from repeats; (b) ownership of produc-tion facilities in Hollywood; (c) future earnings if it fails to retain its ITV franchise; and (d) becoming more than just a ITV regional company.

By 1989 the prospects for TVS looked bleak: in the year to October 1989, MTM recorded a $45 million loss and had few programmes to replace its earlier classics. Media experts argue that the potential for endless repeats of MTM programmes was limited by their semi-documentary nature. It is therefore unlikely that 'Hill Street Blues' will enjoy the longevity of 'Bilko' or 'I Love Lucy'. The consequences for TVS shareholders were extremely worrying: share prices fell from 330p to 192p, pre-tax profits fell by one-half to £12 million, earnings per share were 7p and the PE ratio was 27.

(Source of information: W Phillips: *Investors Chronicle* 29 September, 1989).

---

1 What do you understand by the word 'franchise'? Compare and contrast an ITV franchise with other franchise operations.
2 If the pessimism about MTM is correct, what does it tell us about the motive for mergers?
3 Why is the South-East a lucrative ITV region?
4 Explain the terms 'earnings per share' and 'PE ratio'. What does a PE ratio of 27 mean?

CASE STUDY 2
Rail transport projects

Integration of EC countries into a single market will be greatly enhanced by railway developments currently being constructed or planned in Europe. These include:

- the building of high-speed rail links between major centres;
- the development of high speed trains such as improved versions of France's TGV;
- a bridge and tunnel linking Zealand (on which Copenhagen is sited) with the Danish and, therefore, European mainland;
- a proposed bridge and rail link from Copenhagen to non-EC countries like Sweden and Norway; and
- the tunnel under the English Channel.

The latter is variously perceived as a triumph of the imagination and engineering skills and a disaster in terms of both a threat to the environment and escalating costs. The tunnel is a private enterprise project for which permission was granted by the French and British Governments to an Anglo-French company known as Eurotunnel. This company will own the tunnel and has permission to operate it for 55 years (that is until 2050). The tunnel is being constructed by an engineering consortium known as Transmanche Link (TML). At the end of 1989, with 25 per cent of the project completed, relations between Eurotunnel and TML had deteriorated, not because of delays but because of the way in which costs were overrunning.

Eurotunnel have revised its original cost estimates upwards by £1.6 billion to £7 billion. TML claim that costs will be at least £7.5 billion while bankers, on whom Eurotunnel relies for finance, fear it could be even higher.

The controversy in late 1989 reached the point where Eurotunnel was even considering terminating the contract with TML although this might have been part of the negotiating tactics. Whatever happens, Eurotunnel will have to raise additional finance of at least £1 billion. Seventy-five per cent of this will come from banks who, in the opinion of *Fortune Magazine*, have little choice but to go along with the request since they are such heavy backers of the project. The balance of finance will come from a rights issue. Market analysts still have confidence in the financial success of the project, and in the opinion of an analyst from UBS Phillips and Drew, 'The project's return on equity will drop from 17 per cent to 13 per cent. But it can still be successful if there are no more cost overruns'.

(Sources of information: *The Observer* 8.10.89 and *Fortune* 20.11.89)

1 Why are improved transport links essential if the Single Market is to be a reality?
2 The Channel Tunnel is a private enterprise project partly at the insistence of Mrs Thatcher. What is the economic justification for insisting that it should be built with private capital?
3 How would you set about estimating the cost of a project like the Channel Tunnel?
4 Why do you think costs escalated?
5 Why have European bankers 'little choice but to go along' with the request for further loans?
6 What is meant by the project's return on equity?
7 What lessons for the proposed Scandinavian links does the Eurotunnel experience provide?

8 Why was the tunnel, and the high speed link to Folkestone, opposed on environmental grounds? What contrary environmental points can be made in defence of the link?

9 Why is construction in the hands of a consortium of companies rather than a single company?

CASE STUDY 3
Expansion

Carol owns a successful, sole trader dress shop in a suburb of Easthampton. Her sales revenue has risen by 10 per cent per year over the last three years. Profits are currently running at £30 000 per year before tax and before Carol draws her personal expenses out of the business. Her current balance sheet shows the net asset value of her business is currently £150 000.

Carol is interested in expansion by acquiring a second shop. After much investigation she has identified four possible premises:

• In another part of Easthampton there is a small shop in a suburban shopping centre. It is in a 'working-class' area with little passing trade other than local residents.

• A second possibility is a larger shop in nearby Southleigh. This is a rapidly growing commuter town for Easthampton and has prospered with growing numbers of 'middle-class' commuters. Unfortunately, its citizens tend to travel to Easthampton for specialist shopping.

• There are also suitable premises in nearby Southcester. This is an historic town enjoying great prosperity as a result of a large and growing commuter population. In addition it is a major centre for tourists and can be assured of attracting passing trade in the summer.

• Finally, in the centre of Easthampton there is a vacant shop close to the major chain stores. As Easthampton is a large and prosperous city, she is attracted to the idea of acquiring these premiscs although she realises that costs are greater and competition is fiercer.

With the aid of her financial advisor, Carol calculates the costs and returns associated with these various options:

Item	Easthampton Suburb	Southleigh	Southchester	Easthampton City
Lease (for 5 years)	10 000	15 000	30 000	40 000
Furniture & fittings	10 000	12 000	15 000	16 000
Advertising	5 000	5 000	10 000	10 000
Stock	30 000	40 000	50 000	50 000
Start up Costs	55 000	72 000	105 000	116 000
Expected annual profit	20 000	25 000	35 000	40 000

1 Assuming that Carol has reserves of £20 000 and taking both marketing and financial considerations into account, advise her on the most appropriate investment.

2 Suggest sources of additional finance for Carol.

EXERCISE ● ● ●

● 1 A small firm of accountants is considering the purchase of a computer which, together with software, staff training and installation costs will involve an initial outlay of £20 000. The computer will enable the firm to reduce its staff by one clerical worker whose annual salary is £8000. However, another clerical worker employed by the firm is to be regraded and given a £1500 a year pay rise to operate the equipment. In addition, insurance and maintenance will add £500 to the firm's annual costs. At the end of five years the firm expects to sell the computer for £5000.

Using the discount factors below calculate the net present value of the return on this investment:
  Year 1 – 0.91
  Year 2 – 0.83
  Year 3 – 0.75
  Year 4 – 0.68
  Year 5 – 0.62

● 2 The following data relates to a large public company:

	Year X
Sales revenue (£m)	700
Operating profits (£m)	80
Price-Earnings Ratio	14
Earnings per share (p)	35
Interest cover	3.8
Dividend cover	10
Dividend per share (p)	11p

From this information calculate:
(a) Market price of share
(b) Dividend yield
(c) Profit margin
(d) Interest payable by the firm

● 3 Research and development is essential for the growth and long-term profitability of industry. Britain's main overseas rivals have long realised that higher R and D produces higher rates of sales growth. Unfortunately, R and D is expensive, results are uncertain and the return is enjoyed only after a considerable delay. In Britain it is frequently neglected in favour of short-term profitability.

Short-termism was labelled as our 'national ailment' by former Chancellor Nigel Lawson. This short-term mentality is particularly prevalent among the managers of pension funds. They manage funds on behalf of other people and are anxious to achieve good current results. It is alleged that the quarterly reporting of the performance of funds adds to short-termism.

Both the Department of Trade and Industry and the National Association of Pension Funds have established committees to make recommendations on procedures and practices necessary to encourage fund managers to take a long-term view. Among the suggestions is a reduction in the frequency of reporting and changes in the manner in which fund management is assessed. One positive move already implemented is SSAP 13 which requires companies to declare their expenditure on R and D.

(a) What is meant by investment? In what way is investment in R and D
  (i) similar; and
  (ii) different
  from investment in real assets?
(b) What is short-termism and what forms can it take, other than neglect of R and D?
(c) Why should the frequency of reporting the performance of pension funds have any bearing on choice of investment?
(d) How should we judge the performance of a company?
(e) What are SSAPs?
(f) Why is R and D essential?

4   Three projects are currently under consideration by Kirby Air Filters Ltd. Only one project can be undertaken and the expected cash flows associated with each are as follows:

Time (years)	A	B	C
0	−100	−100	−100
1	+100	+ 10	0
2	+100	+ 10	+ 10
3	0	+100	+ 10
4	0	+100	+100
5	0	0	+150
(All figures in £000)			

Calculate the net present value of the cash flows based on an eight per cent discount rate. (Discount Factors 0.92, 0.86, 0.79, 0.73, 0.68).

5 Read the article on Asda and answer the following questions:

Asda's First-Half Profits Slump By A Quarter

Asda's profits drop shocked the market despite a warning. The second half does not look any brighter

FOOD RETAILING group Asda hoisted the storm warning cones very visibly a fortnight ago, but the 24% slump in first-half profits was still a shock, and the shares dropped a further 3p, to 103p, on the results. This means they have halved so far this year.

Turnover rose by 18%, but was boosted by acquisitions. The volume picture is much less happy. While food is proving predictably resilient to the present downturn in consumer spending, volume growth of about 4% is hardly impressive. And sales of non-food items such as clothing were being definitely squeezed, with volumes down by 7% in Asda stores.

Volume, however, is the least of Asda's difficulties at the moment. First, the problems associated with the launch of the new distribution system, which prevented supplies of fresh foods getting on the shelves, has cost Asda about £20m. These problems lasted for eight weeks in the summer, leading to a loss of £9m in the first half.

Although they have now been resolved, and stock levels are up to scratch in the stores, Asda has had to carry a higher level of costs, so there will be a further loss of more than £10m in the second half.

There were difficulties elsewhere too, with profits at Allied Marples, the furniture and carpet retail subsidiary, almost halved to £3.8m, while MFI, in which Asda now has a 25% stake following the management buy-out two years ago, contribute a loss of £2.8m against profits of £6.1m in the previous first half.

The purchase of 61 stores from Isosceles is clouding prospects, too. First, the deal's later-than-expected completion means that Asda will have to bear the full costs of financing it in the second half, with little or no benefits from trading. In any case, the high cost of financing the deal means that profits next year are likely to be diluted by anything up to £15m.

And investment managers have yet to be convinced that the Gateway stores will be easily assimilated into Asda, or will do all that much

to improve the group's geographical and sales spread.

28 weeks ended November 11		
	1989	1988
Turnover (£bn)	1.59	1.35
Pre-tax profits (£m)	83.5	109.3
Fully diluted eps (p)	4.76	6.12
Dps (p)	1.85	1.85

The upshot is that Asda is heading for a sharp fall in full-year profits, from £247m to £177m, forecasts Barclays de Zoete Wedd, with only very modest recovery visible, to about £195m in 1990/91.

On this basis, the shares are selling on a prospective multiple of 11 times likely earnings this year, and 10 times next year's. The scale of the problems facing UK retailing, which have been uncovered in the past six months, especially in buy-outs such as Lowndes Queensway, MFI and Magnet, means that Asda is unlikely to be a bid target at its present price.

So, there is probably some further downside in the share price yet.

ANTHONY LUGG

(Source: *Financial Weekly*, 21 December 1989–11 January 1990)

(a) Explain why turnover rose by 18 per cent whereas volume of sales grew by four per cent in the case of food and seven per cent in the case of non-food.

(b) Why is it essential to maintain stock levels in retailing?

(c) What is meant by:
   (i) a management buy out;
   (ii) investment managers;
   (iii) assimilated;
   (iv) geographical and sales spread.

(d) Why is Asda an 'unlikely bid target'?

(e) Explain
   (i) e.p.s. (earnings per share); and
   (ii) d.p.s. (dividend per share).

(f) 'The shares are selling on a prospective multiple of 11 times likely earnings this year . . .'
What does this mean and why is it significant?

6   A company wishes to raise £2 million to finance expansion. It estimates that the investment will generate an increase in cash flow (net of operating expenses) as follows:

Year 1	Income (£000)
1	150
2	180
3	200
4	220
5	240
6	250

The Board of Directors are contemplating raising the finance in one of two ways:
- £0.5m share issue coupled with a £1.5m loan at 10 per cent.
- £1.5m share issue with £0.5m loan at 10 per cent.

(a) For each of the two methods of financing the expansion calculate the annual earnings per share as a percentage of equity capital.
(b) Prior to the expansion the capital value of the business was £10 million, with £6 million in the form of equity and the remainder as long term loans.
Calculate the gearing ratios.
     (i) before the expansion
     (ii) after expansion, using option A
     (iii) after expansion, using option B
(c) Why is the choice of method significant:
     (i) for existing shareholders;
     (ii) for directors;
     (iii) for company's ability to raise loans in the future?

EXAMINATION QUESTIONS ■ ■ ■

■ 1   (a) What do you understand by the term 'gearing', and how might it be measured?
       (b) How might a finance house use gearing ratios when considering an application from a medium-sized manufacturing company for a loan of £5 000 000 for expansion purposes?
       (c) What alternative source of funds might the firm examine?

(Cambridge, June 1987)

■ 2   (a) What is the role of the Average Rate of Return when evaluating investment projects?
       (b) When might the Pay Back Period be a better technique?
       (c) What advantages and disadvantages would the Discounted Cash Flow technique have over other methods when evaluating investment decisions?

(Cambridge, June 1986)

3   The following is an extract from the balance sheet of a public limited company.

	£
Ordinary shares	800 000
Authorised 800 000 at £1 each	
Issued and fully paid 700 000 at £1 each	700 000
General reserve	50 000
Long term borrowing	
Debentures 10% (2010)	250 000
Capital Employed	£1 000 000

The Company now wishes to raise an additional £500 000 to finance the development of a new product. Assess the implications of the relevant alternative sources of finance.

(AEB, June 1986)

4   How would you suggest that a well-established computer manufacturer with
(a) turnover of £25 million
(b) low capital valued fixed assets accurately represented in the Balance Sheet, and
(c) a high debt/equity ratio
might find £5 million to manufacture and launch micro-computers?

(Cambridge, June 1984)

5   Analyse the likely consequences of the extension of share ownership.

6   'Decision trees and discounted cash flow techniques involve sophisticated mathematics, but are based on guesses. Pay back is a crude method of investment appraisal, but is sometimes more appropriate'. Discuss.

FURTHER READING

FINANCE

D A HARVEY AND E MCLANEY *Finance* (Mitchell Beazley/Northcote)
D R MYDDELTON *Financial Decisions* (Longman)
E MCLANEY *Business Finance* (Pitman)
J EVE AND A LANGLOIS *Finance* (Oxford UP)
D DAVIES *The Art of Managing Finance* (McGraw-Hill)
S HUGHES *The Capital Market and the Finance of Industry in the UK* (Longman)
M G WRIGHT *Financial Management* (McGraw-Hill)

CHAPTER 11
Pricing Policy

Pricing decisions are crucial to the success of the firm and its product. In this chapter we will be concerned with pricing strategies adopted by business organisations and the methods by which prices are set.

OBJECTIVES

1 To understand the objectives of pricing policy.
2 To investigate the nature of costs of productions.
3 To understand the cost basis of pricing.
4 To understand know when marginal cost pricing is appropriate.
5 To investigate the influence of demand and competition on pricing policies.
6 To appreciate the constraints on business making pricing decisions.

The contribution of the social sciences

Before dealing with the mechanics of pricing decisions, it would be useful to refer to the way in which price is dealt with in the social sciences.

The theory of demand in economics informs us that there is an inverse relationship between quantity demanded and price (other things remaining equal). Consequently, a rise in price is likely to result in a contraction of demand. Moreover, if demand is elastic the fall-off in demand will be sufficient to cause a decline in sales revenue, as shown in Table XXI.

Table XXI

Price (£)	Quantity Demanded (000)	Sales Revenue (£000)
9	11	99
10	10	100
11	9	99
12	8	96
13	7	91

EXERCISE ● ● ●

● 1 To prove the relationship between elasticity and sales revenue, from the data in Table XXI calculate price elasticity of demand when price rises:
   (a) from £9 to £10.
   (b) from £11 to £12.
   (c) from £12 to £13.

Economists' theory of the firm informs that the more monopolistic the market the greater the firm's discretion over price. In the theoretical ideal of perfect competition, firms are merely price takers. Typical markets, however, are some way between the two extremes. Oligopolists often choose not to compete over price, but to compete in other ways, for example, product differentiation, promotion, distribution, packaging, additional services. They attempt to increase profit by cost reductions rather than by price rises.

Economic theory makes a major contribution to our understanding of markets and pricing but it does have severe limitations. Not only does it not deal adequately with the process of decision-making within the firm (including the mechanism whereby firms actually decide their prices) but it does not really explain why people buy goods and who buys the goods.

In economic theory, the customer is assumed to possess perfect knowledge of the market and of the product. The customer is able to evaluate the product and its quality and decide on the evidence whether it is worth committing money to the purchase of the product. However, this is not always the case in real life. Many of the products we purchase are too complex for us to evaluate fully before we commit our hard-earned money. Many products are wrapped in a way which prevents us inspecting the goods until we get home. When we make our choices, we have imperfect information. We rely upon the reputation of the supplier, the claims made for the product, recommendations, general appearance and instinct. Because we lack perfect knowledge, we frequently judge quality in terms of price. Hence, we end up assuming that high price means high quality.

Economic theory suggests that people are likely to buy more of the product as price falls. Our instincts tell us that we should be suspicious of low price since it probably means low quality. The lesson for those involved in marketing is two-fold. First, price must 'fit' the other aspects of the marketing mix. Arthur Daley, the archetypal seller of dubious secondhand cars, would find it difficult to sell a perfectly genuine new Rolls Royce at the knock down price of £20 000. Not only is the price suspiciously low, but the other features of the mix are not consistent with the quality of the product. Second, customers have a perception of what the price should be. Hence, when we say that firms have discretion over price, the discretion is within a limited range as shown in Fig 11.1. The closer

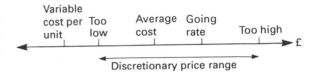

Fig 11.1 Customers' perception of value

price is to the limit of the discretionary range the greater the marketing effort required to sell the product (see Fig 11.2).

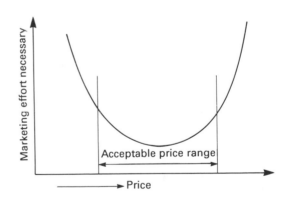

Fig 11.2 The acceptable price range
Note: The marketing effort has to be increased if price is too low or too high.

In marketing it is assumed that the firm does have some discretion over price, but that price is but one element of the marketing mix. The other three 'Ps' equate with economists' non-price competition.

Pricing objectives

Rational decisions can only be made after objectives have been clarified. Firms will choose one of the following objectives in pricing decisions:

PROFIT MAXIMISATION

In private enterprise firms, profit remains the overriding objective. Economists assume that firms are profit maximisers and in the theory of the firm it is demonstrated that profits are maximised when marginal cost equals marginal revenue. That is, when the cost of producing an additional unit of output is equal to the revenue derived from selling an additional unit of output. This is very attractive theoretically but it does not explain how prices are set. Moreover, there are likely to be other objectives influencing the pricing behaviour of firms.

MARKET SHARE

Firms may seek to increase their market share even to the extent of sacrificing short-term profits. Penetration pricing is particularly successful when demand is elastic. By building up sales, and therefore market share, the firm will benefit from greater discretion over price in the long run. Hence, the market share objective involves a sacrifice of profits in the short run to enjoy higher profits in the long run.

RETURN ON CAPITAL

Prices are set to earn a target return on capital employed (e.g. 20 per cent). This is illustrated by means of a break-even chart shown in Fig 11.3.

PROMOTIONAL PRICING

The objective here is not to increase profit, overall sales revenue or overall market share, but to enhance the sales of a particular product within the range. Again, this points to one of the

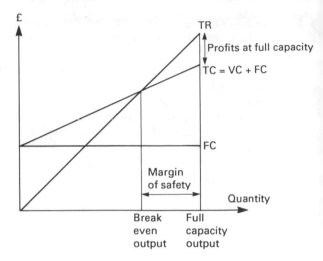

Fig 11.3   A break-even chart

deficiencies of economic analysis which implicitly assumes that suppliers are single product firms.

SALES REVENUE

Firms may choose to set prices to maximise current sales revenue especially if they seek an early recovery of cash.

PROFIT MARGIN

This is pricing to maximise profit margin on each unit sold (rather than overall profits). This objective, which is seen in skimming, is based on the assumption that (a) buyers are still prepared to purchase the goods despite the high price (i.e. demand is inelastic), and (b) the firm has sufficient lead over rivals so that there is little danger of high prices attracting competitors in the immediate future.

RISK MINIMISATION

Economics is based on assumption of rational behaviour which in traditional economics meant maximisation of profits (or income). However, action to minimise risk is also rational. Firms may, in the short run at least, set prices to minimise risk and maximise survival. After all, long-term profits are only possible if the firm continues in existence.

Costing

Just as there are product and market-orientated firms we can make a parallel distinction in terms of pricing policy. Cost-based pricing involves the setting of price by calculation of cost with an added element for profit (e.g. cost plus pricing). Market-orientated pricing sets the price in relation to market demand while ensuring that costs are covered (or at least taken into account). Whether pricing is cost-based or market-orientated, the decision-makers must ascertain the cost of production before setting prices. The calculation of the cost of production is known as costing.

Economists distinguish between fixed costs (rent, interest payments, etc.) and variable costs (cost of energy, materials, labour). The former remain the same in the short run, irrespective of the level of production. Clearly, no costs are fixed in the long run but in the short run, interest on debts has to be paid whether production is high, low or even zero. Variable costs vary with the level of output. Hence, the greater the output, the greater the quantity of materials used.

Cost accountants use an alternative classification which cuts across the fixed/variable classification. Direct costs are wholly and exclusively identified with a particular cost unit (e.g. a unit of output). Hence, labour and material used to produce jam tarts in a bakery are direct costs of jam tart production. However, there are other costs which are not directly linked to jam tart production, e.g. the cost of employing administrative staff or the heating and lighting bill for the bakery. The matrix in Table XXII is intended to demonstrate that (a) fixed and indirect costs, and (b) variable and direct costs are not synonymous. Depreciation and rent are both fixed costs yet the former can be identified with a particular product, whereas this is not the case with factory rent.

Absorption (or full) costing involves an attempt to identify all business costs associated with a

Table XXII

	Direct	Indirect
Fixed	Depreciation on dedicated machinery	Factory rent
Variable	Raw materials	Energy

particular activity. It is relatively easy to calculate the direct costs, but more difficult to decide how much of the indirect costs (or overheads) should be identified with the activity. In essence, to the directly attributable costs is added a share of the overhead costs, which are apportioned on an equitable basis for example:

Overhead	Basis of apportionment
Rent	Area taken up by the activity
Heating costs	Volume occupied
Cost of personnel administration	No. of employees involved
Indirect labour used	In proportion to direct labour
Fire insurance	In proportion to value of capital

After overheads are apportioned to, say, jam tart production, it is then necessary to calculate what share of these apportioned overheads should be absorbed by each box of jam tarts.

Direct or **marginal** costing assigns only variable costs to the production and therefore excludes fixed costs. By ignoring fixed overhead costs it is possible to concentrate on those costs that rise as output rises. Marginal costs are defined as incremental costs or the change in cost resulting from the production of an additional unit of output. Although costs are not fully covered, there are circumstances (described later in this chapter) when marginal cost should be used as the basis for pricing decisions. However, before we investigate full and marginal cost pricing, we should understand a simple graphical technique known as break-even analysis.

Break-even analysis

This simple graphical technique acts as an aid to decision-making. Let us assume that the firm makes a single product. Costs can be divided into variable costs such as materials, fuel and labour costs (which rise and fall with output) and fixed costs, for example, rent, interest charges (which remain the same, irrespective of the level of output). If we assume a linear (straight-line) relationship between quantity and both costs and revenue, we can calculate the output at which the firm exactly covers costs with revenue received.

In Fig 11.3, fixed costs are represented by a horizontal line with variable costs superimposed on top. As output rises, variable costs (and, therefore, total costs) rise. The vertical distance between fixed costs and total costs represent variable costs at each level of output. Total revenue can be calculated by multiplying price by the quantity sold. We can now draw a total revenue line and discover the point at which total revenue equals total costs (the break-even point). Any output in excess of break-even output generates profit for the company. This is shown by the

vertical distance between the TR and TC lines. Maximum available profit occurs at the full capacity level. The horizontal distance between break-even level and current level of output is known as the margin of safety. Where break-even output is a high percentage of current output the margin of safety and scope for profit is small. One way to increase both is to raise prices. This results in a new total revenue line (TR_1 in Fig 11.4) and a lower break-even output (B_1 rather than B).

We will return to this notion of contribution later in the chapter.

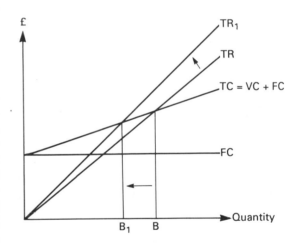

Fig 11.4   A break-even chart depicting a rise in price and a lower break-even output

EXERCISE ● ● ●

● It is possible to calculate break-even output without the use of graphs. This involves the notion of **contribution** which can be defined as the excess of price over variable costs. If

    (i)   fixed costs were £500 000;
    (ii) the variable cost per unit amounted to £1;
    (iii) the selling price was £5 per unit; and
    (iv) full capacity production came to 200 000 units per year:

Calculate
    (a) Break-even output;
    (b) Profit at full capacity; and
    (c) The margin of safety.

ANSWERS ● ● ●

● (a)   Each unit is sold for £5 but variable costs amount to £1 per unit. Consequently, each unit sold contributes £4 to fixed costs which are £500 000.

Break-even occurs at $\dfrac{£500\ 000}{£4} = 125\ 000$ units

To calculate break-even output, divide fixed costs by the contribution per unit.

(b)   At full capacity, costs amount to £500 000 plus £1 × 200 000 = £700 000.
Revenue amounts to £5 × £200 000 = £1 000 000.
Therefore, profits at full capacity are £300 000.

(c)   The margin of safety is the current output minus break-even output. In this example it is 200 000 minus 125 000 equals 75 000 units.

Break-even occurs at five eighths or 62½ per cent of current output. The margin of safety is three eighths or 37½ per cent of capacity.

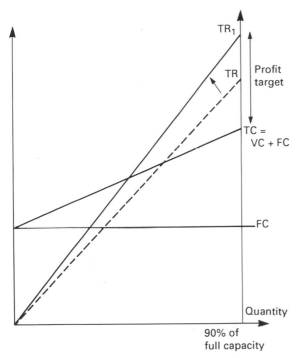

Fig 11.5   A break-even analysis involving a profit target

11.5, the firm wishes to achieve a target level of profits working at 90 per cent capacity. The price which produces total revenue curve TR will not produce profits at the target level. Consequently, it is necessary to raise price to produce a new total revenue line TR₁.

Break-even charts may provide a useful way of looking at cost-output and revenue relationships. However, they suffer from a number of limitations:

1   Fixed costs are likely to change at different levels of activity. Perhaps it would be more accurate to represent fixed costs as a stepped line.
2   Neither variable costs nor sales revenue are likely to be linear. Discounts, overtime payments and special delivery charges all contribute to non-linearity. Economists would depict the break-even chart as revealed in Fig 11.6.
3   Break-even charts show short-term relationships which makes it inappropriate for long-term planning purposes.

Break-even analysis can be used in pricing decisions: for instance, if the firm had a target rate of return or a target for profit, it could calculate the price at which the target would be achieved at full capacity (or any other level of capacity). In Fig

Full cost (cost plus) pricing

Full cost pricing involves the calculation of the full cost of producing or providing each unit of output. Both direct and indirect costs are included in the

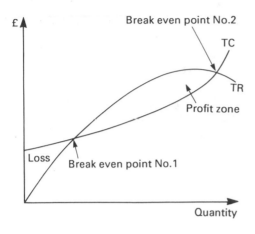

Fig 11.6   Non-linear break-even
Note: (a) As output rises beyond a certain point, costs rise disproportionately;
(b) To increase sales volume, it is necessary to reduce prices, leading eventually to a TR curve which dips downwards;
(c) Profits are maximised at the output where the vertical distance between TR and TC is greatest.

calculation to which is added a fixed percentage mark-up for profit. High turnover items will carry a low mark-up, whereas slow-moving items carry a high mark-up. It is said to be a fair and logical method of pricing to recover overhead costs and maximise long-run profits. As demand is uncertain there is much to be said for a pricing strategy based upon known costs.

However, it is easier to calculate full unit cost when the firm produces a single product than when the firm produces a multitude of products. In the case of the latter firm, there are major decisions to be made about the allocation of overhead costs betwen the different products. The apportionment of overheads follows certain conventions but is of necessity arbitrary: for instance, rent and rates may be apportioned in terms of the area occupied by different departments within the firm. Personnel costs are apportioned by reference to the number of employees in each department. By devising complex formulae, it is possible to ensure the absorption of all overhead costs.

Full cost pricing can be criticised on the grounds that:

- it ignores demand and the price elasticity of demand;
- it ignores the competitive situation;
- it does not take advantage of the market potential;
- it is inflexible in the face of demand changes;
- it exaggerates the precision with which costs can be allocated;
- it does not distinguish between out-of-pocket and 'sunk' costs (those which are spent, regardless of the level of production);
- it ignores capital requirements and the return on investment;
- many costs vary with volume of output, and volume of output depends on price charged;
- it can result in underpricing or overpricing.

Marginal pricing

To understand marginal or contribution pricing, consider the following situation. A firm which produces aerosol products is currently operating at 90 per cent of its capacity. It has fixed costs of £1 million per year. A large supermarket chain wishes to place an order for 200 000 cans of 'own brand' air freshener for which it is prepared to pay 40 pence per can. The aerosol company calculates that this special order will add £40 000 to labour costs, £20 000 to the cost of materials, with additional overhead costs of £10 000. By taking on this special order, the aerosol company can now operate at full capacity. Should it accept the order? The answer is yes, but with certain qualifications.

The special order generates additional revenue of £80 000, whereas costs rise by £70 000. Hence, the special order provides a contribution of £10 000 towards fixed costs and profit. In evaluating this deal the £1 million of fixed cost is irrelevant. These are costs that will be incurred whether or not the special order is accepted. These costs will be covered by the firm's regular production. Provided additional (or marginal) revenue covers additional (marginal) cost, the special deal is worthwhile. The additional cost of the own brand air fresheners works out at £70 000 or 35 pence per can. Any revenue above 35 pence per can will make a contribution.

Marginal cost pricing is only suitable where the firm

(a) has spare capacity

(b) cannot put its resources to more profitable use

(c) is able to segment its market to avoid a diversion of its regular custom to the low price alternative. Fortunately for the aerosol producer the supermarket own brand air freshener is usually perceived to be a different product by customers even if in fact it is identical to the aerosol firm's branded product. Marginal pricing should never be used if it will set a precedent for the future or if it commits the firm to extra capital costs.

Marginal cost pricing is widely employed in those service industries such as public transport, hotel and holiday firms that suffer from daily or seasonal fluctuations in demand. Peak pricing, with off-peak prices reflecting variable rather than full costs, has as one of its aims the reduction in demand fluctuations.

Demand-orientated pricing

This is pricing based upon demand for the product and customers' perception of value rather than the cost of production. Perceived value pricing is used to 'position' the product in the market. As quality is informally assessed by the price charged it is important to choose a price which is consistent with the image of the product and the other elements of the marketing mix.

If the market is segmented it is possible to charge different prices to different segments of the market. This practice is called **price discrimination** if different prices are charged for goods (or services) which are identical in every respect. Where there are slight differences in the product

sold to different segments (e.g. brand names, slight differences in quality, or the timing of a service) the practice is known as **differential pricing**.

The price discriminator will charge a higher price in segments where demand is inelastic, but reduce price for the segment where demand is elastic. The principle can be illustrated by the InterCity rail fares. The commuter and business traveller will make the journey irrespective of price. Hence, full fares are charged when these people travel in the early morning or late afternoon. The social traveller is more sensitive to price and will be unable or unwilling to pay the full fare, but will be attracted by reduced fares. To prevent commuters taking advantage of the lower fares they are only available after 9.30 am. The time restriction separates the two segments of the market. This practice is useful in shifting some trade to off-peak in an attempt to even the flow of travellers.

Pioneer pricing

There are special problems associated with the pricing of a new product especially one that is very different from any previous product. A cost-based approach to this problem is to base price on standard cost. A market-orientated solution is to consider the nature of the market, its customers and potential rivals. One of two strategies could be used.

Skimming v penetration

Skim pricing involves entry to the market at a high price which is later reduced (in real if not in money terms) as the product becomes more acceptable and the volume of sales increases. With an increase in sales volume the firm will enjoy economies of scale and can, therefore, afford to reduce prices. The opposite strategy is known as penetration pricing. By introducing the product at a low price the firm can penetrate deep into the market. As volume increases price is raised. These strategies are shown in Fig 11.7.

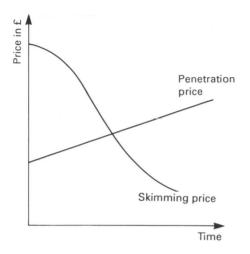

Fig 11.7   Pioneer pricing

Skimming is the preferred strategy with many radically new products (e.g. colour televisions in the early 1970s, video recorders later in the decade). Skimming allows for early recovery of research and development costs. A high profit margin on each unit sold reduces the need to sell a large volume. The strategy will succeed if:

1 through patent rights or technological lead, there is little danger of rivals entering the market in the short term;
2 unit production and distribution costs are not substantially greater for small quantities than for large quantities; and
3 there are sufficient buyers prepared to pay the high skimming price.

The trendsetters, who are the early buyers of an innovative product may actually be attracted by the high price, which creates the impression of a superior product.

Penetration pricing is superficially an attractive way to obtain a large volume of sales and a major market share. However, it is a high risk strategy. It is only suitable when the firm possesses the capacity for high sales volume and when a low price generates sufficient sales to compensate for low profit margins. If the product is expected to have a short life cycle, penetration does not provide sufficient time to recover R and D costs. It is not surprising that many firms choose skimming as their pioneer pricing strategy.

Competition-orientated pricing

Here prices are related not to cost or to customer demand but to prices charged by competitor firms. The more competitive the industry and the more homogeneous the product, the greater the pressure to keep in line with competitors. In the economists' model of perfect competition all firms charge the same price since they are all price takers.

Oligopolists also carefully study rivals when setting prices. A price truce with recognised price leaders is common in oligopolistic markets. It is less disruptive to follow the lead set by competitors than engage in mutually harmful price warfare. Occasionally the truce breaks down and price warfare breaks out. Competitive price cutting is designed to weaken and destroy smaller and less efficient rivals. Price wars are used as a way of forcing out rivals or weakening them prior to take over. Sir Freddy Laker alleged that the larger airlines conspired together to force Laker Airways out of business by a price war. Once the competitor is removed, the oligopolists can resume their previous policy of informal collusion to keep prices high and competitor firms in harmony.

Table XXIII   Summary of pricing policies

Cost-orientated pricing

(1) Full cost or cost plus pricing involves the addition of a mark up to unit cost.
(2) Target pricing sets prices to achieve a target return on investment.

Demand-orientated pricing

(3) Marginal pricing applies in situations where spare capacity exists. Provided variable costs

are covered it is worthwhile producing goods and services that make a contribution to fixed cost. Variations on the theme include peak and off peak pricing and discriminatory pricing in different segments of the market.

(4) Penetration pricing involves low prices and the sacrifice of short term profits to increase market share.

(5) Skimming entails the setting of high prices to yield high profit margin in the short term.

Competition-orientated pricing

(6) Destroyer pricing aims to eliminate rivals in a price war.

(7) 'Follow the leader' is common in oligopolistic markets where firms are reluctant to engage in open price competition.

Conclusion

There is no pricing strategy suitable for all circumstances. Instead, firms must choose the strategy that is appropriate in view of their objectives, the situation in the market and their capacity utilisation. Marginal pricing or penetration pricing is only appropriate where the firm has the capacity to increase output to satisfy the demand that emerges with low prices. Skimming is only appropriate where the firm enjoys a lead over its rivals and is able to enjoy a temporary monopoly position in the market. Full cost pricing is only appropriate when the resulting price is within the customers' perceived range of value.

CASE STUDY
The West End Theatre

Staging a play or a musical in the West End is an expensive business. The average straight play costs £150 000 to £200 000 to set up. £1 million is a typical figure for a musical and in the case of a big production like 'Miss Saigon' development costs are as high as £3 million. These are costs that are incurred before the production opens.

To increase the chances of commercial success, promotional activity is considered necessary. The promotional budget for a typical play is £50 000, but for a musical it is common to have a budget of three times that amount. The objective is to create awareness of the production. In the case of a big musical, advance bookings are important in securing a cash inflow. 'Miss Saigon' had advance bookings of £4 million before it opened. As well as creating awareness amongst British residents it is also important for the commercial success of many productions to secure bookings from overseas visitors. Thirty-six per cent of West End theatre audiences come from overseas, with Americans forming the bulk of this overseas contingent. Up until now the West End has rather neglected European visitors and has not tried to attract them in the way they seek American theatregoers. However, even with promotions and 'big name' stars a play or show will not succeed unless it is of high quality and appealing.

The break-even point will vary with the size of the theatre, scale of production and status of the star. One recent play was reported to need takings of £30 000 per week to break even. Fortunately it was currently taking £50 000 per week and expected to recover development costs in 12 weeks. A failure to reach the weekly break-even point would result in premature closure even though it might mean a total loss of development costs.

However, even if the show breaks even on running costs, it might still be forced to close. The fact is the producer of the show has to rent one of the 40 or so West End theatres. The rent is not a fixed sum, but is usually a percentage of ticket sales (e.g. 20 per cent), subject to a guaranteed minimum payment. As theatre owners receive a percentage (rather than a fixed sum) they are keen to attract successful production into their theatres. The opportunity cost of allowing a mediocre production into their theatre is the revenue they would have received from a more popular show.

1 What do you understand by:
   (a) promotional activity, and
   (b) a promotional budget?
2 Suggest methods of attracting European audiences to the West End.
3 Distinguish between fixed and variable costs. How would you classify the rent payable on the theatre?
4 A musical production cost £1 million to stage. Its weekly break even point is £100 000 and it is expected to recover its development costs in 50 weeks. What are its weekly takings?
5 Compare the attitude of theatre owners to the success of the show when:
   (a) they receive a fixed rent
   (b) they receive a percentage of takings.

EXERCISE ● ● ●

● 1 The Richardson Pen Company produces a range of products including a popular brand of steel-tipped pen. It has the capacity to produce six million such pens per year, although at present it is operating at less than full capacity. The pens are sold to wholesalers at 50 pence each. The production of each pen involves variable costs of 30 pence. Fixed costs at the current output level of five million pens are 10 pence per pen.

   (a) From the above information, construct a break-even chart.
   (b) Calculate the contribution per pen, defining clearly what is meant by the term.
   (c) Using arithmetic rather than graphical means, calculate:
        (i) the break-even output;
        (ii) the margin of safety;
        (iii) profit at full capacity.
   (d) A hotel chain wishes to place a bulk order for 500 000 pens and is willing to pay 35p per pen. The Richardson Pen Company calculates that this special order will involve an additional £10 000 of fixed costs to stamp the hotel logo on the pens. Should the pen company take the order?
        Explain your reasoning.

● 2 A firm sells its product at the price of £4. Its fixed costs are £20 000 and its variable costs are shown in the schedule below.

Output (units)	Variable costs (£)
1000	1000
2000	1600
3000	2000
4000	2300
5000	2400
6000	3000
7000	4000
8000	5500
9000	7200
10000	9000
11000	13000
12000	19000

   (a) On graph paper construct a non-linear break-even chart.
   (b) To the nearest 100 units, at what level of output does break-even occur?
   (c) At what level of output are profits maximised?
   (d) Suggest reasons why costs rise rapidly at the higher levels of output.

● 3 Sally produces a range of dresses sold under her own designer label. She has built up a good reputation with both retail chains and customers and so far has always been able to sell her entire output.

   One of the dresses in her Autumn Collection proved very popular with buyers from a number of large retail chains and they placed pre-production orders for this dress for 50 000. Sally decided to produce 80 000 dresses of this design confident of obtaining orders for the other

30 000. Each dress incurred direct costs of £25 and each was required to make a £15 contribution to indirect costs. Sally sold each dress direct to retailers for £45. They in turn priced the dresses at £80 each.

Unfortunately for Sally the dress did not sell very well especially in south-east England. In part its failure could be attributed to high mortgage rates which have a disproportionate impact on the south-east. Sally was now faced with the dilemma of what to do with the remaining dresses. One possibility is disposing of them at a discount, although she is anxious not to undermine her reputation in the clothes trade. Her marketing manager believes that sales at various discount prices would be as follows:

Price (£)	Sales (000)
45	0
40	5
35	10
30	15
25	20
20	25
15	30

(a) Why was Sally's business affected by high mortgage rates?
(b) Why was the impact of mortgage rate rises greatest in the south-east?
(c) Explain the dilemma that Sally faced and, in particular, the disadvantage of selling her dresses at a discount.
(d) From a short-term financial point of view what should Sally do? Explain your reasoning and your assumptions about her objectives.

● 4 Complete the table below, using the clues that follow.

Output (000 tonnes)	Total Cost £	Fixed Cost £	Variable Cost £	Average Cost £
100				
150				
200				
250				
300				

(a) When output is 400 000 tonnes, average fixed costs are £2.
(b) At 100 000 tonnes of output, average variable cost is £1.
(c) As output rises to 150 000 total costs increase by £50 000.
(d) The average variable cost of 200 000 units is £1.
(e) When output rises to 250 000 average cost is £4.08.
(f) At 300 000 tonnes units of ouput variable costs are £415 000.

5   The TCT Soft Toy Company produces three types of soft toy: a teddy bear, a rabbit and a penguin. The profit and loss account for the year just ended shows that the penguins made a loss and it has been suggested that they be discontinued.

(£000)	Bears	Rabbits	Penguins
Sales	500	350	650
Direct materials	150	80	250
Direct labour	100	100	250
Variable overheads	50	40	60
Fixed overheads	100	80	110
Total costs	400	300	670
Profit/Loss	100	50	(20)

(a) Should the penguin be discontinued? To answer this question it is necessary to calculate the following:
    (i) The variable cost of producing each of the three types of toy;
    (ii) The contribution from each;
    (iii) The overall level of profits; and
    (iv) Total fixed costs.
(b) If the penguin is discontinued and we assume that it does not affect sales of the other products, what is the impact on the company's overall profit?

6   The variable cost of the electric kettle manufactured by Fair Oak Domestic Appliances Ltd is £4. The company, which sells its kettles direct to retailers for £10, expects its net profit for the year just ending to be £270 000 after allowing for fixed costs of £90 000. The productive capacity of the company is under-utilised and the marketing manager suggests that a 10 per cent reduction in selling price will bring about a 25 per cent increase in sales.
(a) Define the term 'contribution'. What is the contribution per unit in the above case?
(b) What level of sales is necessary to break even?
(c) If profits are £270 000 after allowing for fixed costs of £90 000, what is the current volume of output and sales?
(d) Calculate:
    (i) sales revenue at this volume of sales; and
    (ii) sales revenue resulting from the implementation of the marketing manager's proposal.
(e) As a result of the increased volume, by how much has
    (i) revenue changed; and
    (ii) costs changed?
(f) Should Fair Oak Domestic Appliances reduce their selling price by 10 per cent?

● 7   Read the article on petrol prices and answer the following questions.

A tankful of trouble

FINGERS crossed, a weighty document from the Monopolies and Mergers Commission (MMC) on Britain's petrol-retailing market will thud onto the desk of Mr Nicholas Ridley, the trade and industry secretary, on December 20th. It will be a last-minute rush: this week the MMC was still mulling over evidence from the oil companies (which directly own a third of the country's petrol-stations) and, among others, the Petrol Retailers Association, which represents the independent retailers and is the biggest thorn in the oil industry's side.

Britain's motorists spend £12 billion a year on petrol. Are they paying too much? When wholesale petrol prices rise, the big oil companies swiftly raise their pump-prices, more or less in tandem. Just shows how competitive the market is, say the oil companies. Well, perhaps; but it could be a sign of an oligopoly, or even of collusion. When wholesale prices fall, pump-prices invariably edge down much more slowly.

There are other worrying signs. Pump prices (before tax) are now higher, relative to wholesale petrol prices on the Rotterdam spot market, than they were during the first half of the 1980s. And the oil companies make rather more profit from a gallon of petrol sold in Britain than they do from one sold in, say America. This is a discrepancy both the oil companies and the MMC are finding hard to explain.

Worse, the oil companies selectively support retailers' profit margins – a system which has led to charges of *de facto* retail-price maintenance (which would be illegal). If a petrol-station owner unilaterally cuts prices, nearby rivals will usually match the cut (with oil-company financial support). In a truly competitive market, petrol stations offering full service and a range of facilities would charge high prices; those simply selling self-service petrol would price it cheaply.

The oil companies claim that they make a paltry profit from selling petrol (although some of them seem not to know exactly how much). But the MMC should remember that this is only half the story: big, integrated oil companies make money from refining petrol, too. And if selling petrol is so unprofitable, why are oil companies spending so heavily sprucing up existing petrol stations and buying new sites?

The MMC is likely to recommend that contracts which currently bind about a fifth of Britain's petrol stations to their oil-company suppliers should be scrapped and replaced with arms-length tenancy agreements. It is also set to recommend the abolition of "margin support". But what is surely needed is a way to ensure that petrol-retailers in Britain genuinely compete. The Office of Fair Trading does not want the job of making that happen. So expect the MMC to recommend the establishment of an Office of Petroleum Supply.

(Source: *The Economist*, 16 December 1989)

(*a*)   The Thatcher Government believes in the free market. Why then do we have a Monopolies and Mergers Commission?

(*b*)   Explain:
   (i)   oligopoly;
   (ii) collusion;
   (iii) Rotterdam spot market;
   (iv) retail price maintenance;
   (v)   'integrated oil companies'.

(*c*)   The second paragraph of the *Economist* article implies that similarity of prices reflects either a competitive situation or collusion.
      Explain.

(*d*)   Why do oil companies 'selectively support retailers profit margins'? Why should this support be abolished?

(*e*)   Why is the MMC critical of present tenancy agreements?

8   A firm produces a good, the demand for which extends as price is reduced. The demand schedule is shown in the first two columns below.
   It is known that the fixed cost of producing the goods is £1 000 000 but in addition there are variable costs related to the level of output. Variable costs are shown in the third column.

Price £	Quantity demand (000)	Variable Costs (£000)
20	100	1000
19	110	1040
18	120	1050
17	130	1020
16	140	1120
15	150	1200
14	160	1300
13	170	1500
12	180	1800

(a) For each level of output calculate (i) total revenue and (ii) total costs.
(b) Assume that the goods can only be produced in batches of 10 000. Which price-output combination would (i) maximise total revenue, and (ii) maximise profits?
(c) Marginal cost is the extra cost incurred when increasing the level of output (in this case by 10 000). Marginal revenue is the extra revenue resulting from the increased level of output.
    Calculate the marginal cost and marginal revenue from each successive increase in output. What do you notice about MC and MR as we approach profit maximisation?
(d) This analysis was developed by economists to explain the behaviour of profit maximising monopolists. Comment on its usefulness to firms in setting prices.

9   Study the following data extracted from a profit and loss account and answer the questions that follow:

	£000	£000
Sales (50 000 units)		1000
Variable costs	800	
Fixed costs	300	
		1100
Loss for the year		(100)

(a) Calculate the selling price.
(b) The marketing manager suggests that a 10 per cent reduction in price would lead to a 20 per cent increase in the volume of sales. Assuming a linear relationship between output and variable costs, calculate the impact on the firm's losses.
(c) The production manager points out that, to achieve this higher level of output, it is necessary to increase direct labour wage rates from £4 to £5 per hour as part of a

productivity deal. Assuming that direct labour accounts for 40 per cent of variable costs, calculate the impact on the firm's losses of implementing both the suggestions of the marketing and production manager.

10 You are given the following information about the pricing of a new consumer product.

- The product will be sold at a retail price of £3.00 which includes distributors margin of 33⅓%.
- Similar but inferior goods produced by competitors currently retail for between £2.50 and £2.75.
- The product is expected to achieve an annual sales volume of 100 000.
- At this level of output variable costs will be £100 000 per year.
- To produce the goods, the firm has invested in dedicated plant costing £400 000 to be depreciated over ten years (assume no residual value and the use of the straight line method).
- General overheads amount to £1.8 million and the product will account for 10 per cent of the company's overall volume of sales.

Comment on the price charged by the manufacturer.

11 A manufacturer of dining tables incurs the following expenses:

	£
Annual rent and rates	5000
Interest payments	1000
Tax and insurance for delivery van	800
Materials used per item manufactured	450
Petrol for the delivery van per item	20
Wages per item	150
Workshop insurance	500

(a) Calculate average fixed costs per item for each of the following levels of output:
(i) 20; (ii) 50; (iii) 10 000.
What conclusion can be drawn about average fixed costs?
(b) For each of the above levels of output, calculate the profit (or loss) when each table is sold for £750.
(c) Calculate level of output necessary to break even.
(d) Assuming that costs remain unchanged, what price would the firm have to charge to break even at an annual output of 30 tables.

EXAMINATION QUESTIONS ■■■

1 Explain why different pricing tactics may be used in a marketing campaign when economic theory might suggest that price is determined solely by demand and supply.

(AEB, November 1988)

EXAMINATION QUESTIONS ■■■

■ 1 Explain why different pricing tactics may be used in a marketing campaign when economic theory might suggest that price is determined solely by demand and supply.

(AEB, November 1988)

■ 2 A business is about to launch a new product. Identify and discuss the information it will require before deciding on a pricing strategy.

(AEB, June 1985)

■ 3 If a firm's pricing policies are to be effective, they must be market-orientated. Outline critically the types of pricing policy implied by this statement.

(AEB, June 1982)

■ 4 (a) What is meant by 'full cost pricing'?
   (b) In what circumstances would you advise the use of marginal cost pricing, and why?
   (c) Why is the profit earned on a product important?

(Cambridge, June 1985)

FURTHER READING

PRICING

For further information on costing the reader should refer to the works mentioned at the end of the chapter on accounting. The marketing aspects of pricing is dealt with in the books on marketing.

THE ECONOMICS OF PRICING POLICY

L DAVIES & S HUGHES *Pricing in Practice* (Heinemann)
B HARRISON *Pricing and Competition in the Private Sector* (Longman)
N BRANTON & J LIVINGSTONE *Managerial Economics in Practice* (Hodder and Stoughton)

CHAPTER 12
Management and Organisational Theory

In this chapter we will look at people in organisations, starting with an investigation of the development of theory relating to management and organisations. In the subsequent chapters we will look at practical issues relating to people in organisations.

OBJECTIVES

1 To understand the role of managers.
2 To outline the development of management theory in the 20th Century.
3 To understand the nature of the formal and informal organisation.

Management

Management is the process of achieving objectives by the utilisation of resources (manpower, material, machinery and money). Writers have long argued about the essential tasks performed by managers. Fayol identified five management tasks: forecasting and planning, organising, commanding, co-ordinating and controlling. An alternative classification of tasks is known as POSDCORB which stands for:

1 PLANNING: a plan is a pre-determined course of action designed to give sense and purpose to an undertaking.

We can make a broad distinction between a strategic plan and an operational plan. The former is a long-term plan which describes the way in which it is intended that the organisation should develop. Operational plans are concerned the achievement of immediate goals with an emphasis on efficiency and profitability today rather than developing future potential.

The corporate plan attempts to answer the following questions:

(a) Where are we now? This is known as a situational audit.

(b) Where do we want to go? This refers to organisational objectives.

(c) What do we have to do to get there? This is concerned with strategy and tactics.

(d) How are we getting on? All plans should include a system of control and evaluation of performance.

The situation can be assessed by SWOT analysis.

Strengths and weaknesses are internal and can be expressed in terms of sales volume, market share, product range and development, and human and other resources at the disposal of the organisation. An organisation might enjoy strength in terms of the range of its products but be weak in terms of export performance. Opportunities and threats exist in the external environment. Demographic changes might provide an opportunity for future development whereas new product development by rivals might pose a threat to the future profitability of the organisation.

We have already encountered the Boston Matrix which is a useful way of assessing an organisation's product range. Dogs (products with low market share, low growth rate) should be eliminated in the strategic planning process. On a larger scale, an organisation which owns a diverse range of companies might use SWOT analysis to identify the parts of organisation to sell off.

Under the umbrella of the overall corporate plan, there will be operational plans for each of the functional areas within the organisation, e.g. production, marketing, manpower, finance and investment. Although not as wide ranging as the strategic plan, they conform to the same pattern as outlined above.

2 ORGANISING is the establishment of a formal structure by which work is divided up, defined and co-ordinated. A formal structure is considered necessary to establish authority and responsibility, to gain the advantage of specialisation, to enable the individual to relate to a sub-unit of the organisation and provide for the flow of information. The classical writers were preoccupied with the formal structure to the neglect of the people within the organisation.

3 STAFFING refers to organising the human resources to ensure that the right person is in the right job and at the right time and place.

4 DIRECTING is the continuous task of decision-making and embodying those decisions in orders and instructions or by inspiring the workforce. In the past the emphasis was on giving orders and directing people towards the achievement of organisational goals. Today, the emphasis has switched to inspiring or leading the workforce giving general guidance, but allowing the worker considerable freedom for initiative.

5 CO-ORDINATION means bringing the various parts together to ensure that they work in harmony and balance. For instance, the achievement of marketing objectives is dependent upon co-ordination with other functional departments. Unless the production department acquires sufficient inputs, it will not be able to produce the goods, and without the goods, the marketing department will not be able to satisfy customers.

6 REPORTING is necessary if senior management is to be kept informed of progress towards the goals. This links up with Fayol's control function which is concerned to see that everything happens in conformity with the plans.

7 BUDGETING. A budget is a financial or quantitative statement relating to income, expenditure and the employment of capital. It is expressed in terms of a specific quantitative target to be achieved within a particular time frame.

Table XXIV Development of management theory

School	Key ideas	Writers
1 Scientific management	Plan workers movements in the most efficient and least tiring way.	Taylor
2 Classical management	Formal structures. Technical requirements. Set of principles. Bureaucracy.	Fayol Weber

3 Human relations	Informal organisation. Psychological and social needs.	Mayo
4 Neo human relations	Personal adjustment of the worker. Group relationships. Leadership.	Maslow Herzberg McGregor Argyris McClelland
5 Systems	The task of managers to maintain a system of co-operative effort in a formal organisation. Integration of formal and informal organisation. Socio-technical approach. Open systems interacting with the environment.	
6 Contingency	Rejection of one best way. Structure is dependent upon circumstances.	Woodward, Burns and Stalker

Classical management theory

Classical theory is frequently confused with scientific management mainly because they both emerged in the first decades of the 20th Century and both saw man as a rational economic animal. Scientific management attempts to improve work methods and to measure work as a means of paying employees by performance. Classical management theory deals with the formal structure of organisation. It seeks to formulate principles of sound effective management which have universal validity. Classical theorists recognised the benefits of division of labour and sought to discover the most effective means of achieving co-ordination, direction and control of the various sections of the organisation.

Henri Fayol (1841–1925) was a French industrialist whose ideas on management were expressed in his book *Administration Industrielle et Générale* (1916). The role of the manager was to (1) forecast and plan, (2) organise, (3) command, (4) co-ordinate and (5) control. The task of management is to steer the organisation to the achievement of a set of objectives. This is best accomplished by the adoption of the following principles:

1   DIVISION OF WORK to increase efficiency and output.
2   AUTHORITY AND RESPONSIBILITY. Authority means the right to act, whereas responsibility refers to the duty to act. Managers with responsibility for carrying out a task should be given the requisite authority to undertake the task. When authority and responsibility are delegated to a subordinate, he or she becomes accountable for ensuring the task is carried out.
3   DISCIPLINE. Fayol saw discipline 'as respect for agreements which are directed at achieving obedience, application, energy, and the outward marks of respect'. Discipline requires good supervisors.
4   UNITY OF COMMAND. Each subordinate should have a single superior.

5 UNITY OF DIRECTION was necessary to ensure all people within the organisation work towards the organisational goal.

6 SUBORDINATION OF INDIVIDUAL to general interest.

7 The DEGREE OF CENTRALISATION (the extent to which authority is concentrated or dispersed) will vary with the circumstances of the organisation.

8 SCALAR CHAIN. A hierarchy is necessary for unity of direction.

9 A fair system of REMUNERATION should be devised affording satisfaction to both employer and employees.

10 ORDER. 'There is a place for everything, and everything in its place'.

11 EQUITY. Kindliness and justice are necessary to obtain loyalty and devotion from the workforce.

12 STABILITY OF TENURE. Fayol argued that a high turnover of staff was costly and was both the cause and effect of bad management.

13 Subordinates should be allowed to exercise INITIATIVE.

14 ESPRIT DE CORPS. Believing that there is strength in union, Fayol emphasised the need for teamwork and the importance of good communication.

Lyndall Urwick (1952) produced a further set of principles which, if adhered to, would result in effective and successful management. These included:

1 The PRINCIPLE OF CORRESPONDENCE which means that authority (the right to make decisions) should be commensurate with responsibility (duty).

2 The PRINCIPLE OF DEFINITION means that the duties and relationships associated with jobs should be clearly defined.

3 The SPAN OF CONTROL refers to the number of direct subordinates for which a manager is responsible. Urwick argued that it should not exceed six.

4 The PRINCIPLE OF RESPONSIBILITY is such that even when authority is delegated, the superior remains responsible for the delegated actions of subordinates.

5 The PRINCIPLE OF THE OBJECTIVE refers to the overall purpose which is the raison d'être of the organisation.

The other major contribution to classical organisational theory came from the German sociologist Max Weber (1864–1924) in his book *The Theory of Social and Economic Organisations*. Weber developed the idea of bureaucracy as the most appropriate administrative form for the rational and efficient pursuit of organisational goals. Whereas today we use the words bureaucracy or bureaucratic in a pejorative sense to mean inflexible and impersonal, Weber saw bureaucracy as the ideal organisational form. For Weber bureaucracies had the following characteristics:

1 A high degree of SPECIALISATION based on functional specialisms.

2 A HIERARCHY with well defined levels of authority.

3 Duties carried out IMPERSONALLY and employment and promotion based on **qualifications** and **merit**.

4 A CONSISTENT system with formal rules, and procedures.

5 WRITTEN RECORDS of decisions taken.

Studies since Weber have highlighted the problems associated with rigid bureaucracies. Bureaucracy can result in inflexibility with ritualistic adherence to rules. Bureaucratic organisations can be slow to adapt to changing circumstances and leave little scope for personal growth and development. Moreover, Weber (like the classical management writers) ignored the informal organisation.

Organisational concepts

The organisational chart

An organisational chart depicts relationships between personnel within the formal organisation.

This is the official or planned structure of the organisation and is the only structure which classical theorists recognised or were interested in. From the organisational chart we can identify:

(a) lines of communication

(b) delegation of authority
(c) accountability
(d) span of control
(e) the way in which the work of the organisation is grouped (see Fig 12.1).

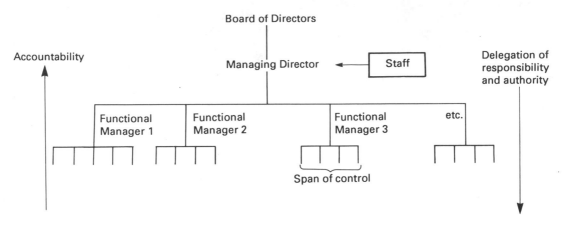

Fig 12.1   A chart of the formal organisation

In all organisations (other than the very smallest) it is necessary to organise or group the work and employees in order to:

- benefit from specialisation;
- simplify the task of management;
- maintain control.

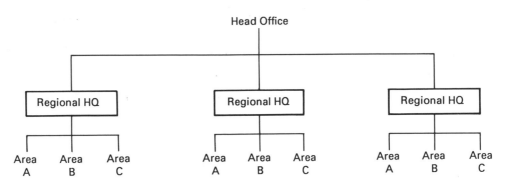

Fig 12.2   A geographically based organisation

In some organisations the grouping of work is based on geography with managers having responsibility for specific geographical areas (Fig 12.2). Retail and banking chains which are geographically dispersed but relatively homogeneous in function tend to be organised geographically. An organisation which is departmentalised on a functional basis (e.g. production, sales, advertising, etc.) will gain the benefit of specialisation of managerial function (see Fig 12.3). Alternative methods of organisation are by market (e.g. retail, industrial, export) or by product (especially in the case of a group of companies producing a diverse range of products (Figs 12.4 and 12.5).

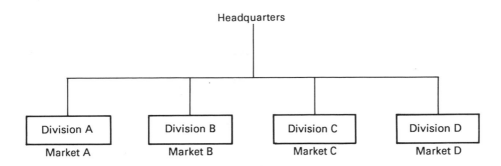

Fig 12.3 A market-based organisation

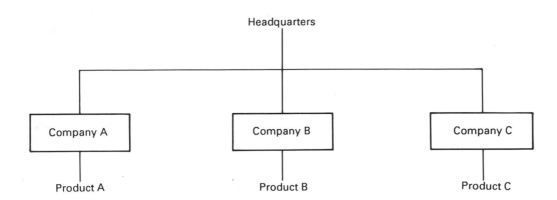

Fig 12.4 A product-based organisation

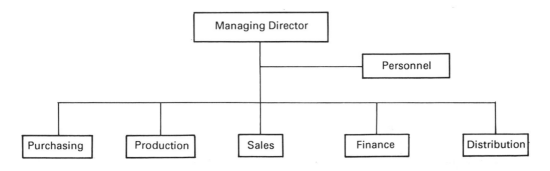

Fig 12.5 A functionally based organisation

A matrix structure breaks down rigid hierarchies by combining the functional manager principle with managers appointed to supervise particular projects. Some colleges are based on the matrix system with some members of the senior management responsible for functional areas such as student admission, pastoral care, staff development and finance whereas others are responsible for specific student courses or teams of teachers (*see* Fig 12.6).

Fig 12.6 A matrix structure

Authority

Authority refers to the legitimate exercise of power which in turn is the ability to exercise influence over objects, persons and situations. It is, therefore, possible to possess power without authority (and vice versa). Weber, the German sociologist whose ideas on bureaucracy we have already encountered, believed that authority was derived from tradition (e.g. choice of tribal chiefs), charisma (seen in the rise of dictators) or from a rational legal basis. In the case of the latter, authority is given to those appointed by the recognised, legitimate procedure. This is the classical view of authority, it originates high up in the organisation and is lawfully passed down. Under the capitalist system, the risk-taking owners have the authority to make decisions which they may choose to delegate to paid professional managers.

The modern view of authority is the acceptance view. Acceptance of authority is necessary if the communication is to carry authority. The authority of the superiors is more acceptable if they are respected.

Delegation

To enable top management to concentrate on major issues, it is necessary to delegate decision-making and other tasks to subordinates, especially as the organisation grows in size and complexity. Delegation is the act of assigning duties to subordinates and it has the additional virtue of enlarging and enriching the experience of the subordinates and providing training opportunities to enable them to advance their career.

To enable subordinates to carry out the delegated task, it is necessary to confer on them sufficient authority (i.e. the right to make decisions). It would be unfair to impose an obligation on subordinates unless they have the means to carry out the task. The subordinates are responsible for carrying out the task and to this end are made accountable to their superior. Responsibility and authority should be equal in amount, but a major problem is that delegated responsibility does not negate the responsibility of the superior: this is why some managers are reluctant to delegate. The superior remains responsible for the work carried out under delegation. Effective delegation requires that (1) the objectives be defined and understood. (2) the subordinate has sufficient authority to match their responsibility and (3) the task is properly understood.

Within an organisation the degree of delegation depends upon:

1 its size;
2 its history;
3 the quality of staff (although unless staff are given responsibility, they cannot demonstrate or improve their capabilities);
4 the cost of decisions (top management will be reluctant to delegate if mistakes are costly);
5 the quality of top management (insecure and ineffective managers are reluctant to delegate);

6 the need or desire for uniformity within the organisation. An organisation with a concentration of decision-making at the top is a centralised organisation. One in which it is delegated far and wide is said to be decentralised.

Span of control

This is the number of people directly responsible to a manager. Early management writers argued that any span in excess of six would result in ineffective supervision. However, the effect of operating a small span is to increase the number of tiers within the organisation. The resulting 'tall'

organisation suffers from problems of communication and the stifling of subordinates.

Modern writers dismiss the idea of a single ideal span of control. The number of subordinates that can be effectively supervised depends upon:

1 the nature of the task with repetitive work permitting the supervision of larger numbers of subordinates;
2 the ability and experience of the people concerned;
3 the effectiveness of communications;
4 the cohesiveness of the team;
5 the degree of delegation exercised; and
6 physical condition such as proximity of the people concerned.

Table XXV   Tall and flat organisations

Tall	Flat
Decentralised authority	Centralised authority
Many authority levels	Few authority levels
Narrow span of control	Wide span of control
High delegation	Low delegation
Long lines of communication	Easier communication
High degree of functional specialism	Low degree of functional specialism
Bureaucratic	Easier co-ordination

(Adapted from P W Betts: *Supervisory Studies*, Pitman)

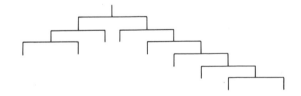

Fig 12.7 A 'tall' organisation
A small span of control results in a
multiplicity of layers.

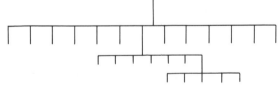

Fig 12.8 A 'flat' organisation
A wide span of control reduces the
number of layers.

Relationships

The organisational structure is likely to contain three types of relationship.

1 LINE RELATIONSHIPS exist between vertical

levels in the organisation. A line organisation incorporates Fayol's principle of unity of command and the scalar chain. Authority is delegated from highest to lowest and each superior within the hierarchy has authority and responsibility for all that occurs lower down the chain. Production managers are line managers responsible for the work of the production department.

2 STAFF RELATIONSHIPS. When planning a battle, generals from Marlborough to Eisenhower receive advice from specialist staff officers. Hence, staff has come to mean advisory. They have no line authority and cannot implement decisions. Instead they advise the line manager. In the words of Mrs Thatcher, 'Advisers advise and Ministers (line managers) decide'.

3 FUNCTIONAL RELATIONSHIPS arise when a specialist is allowed to take over a limited, defined function. The line manager, or managers, delegates authority to a specialist to carry out the task.

The line relationship is the backbone of the whole organisation, with the other two supplementing the line. Table XXVI summarises the merits of the three organisational relationships.

Table XXVI   Advantages and disadvantages of the three organisational relationships

Advantages	*Disadvantages*
Line Relationships	
1 Simplicity	1 Neglects specialists
2 Clear division of authority	2 Overworks key people
3 Facilitates rapid action	3 Depends upon retention of a few key staff
Staff Relationships	
1 Specialists give expert advice	1 Confusion if functions are not clear
2 Frees the line executive of detailed analysis	2 Tends towards centralisation
	3 Resentment and frustration
Functional Relationships	
1 Relieves the executives of routine, specialist decisions	1 Complex relationships
2 Expertise	2 Problems of co-ordination
	3 Confusion over limits to authority
	4 Centralising tendency

Centralisation v decentralisation

Centralisation refers to the amount of control exercised at the centre compared to that delegated to the periphery of the organisation. It is not necessarily related to the extent to which an organisation is spread out geographically. Hence, a multi-plant firm can be very centralised whereas a single site organisation can be decentralised if decision-making is delegated downwards. It is possible for an organisation to be totally centralised but complete decentralisation is not possible. The centre must retain some control over the planning process. As we saw earlier, authority can be delegated downwards but top management cannot abdicate all responsibility.

Decentralisation can be on a functional basis in which case authority is delegated to specialist functional departments. Alternatively, it could be on a federal basis, where departments or divisions are responsible for a range of products and operate as autonomous businesses (or profit centres). The advantages and disadvantages of centralisation and decentralisation are summarised in Table XXVII.

Table XXVII Centralisation v decentralisation

Advantages	Disadvantages
Centralisation	
1 Greater control	1 Excessively bureaucratic
2 Economies in staffing	2 Rigidity
3 Economies of specialisation	3 Delays in decision-making
4 Easier communications	4 Loss of initiative
	5 Stifles personal development
Decentralisation	
1 Decisions made where the action is	1 Loss of control
2 Recognise local conditions	2 Loss of some economies of scale
3 Improved morale	3 Development of a narrow departmental view
4 Personal development	
5 More responsive to the environment	

The classical theorists made a vital contribution not least in demonstrating that management was a subject for intellectual analysis. The main criticisms of classical theory is its concentration on formal structures and neglect of the sociological and psychological aspects. Classical theory presents a rather mechanistic, rigid view of organisations which, it is now recognised, need to adapt if they are to survive in a changing environment. Writers such as Fayol and Urwick presented their principles as universal panacea whereas it is now accepted that organisational structure should vary with circumstances.

The human relations school

The human relations school reflects the influence of sociologists and psychologists on the development of management theory. Business organisations were seen not as impersonal formal structures but as social systems in which psychological and emotional factors have a significant influence on productivity. Like all major schools of thought there are major differences between the various writers included within the 'umbrella' but the following strands of thought are present in the works of the human relations school:

1 Performance can be improved by good human relations.
2 Managers should consult employees in matters that affect staff.
3 Leadership should be democratic rather than authoritarian.
4 Employees are motivated by social and psychological rewards and are not just 'economic animals'.
5 The work group plays an important part in influencing performance.

The first significant research undertaken by a member of the human relations school was Elton Mayo's experiments at the Hawthorne Works of the Western Electric Company in Chicago (1923 to early 1930s). Mayo altered the working environment to study the impact on the productivity. He discovered that whatever he did productivity rose. From these results he concluded that people work more effectively and contendedly if the work appears to have meaning and value and if they feel valued within the organisation. The working group affected performance. Classical theory focussed exclusively on the formal organisational structure (defined as that structure rationally and deliberately defined to achieve the organisation's goals). Mayo now focussed on the informal organisation which developed out of the interaction of people within the organisation. The cohesiveness and attitudes of this unofficial self-grouping of workers had a profound effect on efficiency. Strong group cohesion, especially if group objectives are compatible with organisational aims, will enhance the performance of the organisation. Managers should be sensitive to social groupings and need to harness the efforts of such groups to achieve the firm's objectives.

The informal organisation is a network of personal and social relationships. It is not planned or official but arises spontaneously as people associate with each other. The power of the group leader is personal (not related to position) and is given by the group. Behaviour is guided by norms (notions of what is acceptable) rather than rules laid down. The group cannot control by means of financial rewards or penalities but is able to impose sanctions (threat of 'sending to Coventry'). Some of the needs of the individual are satisfied by the informal organisation and this is especially the case when the formal organisation fails to give satisfaction.

Managers should be aware of the informal organisation whose existence can be charted by means of a **sociogram**. This is a diagram in which group members feelings toward each other are plotted by means of lines. (It is the informal organisation's equivalent of an organisational chart.) It is accepted that the informal organisation is both beneficial and disadvantageous to the formal organisation.

The neo human relations school of the post-1945 era has brought a deeper psychological insight into motivation. Maslow's hierarchy of needs has relevance for the understanding of both employee motivation and customer needs. People have needs which are satisfied by action (goal-directed behaviour), and we are motivated to act by the desire to satisfy our needs. We first need to satisfy the basic requirements of continued biological existence. Once these needs are satisfied we seek to satisfy higher level needs. Figure 12.9 depicts Maslow's theory.

Unless and until a lower order need is satisfied, higher order needs do not motivate. It is, therefore, of little use to attempt to motivate through creativity unless people possess the requirements for continued existence. The hierarchy concept suggests that the needs have to be satisfied in turn. As important is the fact that once a need is satisfied it no longer motivates. Hence, once the lower order needs are satisfied, further motivation can only come by giving employees greater scope for autonomy and creativity.

Herzberg distinguished between motivators (which give positive satisfaction) and what he called **hygiene** or **maintenance factors**. The latter do not give positive satisfaction but their

Table XXVIII   The informal organisation

Benefits	Problems
More effective total system	Grapevine
Encourages co-operation	Resistance to change
Gives satisfaction	Negative attitudes
Increases stability	Conflict
Safety valve for workers	Weakens motivation
Improves communication	Conformity to the group
	Outside managerial control

Fig 12.9   Maslow's hierarchy of needs

and include a sense of achievement, autonomy, responsibility and recognition. Translated into practical management, Herzberg's theory led to the notion of **job enrichment**. This involves giving the individual employee greater autonomy by removing some of the hierarchical controls. By enriching the job, management seeks to increase employee motivation.

McGregor's contribution to the study of motivation was to contrast two sets of assumptions about workers' attitude to work and responsibility. **Theory X** depicts the 'economic man' characteristic of Taylor's scientific management. The Theory X employee is a reluctant worker who has to be coerced and be given extrinsic rewards. The **Theory Y** worker is a self-actualising man. He or she prefers autonomy, responsibility and gains a sense of achievement from work.

Acceptance of Theory Y has implications for (a) leadership styles adopted (b) the structure of organisations and (c) the most appropriate ways of rewarding the workforce.

Chris Argyris developed the **'immaturity-maturity theory'**, so named because it is concerned with the conflict between the needs of the individual and the demands of an efficiency-conscious, formal organisation. Man's need for self-fulfilment is frustrated by the unrewarding nature of much work in our modern society. Argyris advocates meaningful work which enables workers to feel a sense of fulfilment.

McClelland was concerned more with differences between individuals than understanding

absence will cause dissatisfaction. If you neglect to clean the kitchen you will eventually suffer the consequences: however, if the kitchen is thoroughly cleaned and therefore hygienic, it does not guarantee good health. Herzberg's hygiene factors equate with the lower levels of Maslow's hierarchy and they include pay and working conditions. These have to be satisfactory to secure effort from the workforce but by themselves they are not enough. In other words, they are a necessary but not sufficient condition for motivation. The motivational factors equate with social needs, self-esteem and self-actualisation in the Maslow hierarchy. The motivators are intrinsic to the work

Table XXIX   McGregor's theories

Theory X	Theory Y
1 People avoid work	1 People enjoy work.
2 Workers are unambitious, irresponsible, lazy and not to be trusted.	2 People seek responsibility
3 Workers have to be controlled.	3 Workers do not wish to be controlled.
4 Concentrate on satisfying physiological and safety needs.	4 Desire to satisfy social and self-actualising needs.

common factors in motivation. He was concerned with three needs:

1 the need for achievement (**n-Ach**);
2 the need for power (**n-Pow**); and
3 the need for affiliation or belonging (**n-Aff**).

The dominance or otherwise of these needs influences the behaviour of the individual. An Olympic gold medallist has a strong need to achieve, whereas other people have greater desire to be 'one of the boys' (n-Aff). N-Ach is a key factor in human motivation and is developed through environment factors (parental influence, education, values of society). People with high n-Ach:

(*a*) seek tasks over which they can exercise personal responsibility;
(*b*) seek tasks which are challenging but within their mastery;
(*c*) want feedback on performance;
(*d*) have a low n-Aff.

McClelland's theory contains both good news and bad news for managers. The fact that n-Ach is developed by cultural or environment factors suggests that with appropriate training schemes it can be fostered within the workforce. On the other hand, people with high n-Ach are not 'good team players'. A high n-Ach is invaluable for those undertaking individual pursuits but can cause frustration for those working in a bureaucratic organisation.

In the brief account of theories of motivation, we have moved from the simplistic view that man is an economic animal motivated by money through the view that man works best in a social setting to the view that man seeks self-fulfilment. Schein classified the various theories of motivation but added a fourth one: man is a complex animal motivated by a variety of factors depending on the situation.

Table XXX   Classification of theories of motivation (from E Schein)

	Motivated by	*Management Strategy*	*Authors*
Rational economic man	Self-interest. Extrinsic rewards	Individual bonus incentives	Taylor Gilbreth
Social man	Social needs. Sense of identity	Group bonus consultation	Mayo
Self-actualising man	Intrinsic rewards. Self-fulfilment. Personal growth	Job enrichment	Maslow Herzberg Theory Y Argyris
Complex man	Motivators vary with circumstances		

So far, motivational theories have concentrated on content without reference to the process by which individuals are motivated. **Expectancy theory** (associated with Vroom and Porter and Lawler) attempts to explain motivation in terms of the path taken (hence it is known as a **path-goal theory**). To understand the theory, consider why athletes train so hard. First, they perceive that there is a link between the amount and type of training and their performance. Training improves performance. Second, there is a link between performance and reward. There is a gold medal for the first across the line but only a silver for the second-placed runner. Third, athletes perceive that the rewards (whether of money, fame, status) are attractive. There is a further factor to consider — likelihood of achieving the goal. Athletes will only train hard if they believe there is a reasonable chance of achieving success.

In expectancy theory, effort is linked not just to

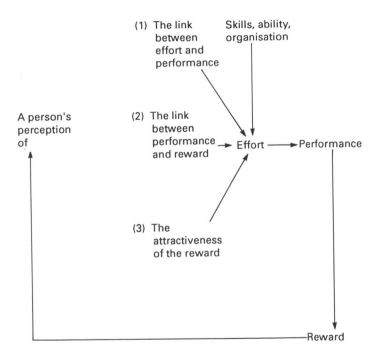

Fig 12.10 Expectancy theory

desire for a particular outcome, but it is moderated by an evaluation (expectancy) that if a particular course is followed, a particular outcome will be attained. The theory can be illustrated in diagrammatical form (*see* Fig 12.10) or in an equation:

Motivational F = fΣExV

Where E = Expectancy or a subjective measure of the probability of success.

and V = Valence or a measure of how much a particular outcome is desired.

The systems approach

Classical theory emphasised the importance of formal organisational structure without reference to the needs of humans within the organisation. The human relations school concentrated on people without reference to organisational structure or technology. In the systems approach (which was developed in the 1950s and 1960s) the organisation is seen as a system composed of sub-systems and responding to the environment.

A system is defined as a set of inter-dependent parts which unite together to carry out some function. We can use a biological analogy. The human body is a system made up of a number of sub-systems – the circulatory system, nervous system, the digestive system, etc. A malfunction in one of the sub-systems affects the other sub-systems and the system as a whole. Katz and Kahn (1966) identify five sub-systems in organisations:

1 **Production or technical** sub-system which is concerned with the basic task of producing.
2 **Support** sub-systems obtain imputs and dispose of outputs.
3 **Maintenance** sub-systems deal with those who work in the organisation.
4 **Adaptive** sub-systems are concerned with change in response to the environment.
5 **Managerial** sub-systems control and co-ordinate the activities of the total system. The essence of management is to control and co-ordinate all the subsystems and ensure that they contribute to the achievement of the goals of the organisation.

A failure in the supportive sub-system to obtain the necessary inputs will prevent the production sub-system from completing the basic task of the organisation which is the production of goods and the provision of services.

Systems theorists have been particularly concerned with the relationship between technology and people in the organisation. The concept of the social-technical system was introduced by Trist and Bamforth (1951) after their famous study of long-wall coal running techniques. This was a mass production system involving miners performing specialist tasks. The new technology brought about the disintegration of the previously close-knit social structure. This led to disputes, absenteeism and low morale. Trist and Bamforth concluded that the work environment was a socio-technical system involving an interaction between the psychological and social needs of the human part of the organisation and the technology and structure of the formal organisation. It was necessary to develop a social system appropriate to the new technical system. Inefficiency will result from disharmony between the social and technical systems.

Business organisations are open systems. They acquire inputs of materials, labour, energy and equipment from outside the organisations. These inputs are then converted into goods and services which are released as outputs to the environment. If the organisation is to survive it has to produce an output that is wanted by other organisations.

Consequently business organisations are engaged in constant interaction with the environment. Increasingly organisations face a 'turbulent field' environment, i.e. a dynamic and rapidly changing environment. The formal, bureaucratic organisation of the classical type is ill-suited to this type of environment and yet, according to research undertaken by Emery and Trist (1965), organisational structures were not becoming more flexible in response to this environment.

In conclusion, the systems approach is a holistic approach to the study of business organisations. It emphasises the inter-relationship between components and the interaction with the environment. Perceptive students will appreciate that this corresponds with the two themes that form the basis of our subject.

Contingency theory of management

A feature of early management theory was the belief that there was a single best way of 'doing things' and that problems would be solved once the universal panacea was discovered. The distinguishing feature of the contingency view which emerged in the 1950s was that there was no single best method appropriate to all situations. The effectiveness of a particular organisational structure is dependent upon its situation, in particular its size, history, environment and technology. An early contribution to contingency theory was Joan Woodward's investigation of manufacturing firms in Essex. She concluded that successful organisations had structures which suited their particular production systems.

In 1961 Burns and Stalker published a famous study of how twenty British electronics firms were adapting to a changing environment. They developed the idea of a spectrum of organisational structures ranging from **mechanistic** to **organic**.

Burns and Stalker believed that the mechanistic organisation was appropriate for carrying out routine tasks in a stable market but that organic

Mechanistic	Organic
Centralised	Decentralised.
Precise functional roles	Tasks continually redefined
Specialist tasks	Whole tasks
Prestige from position	Prestige from performance
Hierarchial	Lateral relationships
Emphasis on productivity	Emphasis on adaptiveness

structure was more capable of absorbing change. For continued success in unstable market conditions organisations ought to become more organic.

Conclusion

We have seen that there are different perspectives on the nature of management and that these have evolved over time. For much of history there was no theory to guide action. Nevertheless the Pyramids of Egypt, the cathedrals of mediaeval Europe and the Taj Mahal in India were outstanding examples of the way in which resources were organised, activities were co-ordinated and the workforce motivated to create something quite extra-ordinary.

The early Industrial Revolution view that the labouring classes had to be forced to work was reflected in the rules, the fines, the threat of instant dismissal and the harsh treatment of paupers in the workhouses. By the end of the 19th Century a more enlightened view prevailed and the 'stick' was replaced by the carrot of incentive payments. The 19th Century concern for order, efficiency, hard work and output provides the background for the development of the classical theory of organ-

isation and scientific management theory. These separate schools of thought are linked by their emphasis on division of labour, and the need to devise the best method of organising and working.

The human relations school reflects the rise of the social sciences. Although fundamentally different from the early schools, there was one thing in common: a belief that it is possible to discover a best method which was universally applicable. Modern theorists are more modest. Contingency theory is based on the proposition that the best method will depend upon (i.e. is contingent upon) the particular circumstances. Management should evolve techniques which are appropriate. In systems theory the emphasis is placed on the process of continual interaction with the environment. Open organisations respond to the environment. They need a degree of flexibility and initiative which is absent in the organisation conforming to classical principles.

Management theory like other areas of human knowledge and understandings proceeds by the process of thesis (an idea), antithesis (a contrary view) and synthesis (combining elements of the two). 'A' level candidates should remember that, although theory has moved on considerably since Fayol, Taylor and Mayo, these early writers made an major contribution and at least some of their ideas have stood the test of time.

CASE STUDY 1
'The empty suit'

In the film 'Broadcast News' a newscaster (known in America as an anchorman) was described by an envious rival as having more flash than substance. This notion of important postholders within the organisation 'cutting a dash' but actually achieving very little has recently been the subject of amusing but deadly serious articles in US business magazines like *Fortune* (November 1989). The American term used for such an executive is, rather aptly, 'the empty suit'.

The empty suit has style, is well dressed, is excellent at presentation and is inclined into talk about vision and his philosophy rather than the details of the matter in hand. He (or she) conforms to the regular practices of the organisation in a ritualistic fashion. However, despite all this, the empty suit achieves very little and avoids taking either decisions or risks. The only thing that saves him from exposure is the remote link between what he does and the actual results of the business. Results are achieved in spite of him rather than because of him.

American management writers have attempted to ascertain the circumstances in which the empty suit can flourish undetected, and have identified the following:

- hierarchical organisations, which do not encourage participation.
- organisations strong on ritual and formality rather than being people-centred.
- organisations which emphasise uniformity rather than plurality.
- organisations that rotate 'high fliers' every 18 months.
- staff (rather than line) posts.
- excessively large corporations.

1 Explain (*a*) why job rotation is usually seen as desirable; and (*b*) why it is conductive to the development of the empty suit.
2 Why does formality and uniformity lead to the empty suit phenomenon?
3 Why is participation likely to expose the empty suit?
4 Explain the difference between line and staff functions and why, despite the danger of the empty suit, staff roles are essential in any large organisation.

CASE STUDY 2
Amstrad plc

Since it was started in 1968 by Alan Sugar, Amstrad has achieved remarkable success, both in terms of profits and growth. In the beginning it sold car radio aerials before moving on to audio and television equipment, personal computers and satellite receiver dishes. For the first twelve years, Amstrad was a private company but was floated on the Stock Exchange in 1980 since when its pre-tax profits have risen from £9 million (1984) to over £160 million (1988).

Amstrad's growth is all the more remarkable because it is organic growth rather than growth through acquisition. In a survey of 'organic growers' contained in the November 1989 issue of *Business* Magazine, Amstrad headed the list of companies that grew without the benefit of substantial acquisitions. Alan Sugar is quoted as saying, 'I am a great believer in organic growth. I don't think that contested takeovers bring half the benefits claimed. All our acquisitions (e.g. the £5 million purchase of Sir Clive Sinclair's computer business) have been careful and logical'. Expressed another way, 'profit is sanity but volume is vanity'.

To sustain the Amstrad growth rate, it was necessary to look beyond the UK market which now only accounts for 43 per cent of its turnover. France is now responsible for 18 per cent of turnover with Germany (12 per cent) and Spain (12 per cent) close behind.

Amstrad prides itself on its market orientation which the company has achieved by keeping a close watch on market trends to identify and anticipate customer needs. Because the electronic industry is so competitive, it is necessary to respond quickly to trends, and this has meant rapid development of high quality products with production costs kept to a minimum. This is achieved by sub-contracting out manufacturing to low cost firms in South Korea. Consequently, Amstrad gains a high sales volume by keeping costs and profit margins low.

A further characteristic of Amstrad is that its workforce remains relatively small (1000). Sugar runs a 'close knit' business arguing that it must remain small and avoid becoming bureaucratic. Although he retains a large equity share in the company, Sugar maintains that Amstrad's success is the result of team work by a small group of senior managers and an enthusiastic and committed workforce.

1 What is meant by 'organic growth' and how is it achieved?
2 Why is 'profit sanity but volume vanity?'
3 What additional problems face a company when seeking overseas markets?
4 Amstrad is a marketing (rather than production) company and a market-orientated (rather than product orientated) firm. Explain these distinctions.
5 Weber saw bureaucracy as efficient and rational. Why does Alan Sugar strive to avoid Amstrad becoming 'bureaucratic'?
6 Alan Sugar is quoted as saying that 'I seriously believe I've got an inborn talent. Some people are born with the talent to be a musician or a doctor. I just have an aptitude for business, trading and dealing. It's something you just can't learn at university, it's just in you'. What special qualities are needed for a successful entrepreneur? Do you agree with Alan Sugar's view that entrepreneurship cannot be acquired?

CASE STUDY 3
Management and strategic planning

The large Swedish company, Stora, is in the forest products industry. Its sales revenue comes mainly from packaging material (25 per cent), fine paper (18 per cent), newsprint (18 per cent), pulp (16 per cent) and sawn timber. Stora grew rapidly in the 1980s to become the world's third most profitable forest product company.

The company owes its recent growth and success partly to three strategic decisions taken in the mid 1980s following a report produced by a leading firm of management consultants. These were:

- to diversify out of a narrow range of products (such as sawn wood) which were sensitive to movements in the business cycle;
- to become more international by the acquisition of foreign companies; and
- to decentralise.

Stora achieved its first objective by the acquisition of (a) companies in the fine paper business, and (b) Swedish Match. The latter produces a range of products such as Wilkinson Sword blades and Swan Vesta matches. It also has substantial interests in packaging and flooring. However, the Swedish Match acquisition proved troublesome for Stora because:

- the product range did not fit with Stora's product mix; and
- Swedish Match was very centralised. Stora now intends to sell off part of Swedish Match, but to retain the flooring and packaging businesses.

To achieve the internationalisation objective, Stora acquired plantations in Chile and Thailand, land in Portugal and a German flooring company. The EC, which is 43 per cent of Stora's market, is the main thrust of its activities on the international front, especially with the Single Market due for completion in 1992. Stora was anxious to obtain a foothold in the EC even if neutral Sweden remained aloof.

The decision to decentralise was prompted by two factors. First, its new Chief Executive was an advocate of decentralisation. Second, integration of the newly acquired companies was only possible if decision-making was decentralised. These new companies were in diverse parts of the industry and some were abroad. Only by delegation of responsibilities to managers of subsidiary companies could they be run efficiently. Major strategic decisions remain with the parent but everything else is delegated. Part of this new approach is the inclusion of workers representatives on the boards of subsidiary companies and the attention given to improving the working environment.

(Source: adapted from *Euro Business* October 1989)

---

1 What is meant by 'sensitive to movements in the business cycle', and why should sawn wood be sensitive to such movements?
2 Why acquire a group of companies such as Swedish Match and then sell off part of the group?
3 Explain the term 'product mix'.
4 Why did Stora want a foothold in the EC?
5 Why is decentralisation (a) desirable and (b) essential in the case of a diversified group?

6 How would the company benefit from the inclusion of workers' representatives on the boards of subsidiaries?

7 Why is the working environment important and what can be done to improve it?

EXERCISE ● ● ●

1 'Euro-Sun' is a large tour operator marketing a range of holidays in Europe and North Africa. At present it has a functional structure with managers responsible for Finance, Marketing, Operations and Personnel reporting to the Managing Director who in turn reports to the Board of Directors. The Marketing Manager has responsibility for a large department which is divided into four sections: Product Development, Promotion, Market Research and Selling. The Operations Manager has sections dealing with 'Euro-Sun' operations in each of Spain, Portugal, Greece, Alpine Areas, France and Germany, and the Rest of the Mediterranean.

In addition there is a small management services section employed in an advisory role and reporting direct to the Managing Director. Euro-Sun is the majority shareholder in British Mediterranean Airways which is run as a separate company.

The new Managing Director plans to restructure the organisation on a product-divisional basis. She aims to create separate divisions for each of the following categories of holidays: Summer Sun, Winter Sun, Ski-ing, Activity Holidays, Short Break Holidays.

(a) From the information provided, construct an organisational chart to show the original structure of Euro-Sun.

(b) What is the role of the Operations Manager?

(c) What is meant by management services? Describe the relationship between the manager of this section and the Finance Manager.

(d) What are the advantages of keeping British Mediterranean Airways separate from Euro-Sun?

(e) Analyse the advantages and disadvantages of changing to a Product Divisional Structure.

(f) Why might the proposed change be resisted?

2 Investigate the organisational structure of your school or college and produce an organisational chart. Analyse:

(a) The departmental structure and division of work.

(b) The span of control exercised by various senior staff.

(c) Lines of authority and responsibility.

(d) The extent to which the organisation conforms with classical principles.

3 Multinational corporations come in different shapes and sizes. Consider the brief account of three multinationals:

● **Corporation A** is an American-owned company which owns a series of overseas subsidiaries. Top management treats these overseas operations as independent businesses which are expected to identify and exploit local opportunities as they arise. Decision-making is decentralised with only loose control from the central. In effect, it is a confederation of separate businesses.

● **Corporation B** is a German multinational. There is much tighter control from the centre especially over key areas of policy but detailed decision-making is delegated to the local management. The overseas operation is seen as something 'bolted on' to the domestic operation in the home country. Overseas subsidiaries are required to adapt and develop the parent company's strategy and abilities.

- **Corporation C** which originated in the USA prides itself on a global mentality. Decision-making is very centralised and all parts of the organisation are required to implement the strategy of the parent company.

Assess the advantages and disadvantages of these three models of multinational corporate activity from:
   (*a*) a marketing perspective; and
   (*b*) an organisational perspective.

EXAMINATION QUESTIONS ■■■

1   Why is delegation so necessary to the success of a business, and why is it so difficult to carry out?
(AEB, June 1988)

2   Over a period of two years the workforce of a single plant manufacturing business increased from 500 to 2000.
   Outline the possible organisational problems presented to management as a result of this growth. Comment briefly on the ways in which these problems may be avoided.
(AEB, June 1981)

3   (*a*) Suggest an organisational structure that might be appropriate for a domestic airline.
   (*b*) How might fluctuations in exchange rates affect the budgeting for operations, and the profitability, of an integrated airline?
(Cambridge, June 1986)

4   (*a*) What do you understand by the phrase 'hierarchy of objectives' as it relates to a business organisation?
   (*b*) Discuss the relationships between objectives and the organisational structure.
(Cambridge, June 1989)

5   (*a*) Compare and contrast what is meant by 'line' and 'staff' relationships within an organisation.
   (*b*) Distinguish between cost centres and profit centres. How do these help organisations in planning and controlling their operations?
(Cambridge, June 1988)

6   'If you dig very deeply into any problem, you will get people'. (J Watson Wilson). Discuss.

7   'In the final analysis profit maximisation remains the ultimate objective of organisations in the private sector.' Discuss.

8   Describe the circumstances under which mechanistic system of organisation is the most appropriate.

9   'Adequate levels of pay are essential if the workforce is to be motivated.' Discuss.

10 Discuss the organisational problems that result from growth in the size of the firm.

11 Discuss the implications of 'Theory Y' for management.

- 12 What is meant by 'span of control' and outline the consequences of a small span of control on the shape of an organisation? Why do modern experts reject the idea of an optimum span of control applicable in all circumstances?
- 13 Strategic management is concerned with the future direction of the organisation whereas operational management is the management of individual business functions. Explain and discuss using appropriate examples.

FURTHER READING

ROGER OLDCORN *Management* (Macmillan)

P BRYANS AND T P CRONIN *Organisation Theory* (Mitchell Beazley/Northcote)

G A COLE *Management: Theory and Practice* (D. P. Publications)

J W D GLOVER AND W G RUSHBROOKE *Organisation Studies* (Pitman)

J L MASSIE *Essentials of Management* (Prentice/Hall)

E C EYRE *Mastering Basic Management* (Macmillan)

H KOONTZ AND H WEIHRICH *Management* (McGraw-Hill)

A COWLING, M S STANWORTH, R BENNETT, J CURRAN, P LYONS *Behavioural Sciences for Managers* (Edward Arnold)

K DAVIS AND J NEWSTROM *Human Behaviour at Work: Organizational Behaviour* (McGraw-Hill)

CHAPTER 13
Personnel Management and Industrial Relations

The previous chapter dealt with theoretical matters. This chapter will concentrate on more practical issues relating to the management of people in organisations.

OBJECTIVES

1 To understand the role of the personnel managers.
2 To investigate key issues relating to the employment of people.
3 To investigate the role of trade unions and the process of collective bargaining.
4 To look at worker participation in decision-making and/or ownership of the organisation.

Personnel management

The personnel department deals with the human resources of the organisation. Its main responsibilities are:

1 INDUSTRIAL RELATIONS, which is dealt with later in this chapter.
2 MANPOWER PLANNING. The main purpose of manpower planning is to forecast the organisation's labour requirements for the future and to devise strategies to ensure that sufficient labour of the appropriate types are available to enable the organisation to achieve its overall objectives. Planning assists management in making decisions over recruitment, training, accommodation, promotion, labour costs and redundancies. The process is summarised in Figure 13.1.
3 RECRUITMENT AND SELECTION OF STAFF. To ensure that the most appropriate labour is recruited it is necessary for the organisation to be clear about its requirements. Job analysis involves an examination of the job to identify the various tasks to be performed.

A job description is a broad statement of the scope, purpose and duties associated with a particular job, and a job specification is a more detailed statement of the physical and mental attributes necessary to perform the job in question. Once the requirements of the job have been clarified, the personnel department will seek to recruit and select staff in the manner most appropriate for the particular job. To avoid later problems, it is important to select the best person for the job (or, failing that, someone who is able to perform the job in a satisfactory manner).

4 TRAINING AND STAFF DEVELOPMENT. Training takes many forms, including attendance on day release or short courses, instruction manuals, induction of new staff, simulations, job rotation and instruction at the work place. The prime purpose is to ensure that the workforce possesses the skills, knowledge and aptitude to undertake the work effectively. In a rapidly changing world, training (or retraining) is a continuous activity. Training is also important to develop employees to enable them to progress. Not

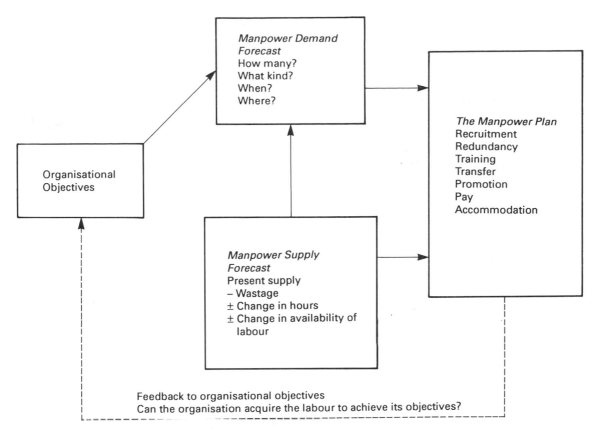

Fig 13.1 Manpower planning

only does this maintain employee morale but provides for succession when the current generation of managers and supervisors leave the organisation. Training is a costly but essential form of investment in human capital. Firms that fail to train staff in case they lose workers to rival firms are short sighted. Continuing success in business is based on responding to the changing environment.

5 HEALTH AND SAFETY. Under the 1974 Health and Safety at Work Act, employers have a legal obligation to maintain a safe working environment. Failure to carry out responsibilities under the Act could render the employer liable to criminal prosecution.

6 WELFARE. Welfare measures undertaken to achieve a harmonious and productive work-force include counselling facilities, social clubs, staff discount schemes and benevolent funds.

7 TERMINATION OF EMPLOYMENT BY EMPLOYERS. Employers seek to terminate the employment of workers for two basic reasons:

(a) redundancy where workers are surplus to requirements; and

(b) misconduct, incapacity or incompetence. However, a major constraint on employers are the rights of employees under various Employment Protection Acts. When an individual considers that he or she was unfairly dismissed there is recourse to Industrial Tribunals where the onus is on the employer to prove that the dismissal was fair. There are five reasons for dismissal that are statutorily fair:

(i) Misconduct;
(ii) Incapacity to do the job;
(iii) Redundancy;
(iv) Continued employment would break the law (hence the dismissal of a lorry driver who lost his driving licence is fair);
(v) Some other substantial reason (e.g. refusal to accept a change in duties or a personality clash).

Even when dismissal is fair and justified, it is still necessary to carry it out in accordance with procedures laid down. Summary dismissal without notice is only lawful in cases of gross misconduct or gross negligence. In other cases, failure to give appropriate notice or warnings can result in action for unlawful dismissal.

Termination resulting from misconduct or unsatisfactory work should be preceded by a verbal warning, a second warning in the course of an interview, a third warning in writing and disciplinary action conducted in accordance with rules of natural justice. To avoid the risk of action for unlawful dismissal, the organisation should clearly state the reasons for the action and allow the employee to be represented, for example, by a union official.

In the case of redundancy, legal protection is given to those with two years' continuous employment with the organisation for more than 16 hours per week (eight if employed for more than five years). The employer has an obligation to consult with workers' unions and pay compensation on a scale related to the number of years service. Individuals can take legal action if they were unfairly selected for redundancy. Consequently redundancy must be carried out fairly in accordance with agreement within the union. Voluntary schemes of redundancy are the least painful but it is conceivable that the most useful workers would opt for redundancy. Compulsory redundancy might be on the basis of last in, first out (often regarded as fairer but it discriminates against young workers) or first in, first out (expensive for the firm, harsh on the loyal members of staff, but enables the firm to retain younger and, perhaps, more productive workers).

Table XXXI Statutory rights of employees (working 16 + hours per week)

1 Written statement of terms of employment.
2 Itemised pay statement.
3 Notice of termination of employment.
4 Time off for public duties.
5 Reasonable time off for union activities.
6 Redundancy compensation.
7 Statutory sick pay.
8 Guaranteed payment of wages.
9 Maternity benefit and right to return to work after pregnancy.
10 To be treated without discrimination.
11 Safe working environment.
12 The right not to be unfairly dismissed.

Major legislation of recent decades

1970 *Equal Pay Act*. Equal pay for men and women performing the same (or broadly similar) work.
1974 *Health and Safety At Work Act*. Employers' obligation to create a safe working environment.
1975 *Sex Discrimination Act*. With some exceptions (e.g. the Church) discrimination on grounds of sex is illegal.
1976 *Race Relations Act*. Discrimination on grounds of race is illegal.
1978 *Employment Protection Consolidation Act*. Termination of employment and statutory rights of employees.

Motivating the workforce

In Chapter 12 we investigated some major theories of human motivation. It is necessary now to see how these theories can be utilised in practice. Modern theorists accept that there is no universal panacea: what acts as motivation in one situation is not guaranteed to do so at other times and in other places. With the extension of education and trade unionism and improvements in living standards, employees demand more than financial rewards. The major factors affecting motivation are:

- pay rates, if only as a hygiene factor
- security of livelihood
- prospects of promotion, advancement and improvement in living standards
- social grouping (the informal organisation)
- style and quality of leadership
- the nature of the work
- sense of challenge in relation to the workers ability
- desire for autonomy and responsibility
- opportunities to participate in decision-making
- working conditions (if only as a hygiene factor).

Modern industrial processes often involve extreme division of labour. Although this has been the route to increased output and efficiency, repetition results in boredom and alienation, the symptoms of which are high labour turnover, low productivity and a general disinterest in work. To increase job satisfaction for the benefit of both the organisation and its workers, management should consider job rotation, enlargement and enrichment.

Job rotation involves moving employees around between jobs. This increases their experience and is a useful method of enriching the job as well as providing for individual training and development. Job enlargement is a technique to motivate employees by increasing the scope of the job. The addition of new tasks will increase the sense of the wholeness of the job, but must not result in the over-burdening of the worker. Job enrichment is designed to increase job satisfaction by giving opportunities for greater autonomy and participation in decision-making. Thus, the employee is able to satisfy social, esteem and self-actualisation needs.

Job satisfaction can be increased by the alternative strategy of changing work schedules. This might mean a compression of the working week, hence motivating the worker by the prospect of increased leisure time. Alternatively, a flexi-time system of working allows the worker, within certain constraints, to choose starting and finishing times. By giving people greater control over their lives, it is hoped that motivation will be increased.

Management by Objectives (MbO)

MbO is a results approach to management developed in the 1950s by Druker. Performance is assessed in terms of achievements rather than activities. This is designed to avoid what is known as the activity trap which is really an inability to see the 'wood for the trees'. Staff can become so engrossed in carrying out tasks that they lose sight of the purpose of the task.

The overall goals of the organisation are broken down into individual goals for each manager. It should be appreciated that in a very large organisation even line managers may feel isolated from senior management. A significant feature of MbO is that managers participate in setting their goals which ensures that goals are feasible and clearly understood by all concerned. It is expected that morale will be improved and managers become committed to the goals. Regular discussions are held to assess the extent to which goals are being achieved.

The problems associated with MbO are that it is time-consuming and, if handled badly, can cause resentment from staff. There are also problems associated with the goals set. For instance, quantitative goals, which are more easily verifiable, may be preferred to qualitative goals. Moreover, it might lead to a stress on short-term issues such as achieving production targets at the expense of maintenance.

Labour turnover

There are a variety of reasons for employees leaving the organisation, which can be categorised as:

1 Separation due to management action (disci-

plinary action, dissatisfaction with performance, redundancy).

2 Involuntary or unavoidable separation (death, retirement, ill-health, pregnancy, marriage, partner's career).

3 Voluntary or avoidable separations (dissatisfaction with the job, pay, conditions, etc.).

It is this third category that should be of concern to management since it suggests a malaise within the organisation. The annual turnover of labour can be expressed as a rate:

$$\frac{\text{Number leaving minus unavoidable separations}}{\text{Average number employed}} \times 100$$

This can be used as an indicator of staff morale, although like all statistics it should be handled with caution. We should not extropolate from a 25 per cent annual turnover that there will be a 100 per cent turnover over four years. It could be the same few posts involved time and again. Another revealing statistic is the stability index:

$$\frac{\text{Number with over one year's service}}{\text{Total number employed one year ago}} \times 100$$

A certain amount of turnover is essential for the health of any organisation. A stagnant workforce is likely to become complacent and set in its ways. For the organisation to respond to the changing environment, an injection of new blood is essential. Moreover, labour turnover is the only way to avoid an ageing workforce. On the other hand, if turnover is too high it will impose a high cost on the organisation. Those costs can be itemised as:

- Lost production while the post is not filled
- Lost production during training period
- Cost of recruitment and training
- Break up of work groups and undermining of morale
- Cost of mistakes made by trainee
- Payment of bonuses to other workers until replacement is found.

It is the responsibility of personnel managers to devise strategies to reduce an excessively high turnover. The first task must be to identify trends, areas of special concern and the reasons for these separations. The major constraint under which they work is that an increase in pay would have to be sanctioned by higher authority. Suitable strategies might include:

1 Improving the process of employee selection, induction and training.
2 Ensuring that employees are being fully utilised.
3 Improving working conditions.
4 Promoting group morale and cohesiveness.
5 Job enrichment, rotation and enlarging.
6 Demonstrating that promotion prospects exist.
7 Overhauling the pay structure.

Industrial relations

Trade unions

Trade unions emerged in the 17th and 18th Centuries as trade clubs or journeymen guilds. Master craftsmen (i.e. employers) who dominated the mediaeval guilds, restricted the number of journeymen who graduated to the status of master. As a result there emerged a class of permanent employees who joined together to negotiate with employers and to petition magistrates to use their powers to fix wages. This historical point is intended to emphasise that trade unions are associations of employees established to negotiate with employers on pay and conditions.

Economists see unions as monopoly suppliers of labour. As a general rule, monopoly is considered undesirable and harmful but the justification for unions is that, individually, workers are in a weak bargaining position, and need the collective support of fellow workers to negotiate with employers. Negotiation to defend and improve pay and conditions remains the prime function of unions. However, we should add to this the following functions:

1 To provide benefits for members (e.g. legal assistance in disputes with employers).
2 To secure participation of employees in

decision-making at firm and industry level.

3 To influence the economic, industrial and social policy of the Government.

To achieve these aims it was considered necessary for unions to work together in the Trades Union Congress which is an association of unions founded in 1868. When this proved insufficient, the union movement joined with socialist societies in the establishment of the Labour Party at the start of the 20th Century.

Unions have had a checkered history with numerous legal and other setbacks. Historically they grew in strength and militancy during periods of high employment but suffered a reversal of fortunes during subsequent slumps. Generally, unions enjoy high membership (in proportionate terms) in trades where workers are permanent, full-time and concentrated in a limited number of large-scale plants. In the past, the union movement was especially strong in male-dominated trades, but remained weak in female trades, but this is less true today. Female and white collar workers provided the growth in union membership in the 1950s and 1960s. Obviously the size of the union and the proportion of relevant workers it represents are the main determinants of union strength. Other factors that should be considered are the commitment of members and their willingness to take industrial action, the level of company profits which can be extracted by unions in the form of increased wages, the extent to which the union can inflict damage on the employer and/or society, and the extent to which labour is capable of being replaced by capital equipment. Against the accusation that unions enjoy unlimited power is the logic of economic theory. An excessive pay rise will reduce the number of members employed. Union negotiators, therefore, have to balance the benefits of pay rises against the danger of job losses.

Workers' pay

We should distinguish between wage rates and earnings. The former is a rate of pay per unit of time (time rates) or unit of output (piece rates) Piece rates are only appropriate if the product is homogeneous, the output of the individual or group can be measured, there is a relationship between effort and output and if workers respond to the prospect of higher pay. In all other circumstances time rates are more appropriate even though a system of payment unrelated to effort and output necessitates close supervision of workers.

In terms of economic theory, wages (which are the price of labour) are determined by the interaction of employers demand for labour and the supply of labour. A shortage of a particular type of labour will force up wage rates, whereas a surplus will depress them. Like all markets the labour market is imperfect. Differences in abilities, skills, intelligence and qualifications result in a market which is broken down into a series of overlapping sub-markets, e.g. the market for electricians in the south-east, the market for shop assistants in Manchester etc. Because labour cannot move freely and easily between jobs and geographical areas (i.e. it is imperfectly mobile) wage differences can persist. The non-monetary elements in job choice (intrinsic job satisfaction, security, pleasantness or otherwise of the job) affect wages via the impact on supply. Hence, it might be necessary to pay high wages to attract people to jobs that are onerous, risky, unpleasant or involve unsocial hours of working.

Trade unions act as monopoly suppliers of labour to force up wage rates. It is a fact that wages tend to be higher in those trades covered by collective bargaining and strong trade unions. Union ability to force up wage rates is constrained by the desire to protect jobs. If wage rates are pushed up there will be a contraction in the demand for labour. However, if the firm is enjoying excessive monopoly profit unions, through solidarity and the negotiating skill of leaders, obtain a share of the profits for their members.

Union pay demands are usually based upon one or more of the following:

1 RISE IN THE COST OF LIVING. Wage rises below the rate of inflation are seen as cuts

in (real) wages. Unions will always bargain to maintain the real wages of members.

2 THE NEED TO PAY WAGES sufficient to recruit and retain adequate numbers of employees of the right calibre.

3 THE NEED TO MAINTAIN PAY DIFFERENTIALS. Pay claims are often based not upon supply and demand within the sub-market, but upon the need to secure pay rises in line with comparable groups of workers and the need to maintain pay differentials in respect to less skilled workers. Although bargaining to preserve the relative position in the wages league is an understandable tactic it should not be allowed to fossilise the wage structure. Pay differentials should change as the nature of the job changes.

4 PRODUCTIVITY RISES. Productivity is defined as output per unit of input (in this case output per man-hour). Productivity bargaining involves a trade-off. In return for wage rises, unions agree to changes in work practices to increase productivity.

Collective bargaining

The Advisory, Conciliation and Arbitration Service (ACAS) defines collective bargaining as 'the process whereby procedures are jointly agreed and wages and conditions of employment are settled by negotiations between employers, or associations of employers, and workers organisations'. The rationale for trade union negotiation on behalf of employees is that, individually, workers are in a weak position and are unable to negotiate on a basis of equality. Employers will be represented by those executives who have the responsibility and authority to conduct negotiations. In some sectors of the economy (e.g. engineering) unions negotiate with associations of employers who again seek strength through collective action.

The ACAS definition highlights the fact that negotiation deals with both procedural and substantive matters. Procedural agreements establish a framework of rules by which substantive issues can be negotiated. Procedural agreements are usually open-ended (i.e. subject to a period of notice if either side wishes to re-negotiate procedural arrangements) and deal with:

1 RECOGNITION (e.g. which unions should be included in bargaining);
2 Arrangements for REPRESENTATION;
3 PROCEDURES for handling disputes;
4 GRIEVANCE procedures;
5 REDUNDANCY procedures;
6 DEFINITION of matters to be dealt with in substantive bargaining.

Substantive agreements usually run for a limited period of time and deal with the terms under which workers are employed. Typically they relate to pay, incentive schemes, working hours, holiday entitlement, pensions, manning levels and sickness pay.

Collective bargaining frequently takes place at three levels. National bargaining involves unions (individually or collectively) and employers' associations. A national agreement usually lays down minimum standards of pay and conditions and is designed to protect individual employers from competitors who might otherwise take advantage of the situation. The national agreement will be supplemented by company and local (plant level) agreements. A company may choose to be more generous over pay and/or conditions than is allowed for in the national agreement.

A local agreement is designed to take local circumstances (e.g. local shortages of labour) into account. Piece-rate systems must always be adjusted to take account of particular local circumstances. At local level, the union will be represented by district officials or by shop stewards. The latter are in a rather anomalous position since they are employees of the firm and not, as commonly believed, paid officials of the union. Shop stewards are given time off from work to conduct union duties. Historically they have a reputation for militancy in excess of the more moderate union officials.

There is a voluntary tradition in British industrial relations. It is beneficial to both sides to retain some flexibility and freedom of manoeuvre by not making agreements which are legally enforceable. Legislation passed in the 1980s has brought the courts of law into industrial relations. Basically, unions only have immunity from the process of law if they conduct industrial action in specified ways. However, although some employers have taken advantage of legislation to sue unions, many others have preferred to continue the voluntary tradition. Free collective bargaining can be contrasted with bargaining that is constrained by government policy and action. Incomes policies, which were common in the 1960s and 1970s, impose a limit on pay rises and thus constrain both sides. Free collective bargaining, where such constraints are absent, is not only preferred by the trade union movement but many managers prefer the freedom to settle the pay of their own workers. In some cases, management is anxious to raise pay rates to motivate the workforce or to acquire and retain staff.

There is clearly a conflict of interest between the two sides engaged in collective bargaining. Employers buy labour and seek to minimise unit labour costs whereas unions, on the other hand, are monopoly sellers of labour and seek to maximise pay and minimise effort of members. Conversely, there are interests common to both sides (e.g. the continuing success of the organisation) and the purpose of bargaining is to reach a mutually acceptable agreement. Walton and McKersie distinguish between:

1 INTEGRATIVE BARGAINING which reflects the unitary perspective on management-employee relations. Both sides seek a mutually acceptable solution and are prepared to compromise.

2 DISTRIBUTIVE BARGAINING which reflects the pluralist perspective. Each side pursues its own interest with success for one side and defeat for the other side being the likely outcome.

Prior to the conduct of negotiations each side has to:
- decide its objectives.
- assess relative bargaining strengths.
- decide on strategy (e.g. under what circum-

stances will they resort to sanctions such as strikes?).
- decide on tactics (e.g. how can the strike be made effective?).

The union side will submit a claim while management will make an offer. Successful negotiation usually involves a compromise which is satisfactory to both sides but less than the original objective. However, before the agreement is reached, one of the sides may seek to test the resolve of the other side. Whether they impose sanctions (e.g. withdrawal of labour by the union or refusal to negotiate further by management) depends upon:

1 THE AVAILABILITY AND LIKELY EFFECTIVENESS OF SANCTIONS: for example, a union which threatens to take action must be sure that members will act. A union will be weakened if its bluff is called.

2 THE RULES OF BEHAVIOUR laid down in procedural agreements.

3 THE ABILITY AND ASTUTENESS OF NEGOTIATORS.

4 THE DEGREE OF TRUST in the relationship. Where trust is substantial there is less likelihood of resort to sanctions.

5 DEGREE OF POWER AND DEPENDENCE. If there is little likelihood of alternative employment management is in a powerful bargaining position. Where the employer relies heavily on key workers whose skills are not present in the immediate external environment, the union is in a strong bargaining position.

To resolve a dispute, one or other side may seek the assistance of the Advisory, Conciliation and Arbitration Service (ACAS) which was established in 1975 to be independent of the Government. The role of ACAS can be seen in its title as it offers advice on industrial relations matters (e.g. grievance procedures, communications within the organisation). When engaged in conciliation, ACAS helps the two sides to reach a mutually acceptable settlement. It brings the two sides together but only when conciliation does not impose a settlement. The arbitration process is semi-judicial with a neutral third party making an award based on the justice of the case. Traditionally this has usually been a compromise between the claim and offer but with 'single union, no-strike' agreements there has been a movement to compulsory, pendulum arbitration. The arbitrator will choose between the union's claim and the management's offer, rather than some compromise between the two. Supporters of pendulum arbitration argue that it encourages both sides to act reasonably but on the other hand the outcome is victory for one side and defeat for the other, leaving a sense of grievance. **Mediation**, which is another ACAS service, lies some way between **conciliation** (bringing the two sides together) and **arbitration** (making an award). The mediator will seek to guide the two sides to a compromise agreement.

Industrial action

Industrial action is a generic term used to cover a variety of trade union actions designed to pressurise employers. Just as 'war is diplomacy by other means', so industrial action attempts to conduct industrial relations by other means. It can take the form of a ban on overtime, a work to rule, non-cooperation, a sit-in or a strike. If the strike is sanctioned by the union it is called an official strike, whereas if it is not sanctioned it is called an unofficial strike. The Department of Employment does not produce statistics of 'strikes', but instead produces statistics of stoppages. Therefore, it does not attempt to distinguish between strikes (where pressure is imposed by the union) and lock-outs (where pressure is imposed by employers). The distinction is sometimes difficult to make, although the stoppage in coal mining in the General Strike year of 1926 was clearly a lock-out rather than a strike. Miners were willing to work at current wage rates but owners locked them out to pressurise them to accept lower wages and inferior conditions.

Strikes are the result of a dispute which is not solved by negotiations. The major sources of dispute concern:

- wage rates;
- methods of payment;
- job security;
- trade union rights and recognition;
- disciplinary matters;
- proposed changes in work practices.

Statistics of stoppages do not support the commonly held view that Britain is a strike-prone country and that this is both the cause and symptom of the 'British malaise'. The fact is that most employers do not suffer strikes. Strikes are confined to a small number of business organisations, and it is possible to identify four variables which affect the degree of strike proneness:

1 LABOUR INTENSITY. Strikes are more common in firms and plants where labour constitutes a high proportion of cost. Employers are more likely to resist pay demands. In a capital intensive firm, labour constitutes a low proportion of costs and employers are reluctant to allow expensive equipment to remain idle. They are less likely to reject pay demands.
2 ESTABLISHMENT SIZE. Strikes are more common in industries with large-scale plants.
3 EARNINGS LEVEL. Strikes are more common in high wage industries partly because dissatisfied workers are unlikely to be able to obtain higher pay by moving to other jobs.
4 THE SEX OF WORKERS. Female-intensive industries are less strike-prone.

Critics of the public sector also add that the public sector is more strike-prone. This is not borne out by statistics, although strikes in essential public services tend to receive more publicity.

The years of greatest strike activity in recent times were 1979 (in the 'winter of discontent') when 29 million working days were lost through strike, and 1984 (the year of the miners' strike) when 27 million days were lost. Twenty-seven million sounds a high figure, although to place it in context, it averages out at just over one day lost per worker. These were exceptionally high figures of working days lost – more typical is a figure of less than five million. The 1984 figure is obviously distorted by the prolonged strike in a major

Industry, hence the statisticians use other mea sures such as the number of stoppages or the number of workers involved. Both fluctuate over the years: in the 1970s, an annual figure of 2000 stoppages were common, whereas in the 1980s it has been less than 1500 per year. In the exceptional year of 1979, 4.6 million workers were involved in stoppages, although a more typical figure is one million or even less. One million means that only one worker in 25 was involved in a stoppage during the year. Apart from 1984/5, there was a decline in the number and severity of strikes in the 1980s.

This partly reflects the high unemployment of the decade, leading to a fall in union membership and enforced moderation.

Strikes are designed to hit the employer although the workers themselves, customers, the public, the Government and the economy will also suffer to a greater or lesser extent. In a prolonged dispute, it often becomes a war of attrition with victory going to the side that can hold out longest. Table XXXII summarises the harmful effects of strikes.

Table XXXII   The harmful consequences of strikes

For employers	Loss of output
	Reduction in sales revenue/profits
	Loss of custom
	Cash flow problems
	Harm to reputation
	Disruption
For customers	Inconvenience
	Shortages
For the economy	Loss of exports
	Import penetration
	Decline in tax yield
	Additional claims on social services
	Loss of foreign confidence in sterling
For strikers	Reduction in income
	Threat to jobs through closure or capital intensification
For other firms	Reduction in local income reduces trade
	Problems in acquiring inputs

Trade unions and the law

Most trade union activity is unlawful under English Common Law, but under Statute Law – in particular the 1906 Trades Dispute Act – unions were granted immunity from legal action if they acted in pursuance of a trade dispute. For over a century, unions had been hindered by the courts of law. Now they achieved a secure position from which they could advance their cause. However, by the 1960s there was a growing belief that unions abused their privileged position. The major criticisms were:

1 Restrictive labour practices led to over-manning and the blocking of new technology.
2 Unions were insufficiently democratic in their procedures.

3 Inter-union conflicts in the form of demarcation disputes inflicted harm on employers.
4 Many strikes were unofficial (called by shop stewards without union sanction) and called without notice (known as **wildcat strikes**).
5 They undermined the competitiveness of British industry, thus contributing to cost-push inflation and/or unemployment.
6 The closed shop interfered with the rights of both non-union workers and employers.

Labour Governments in the 1960s and Edward Heath's Conservative Government of the early 1970s attempted to reform industrial relations in Britain. The voluntary tradition (whereby by mutual consent collective agreements are not enforceable at law) was to be replaced by legal sanctions (e.g. a 'cooling-off' period before strikes could be called). Both Governments failed to curb what many saw as the abuse of union power. The incoming Labour Government in 1974 favoured a 'social contract', wherein unions agreed to moderate their pay claims to combat wage-push inflation, and in return, unions enjoyed enhanced legal status including increased powers to enforce the closed shop and a right to information from management. Like all incomes policies, the Social Contract was successful in the short-run but collapsed after four years. The strike-prone 'winter of discontent' (1978/79) led to the downfall of the Labour Government and the election of the Thatcher Government.

There was a succession of Employment Acts in the 1980s which reduced the legal protection and status of unions. The main provisions of these Acts were:

1 Lawful picketing was limited to the employees' own work place.
2 Lawful disputes are defined as a dispute between workers and their own employers. These two measures outlawed 'secondary action' by removing immunity from legal action.
3 Severe limitations on closed shops.
4 Postal ballots for election to various union offices.
5 Postal ballots to sanction strikes. To retain immunity from legal action, a strike must be supported by a majority of those voting.

In addition, a code of practice for picketing was laid down by the Government. There is no legal right to picket, but action will not be taken against picketers who keep within the code, the main provision of which is to limit official (i.e. union approved) pickets to six at each entrance to the work place.

The position of the union movement changed in other ways during the 1980s. In the immediate post-war period, unions enjoyed strength and influence. They negotiated not just with employers but also with governments and they were consulted by governments over economic, industrial and social policies. A tripartite relationship was established between the state, the union movement (represented by the TUC) and employers (through their associations such as the Confederation of British Industries). This was to change during the Thatcher years. The Government rejected incomes policies and, therefore, abandoned intervention in wage bargaining between unions and private sector employers. Mediation in disputes is no longer undertaken by Ministers and civil servants, but by the (Government-funded but independent) Advisory, Conciliation and Arbitration Service (ACAS). Although unions are still represented on various Government bodies (such as the National Economic Development Council), the warm relationship between Government and unions had broken down in the 1980s.

The trade union movement was unhappy with its changed position, but given the Conservative majority at successive elections and their own weakness at a time of high unemployment, there was little they could do about it. After initial, and costly resistance to the new laws, unions started to accept the changed conditions in what became known as the mood of 'new realism'. The electricians' union, in particular, was prepared to sign single-union, no-strike agreements with multinational corporations that settled in Britain. Single union agreements confer recognition on a single union, although the workforce is not obliged to join it. No-strike agreements commit both sides to arbitration to settle disputes.

Worker participation

Worker participation refers to the inclusion of employees in the decision-making process. Under the capitalist system, the right to make decisions rests with the risk-takers. In large organisations the shareholders delegate authority to directors and paid managers whose legitimacy is enhanced by their expertise. Employees are seen as the 'hired hands' who sell their labour in return for a contractual wage.

Worker participation (and even worker control) was an aim of the socialist movement that developed in the 19th Century under the influence of men like Robert Owen and Karl Marx. When miners went on strike in 1919 for the nationalisation of the mines, they envisaged that state ownership would be accompanied by workers' control. Various attempts have been made to further the cause of workers' participation: for instance, the Bullock Report of 1976 recommended substantial worker representation on the boards of the 800 largest companies. The EC Fifth Directive requires both sides of industry to find acceptable methods of introducing participation. Supporters of worker participation point to the German experience of industrial democracy and sustained economic success. Ironically, the 'democratisation' of German industry was imposed by the western allies after 1945 in an attempt to make Germany more pacific. British industrialists and trade unionists played a key role in the democratisation of German industry. Table XXXIII summarises the case for and against greater participation.

Table XXXIII   Worker participation

The Case For	*The Case Against*
1 Extension of democracy into the workplace.	1 Time consuming.
2 Increased satisfaction and personal development.	2 Workers lack technical knowledge.
3 Improved motivation.	3 Employees take a short-term view.
4 Improved industrial relations.	4 Conflict of interest.
5 Utilises the knowledge and experience of workers.	5 How are workers to be represented?
6 Development of consensus.	6 Decisions should be taken by risk-takers and the experts to whom authority is delegated.

Little has been achieved in the UK in terms of representation of workers at board level, although more limited schemes of industrial democracy have been implemented. These include joint industrial committees, works councils and schemes of consultation.

The Thatcher Government favours worker participation in the ownership of companies. Employees' share ownership schemes have been granted favourable tax treatment, and in the privatisation issues, employees were given bonus shares and were encouraged to buy further shares. A management buy-out involves a coalition of managers, other employees and financial institutions in buying out shareholders. The National Freight Corporation was privatised in the form of a management buy-out. As shareholders, these employees enjoy the normal rights of participation.

Supporters of employee-shareholder schemes argue that workers feel a greater commitment and sense of responsibility to the company. With a greater harmony of interests, labour relations will be improved. It is also believed that the employee will be a long-term shareholder and will be less likely to sell shares in the event of an attempted takeover.

Conclusion

This chapter has focussed on labour which, despite automation, information technology and robotics, remains an essential resource in any business organisation. Capital intensive production may reduce the quantity of labour required but it frequently requires staff of increased quality. Another economic trend of the late 20th Century is the continued advance of the service sector where, again, people are crucial. All this is happening against a backdrop of demographic trends which will result in relative scarcity of labour especially labour new to the market.

It is the personnel manager who is responsible for obtaining the input of labour that is necessary if the organisation is to achieve its production, sales, profit and growth objectives. The personnel manager also has responsibilities for ensuring that the labour force is able to functional effectively and efficiently in a changing world. Getting the most of out of people means guiding and assisting them to fulfil their potential. What makes labour a unique resource is that it has needs and aspirations setting it apart from the inanimate resources. Consequently, it is necessary to devise strategies to motivate the individual: in the words of Professor John Hunt, 'To motivate an individual means creating an environment in which his or her goals can be satisfied while at the same time the goals of the organisation are met'.

Where workers needs are not being met and where they feel the need for protection from the demands of the organisation, they will seek the support of a trade union. Although unions are criticised for abusing their power, it cannot be denied that, given the weakness of the individual, unions have been crucial in ensuring that the workforce has enjoyed the fruits of a modern industrial economy.

CASE STUDY 1
The Post Office

The Post Office, Britain's oldest nationalised industry (although only organised as a public corporation separate from Government since 1968), is comprised of three elements:
- Post Office counters
- parcels
- the letter service.

In the parcel service, the Post Office competes with TNT, DHL and Federal Express as well as firms which operate their own distribution network (e.g. the large mail order firms). These private carriers of parcels were given a significant boost by the prolonged postal strike of 1971.

In the counter service, the Post Office is a retailer, a Government agency and a financial institution. However, most of its activities are routine and provide low profit margins. Sixty-four per cent of the counter business is in the hands of 19 000 sub-offices (compared with 36 per cent in the hands of the Crown post offices). Consequently, the counter service is largely in private hands and the remainder could easily be absorbed by a major bank or retail firm.

The letter service remains central to the Post Office and is the only part of the organisation which continues to enjoy monopoly status. The Thatcher Government has not yet privatised the Royal Mail although some Conservatives see privatisation, coupled with a loss of its monopoly position, as the way to improve the efficiency and performance of the Post Office.

Problems in the Post Office have been attributed to both sides of industry. The 1971 strike lasted seven weeks and lost the Post Office large and important customers. The 1988 strike started with a dispute over pay supplements to workers in the South-East, but because of internal disputes within the Union of Communication Workers, it changed from being a local one-day strike to a two-week total shut down. Local branches were more militant than the national union. The Post Office's plans to revive Sunday collections have also been the cause of dispute. This is an extension to the service that Post Office users have long sought and its revival is seen as a symbol of the Post Office's market orientation.

Management also shares some of the responsibility for its disappointing performance: Post Office executives predicted a decline in the letter trade and consequently failed to invest sufficiently in sorting office equipment. Moreover, many sorting offices are of an unsuitable multistorey design and are sited beside railway stations, rather than motorway junctions (which would reduce the Post Office's dependence upon British Rail). Inadequate investment coupled with staff shortages, especially in the South-East, have led to growing problems in coping with the expansion of mail in the face of the growth of the direct mail promotion industry.

Post Office Chairman, Sir Bryan Nicholson, is also critical of its organisational culture. He is quoted as saying that its 'long and proud tradition had become atrophied. The organisation had been run by the rule book on a central basis, without regard for the economic consequences'.

1 Why is competition seen by many as being conducive to efficient operations?
2 It is said that the Post Office counter service suffers a crisis of identity. Is it a retailer, a Government

agency or a financial institution? Explain what is meant by this statement and what the consequences are.

3 In what sense is the counter service already mainly privatised?

4 Supporters of a nationalised Post Office would argue that it is a classic case of a natural monopoly. What do you understand by this term?

5 Free market supporters would argue that the Post Office's labour relations problems are directly related to its status as a monopolistic, nationalised industry. Explain and discuss.

6 Why did Post Office executives miscalculate the future trends in the letter service?

7 Sorting offices are wrongly designed and located. Why is this a problem?

8 In your own words explain Sir Bryan Nicholson's criticism of the Post Office's organisational culture. As he is Chairman, is this something he is able to rectify?

CASE STUDY 2
The EC Social Charter

In 1989 two issues separated Britain from her partners in Europe. The first was the Exchange Rate Mechanism of the European Monetary System. Britain has not yet joined the ERM because of the Thatcher Government's desire to retain control over economic and monetary policies.

The second issue was the proposed Social Charter, drawn up by the EC Commission led by its President, Jacques Delors, which sets out workers rights within the EC. These include:

- the freedom to stay and work in any member state.
- the regulation of the working day.
- the right to holidays, hygiene and safety standards at the workplace.
- the right to fair pay.
- the freedom to join a union.
- the right of workers to be informed and consulted about their company's practices and plans.
- access to professional training to adapt to changing technology.
- the protection of young workers.
- adequate social security.

Supporters of the Social Charter argue that it is an essential complement to the 1992 Single Market. A minimum set of workers rights is necessary to prevent the movement of manufacturing investment to those states where labour laws are lax. This process is called 'social dumping'. The West German Government of Helmut Kohl is Conservative but, unlike the Thatcher Government, accepts many of the principles of the Social Charter since it corresponds to the West German standards on labour law and industrial relations. The Bonn Government is anxious to protect workers rights, rather than seeing them eroded in the post-1992 competitive situation.

Mrs Thatcher is determined to fight what she calls Brussels' attempts to introduce 'backdoor socialism'. In her famous Bruges speech in 1988 she said: 'We have not successfully rolled back the frontiers of the state in Britain, only to see them reimposed at a European level, with a European superstate exercising a new dominance from Brussels'. During the 1980s, the Thatcher Government legislated to curb the power of unions. With one of the 'most liberal labour regimes' in Europe, foreign investment was attracted to Britain. The Social Charter would strengthen labour and return Britain to what Mrs Thatcher regards as the 'bad old days' before 1979. The Social Charter will also add to industry's costs and thereby undermine Europe's competitiveness in relation to America and the industrial economies of the Far East.

1 'The Thatcher Government's opposition to the Social Charter and its reluctance to join the ERM is symptomatic of a more fundamental disagreement about the EC.' Explain.
2 Why is 1992 likely to result in 'social dumping' in the absence of a Social Charter?
3 Why could 1992 lead to an erosion of workers' rights?
4 What is meant by Britain having 'one of the most liberal labour regimes in Europe'? Is this desirable?
5 How and why has the balance of power been shifted towards management during the Thatcher years?
6 The Social Charter calls for greater consultation with, and participation by, employees. The Thatcher Government favours employee share ownership. Explain the difference.

EXERCISE ● ● ●

● 1   As personnel manager in a large food processing factory in Essex, you have been instructed to produce a report on the unacceptably high level of labour turnover. The problem which has recently increased in severity affects all grades of workers but seems particularly acute among unskilled female workers. You are required to:

   (a) investigate the reasons for the high turnover; and

   (b) make recommendations to reduce the turnover rate (bearing in mind the constraint of the directors refusal to offer more pay). Your account should be in report form for the Managing Director.

● 2   The accounts department of a manufacturing firm is composed of 20 people with a mean average salary of £200 per week. The introduction of a new computer system will necessitate their attendance at a three-day training course held at the computer firm's training centre. Including accommodation, the cost per employee is £500 for the three-day course. It is proposed to send staff in groups of two to the training centre and to employ two temporary members of staff for four months as substitutes. These are obtained from an agency at £300 per week. It is anticipated that to assist the temporary staff, it will be necessary to obtain a total of 30 hours overtime (at £10 per hour) from the permanent staff. Finally, staff attending the training course can claim travel expenses for the journey to and from the centre. It is 100 miles away and the travel expenses amount to 20 pence per mile.

   (a) Calculate the training costs of introducing the new technology.

   (b) What are the advantages of training being undertaken at a separate training centre rather than in-house?

● 3   Study the article on British Steel taken from the *Financial Times* and answer the following questions:

British Steel signs a single-union deal with TGWU

By Michael Smith, Labour Correspondent

THE TGWU general workers' union has signed a single-union deal with British Steel to enable it to represent workers at a new warehousing facility in Sheffield.

The agreement, which gives the TGWU sole negotiating rights on pay and conditions, provides for strict safety safeguards, voluntary arbitration and a comprehensive programme of workforce training, the union said.

The deal meets the Trades Union Congress code of practice on single-union accords, which in effect pro-hibits unions from signing recognition agreements with a no-strike clause. Workers at the plant will retain the right to take industrial action.

British Steel said yesterday that the Sheffield agreement was the first single-union deal it had signed.

The accord would enable it to introduce flexible working practices among the 135 employees working at the site when it is completed in 18 months. It would also enable British Steel to achieve staffing levels comparable with competitors around the world.

The new warehouse is to replace existing British Steel facilities in the Sheffield area. Workers at the warehouses to be closed will be offered jobs at the new site.

Mr Fred Howell, TGWU national secretary for engineering, said: "The agreement ensures both the flexibility sought by the company and the guarantees on safety, training and workers' rights sought by the union."

In accordance with TUC procedures, the TGWU notified other interested trade unions of its plan to sign a single-union deal with British Steel.

(Source: The *Financial Times*, 28 December 1989)

(*a*) The Transport and General Workers Union (TGWU) is a 'general union'. What is meant by this term and explain how general unions differ from craft and industrial unions?

(*b*) Explain the terms:
- (i) 'single union deal';
- (ii) voluntary arbitration;
- (iii) no-strike deals;
- (iv) code of practice.

(*c*) Explain the role of the Trades Union Congress. Why does it lay down procedures regarding single union agreements?

(*d*) Why do some firms seek single union deals?

(*e*) What is meant by flexible working practices?

4 As Regional Officer of the Federation of General Workers you are required to give advice and support to members who have a grievance against their employers. The final decision or action rests with the individual but you have an obligation to give sound, sensible advice and appropriate support. For each of the following circumstances, investigate the legal situation and offer appropriate advice on action to be pursued by the member. In all cases explain your reasoning.

(*a*) *Ray* has worked as a storeman at the local depot of a medium-sized distribution company for ten years. The company plans to close the depot and transfer staff to a depot in a neighbouring town 20 miles away. His colleagues are willing to accept the transfer, especially as travel expenses will be paid. Ray refuses to transfer, arguing that as a non-motorist he is unable to travel the 20 miles particularly at the 'unsocial hours' he is required to work. The company has informed him that he cannot be made redundant since his job is still available.

Ray feels he is entitled to compensation for redundancy.

(*b*) *Mary* is employed at a local food processing factory. She, and a number of her colleagues, resent the lower pay rates on which females are employed compared to male counterparts. When she raised the issue with management she was told the Equal Pay Act did not apply because the heavier work was undertaken by men who alone were employed on the 10 pm to 6 am shift. Mary's argument is that many of the male employees are doing work which is no more taxing than that undertaken by the females.

(*c*) *Mrs Smith* has worked 15 hours per week for three years at a private sports and leisure centre. She has asked for six months' leave because she is expecting a baby. She was told there would be no job for her at the end of the six months.

(*d*) *Gary* has just been given notice of dismissal from his job as assistant storeman in a large garage. He had worked full-time at the garage for five years but his employer said his work was 'just not good enough'. Gary was given one oral warning prior to being given notice.

(*e*) *Sid* received injuries while working as a semi-skilled labourer working in a local cable-making factory. The employer was willing to pay some compensation but claims that:
- (i) Sid disregarded safety instructions; and
- (ii) Sid and colleagues contributed to the accident by 'sky larking.'

Sid argues that he had not received safety training and is entitled to more compensation than that offered.

(*f*) 100 staff were made redundant at a local pharmaceutical plant. It was agreed that redundancy would be on a 'last-in, first out' basis but Molly, with eight years' service, was made redundant despite the retention of more recent workers. Molly suspects that she was selected because of a long-running disagreement with a supervisor. Although the two do not see 'eye-to-eye' with each other, Molly is adamant that she has always carried out the instructions of the supervisor.

5 You are the Personnel Manager at a large factory. The Board of Directors agree to a major reorganisation involving the introduction of new technology and the redundancy of 500 employees. You have been asked to prepare a report on the implementation of the plan. The report should include reference to:
   (i)   the law relating to redundancy
   (ii) principles and procedures to be adopted to preserve good labour relations
   (iii) recommendations on ways to obtain acceptance of new technology
   (iv) the training implications of new technology.

6 As Personnel Manager in a large departmental store you are faced with a number of 'problems' referred to you by various departmental managers. For each of the situations described below explain the legal situation and, stating reasons, decide on the most appropriate action:
   (a) Dave, a young salesman, has been late for work on five occasions in the last three weeks. On each occasion he said it was because of public transport delays. He has not yet received a formal warning.
   (b) Sharon, a trainee sales assistant, is pleasant and hardworking but has been responsible for a large number of errors in giving change. Her departmental manager feels that she is not suitable for shop work.
   (c) Harry, in stores, is an active member of the shop workers union, USDAW. His union work results in time away from his work place. His departmental head considers him to be a 'trouble-maker'.
   (d) Carol is an active member of the local branch of the Anti-Vivisection League. The store has no objection to staff engaging in outside political activity but insists that it be kept separate from work. Carol refuses to take off an Anti-Vivisection badge when working. In her defence she points out that other members of staff wear ties and badges associated with pressure groups (e.g. RSPCA, WWF, etc.).
   (e) Jason is a young assistant in the furniture department. He has always been a pleasant, co-operative and able worker, but recently received a conviction for a public order offence outside a football stadium. It received a good deal of publicity and came to the attention of the Managing Director who considered it harmful to the store's image.
   (f) Delbert is a young Rastafarian working in accounts. He is an excellent employee but the General Manager objects to his dreadlocks, arguing that it harms the store's image.
   (g) John and Mark engaged in a heated and very public argument with their departmental head, Mohammed Khan. John swore at Mr Khan while Mark went further with a racist taunt.
   (h) Clive in the food department was caught pilfering. In his defence he argued that the goods were damaged and were unsaleable. However, the removal of damaged goods was contrary to the store's rules.

7 As the Regional Official for the National Union of Garden Furniture Makers you have been asked to advise the workforce of Smith and Jones Limited on how to present its annual wage claim.

   Smith and Jones Ltd employ 200 manual workers at their factory. One hundred and fifty of these workers belong to your union with the remainder belonging to either the Transport and General Workers Union or no union at all. Following a £2 million investment programme at the factory the productivity of workers rose by 10 per cent. Smith and Jones are anxious to expand output further but are constrained by problems in recruiting labour. Moreover, the factory suffers from an annual 30 per cent labour turnover ratio. Last year profits were £1.5 million and inflation is currently running at eight per cent per year.

As a professional union officer you will attempt to predict and counter the arguments that Smith and Jones will use to keep the pay rise as low as possible. The industry is very competitive and this reduces the ability of Smith and Jones to pass on cost increases. The current high interest rates reduce disposable income and therefore the demand for garden furniture.

Finally, the NUGFM is a moderate union whose members have never been on strike either at Smith and Jones or elsewhere. All the evidence suggests that they would be reluctant to take strike action over this year's pay claim.

(a) In report form, prepare a submission for an appropriate pay claim supporting your case with information from the above account as well as suitable outside material.

(b) In a separate report advise the union committee at Smith and Jones of an appropriate strategy in the event of the claim not being accepted.

8 Read the article taken from the *Financial Times* about performance-related pay and answer the questions that follow:

Assessment role vital in performance link to pay

By Diane Summers, Labour Staff

THE ASSESSMENT and setting of performance is more important than whether pay is linked to performance, says a study of local councils published yesterday.

Performance-related pay schemes often fail when they are set up to improve staff recruitment and retention, the report also states: schemes that are primarily intended to improve the performance of the individual and the organisation have a greater chance of success.

The research, published by Lacsab, the local authorities' employers organisation, was partly funded by the Department of the Environment. A handbook, intended as a practical guide to local authorities,

will be followed in the next few weeks by survey results of over 300 councils in England and Wales.

The survey is expected to show that over 100 local authorities already have performance-related pay schemes and up to a further 200 are considering setting them up. Schemes will be shown to be particularly popular in departments involved in work that, by law, has to go out to tender.

Performance management is the key issue and pay is secondary, said Mr Stephen Taylor, one of the report's authors. When a scheme is set up it should not be regarded as a "go-faster stripe on a clapped-out car but as a new engine," he said.

He saw no reason why performance-related pay should not be employed in the public sector in the same way as it is used in the private sector.

Nalgo, the local government union, said yesterday, however, that it remained opposed in principle to performance-related pay. "You can't measure performance objectively in many of the jobs our members do. How do you measure the performance of a social worker? It's not like selling double glazing," it argued.

Handbook of Performance Related Pay (£9.50); Performance Related Pay in Practice – Case Studies (£6.50); Lacsab, 41 Belgrave Square, London SW1X 8NZ.

(Source: *Financial Times*, 16 January 1990)

(a) What do you understand by performance related pay?

(b) In your own words explain NALGO's case against performance related pay.

(c) Suggest reasons why such schemes fail when they are set up to improve recruitment and retention?

(d) What is meant by 'work that, by law, has to go out to tender'? Suggest reasons why performance related pay schemes are popular in these areas.

(e) Why is the assessment and setting of performance vital in such schemes?

(f) What does Mr Taylor's comment suggest about some of the schemes?

EXAMINATION QUESTIONS ■■■

■ 1   As leader of a Union negotiating team, which has just had an initial pay claim for an 8% increase in wages (3% more than the current inflation rate) rejected by the Board of Directors of a Cross Channel Ferry Line, prepare a discussion document for other members of your team outlining alternative dispute procedures and their likely effectiveness.

(Cambridge, June 1986)

■ 2   A trade union may be defined as an organisation whose main function is to advance and protect the interests of its members.

Identify and discuss the constraints which a trade union may experience in attempting to achieve these objectives.

(AEB, June 1983)

■ 3   Outline the obligations which any business has to its employees and show how they may conflict with its obligations to other groups.

(AEB, June 1985)

■ 4   Outline the areas where conflict exists in business and examine the proposition that such conflict is not only inevitable but also desirable.

(AEB, June 1979)

■ 5   To what extent have such factors as growing industrial democracy, improved communications and protective legislation changed the role of trade unions in today's business world?

(AEB, June 1987)

■ 6   Haywood Engineering employs 250 workers. In the past there were few union members and little union activity, however, as the number of employees has increased, so too has union membership. There are at present three unions representing employees in the company and discussions are going on about whether to ballot for a closed shop.

The owners of this small and traditional firm are unfamiliar with this new situation regarding trade unions in the workplace. As Personnel Officer, write a formal report to the Managing Director including the following points:

(a) The advantages and disadvantages of trade unions to
    (i) the employees (individually and collectively)
    (ii) the employer;
(b) The meaning of a 'closed shop', and the advantages and disadvantages of introducing one.

(AEB, June 1989)

FURTHER READING

PERSONNEL MANAGEMENT

N WORRALL *People and Decisions* (Longman)
G A COLE *Personnel Management Theory and Practice* (DP Publications)
H GRAHAM & R BENNETT *Human Resource Management* (M and E)
P W BETTS *Supervisory Studies* (Pitman)
M ATTWOOD *Personnel Management* (Macmillan)
M H BOTTOMLEY *Personnel Management* (Pitman)

INDUSTRIAL RELATIONS

N WORRALL *People and Decisions* (Longman)
J GOODMAN *Employment Relations in Industrial Society* (Philip Allan)
G D GREEN *Industrial Relations* (Pitman)
P BAKER *Wage Determination and Industrial Relations* (Longman)
R WALTON & R McKERSIE *A Behavioural Theory of Labour Negotiations* (McGraw-Hill)
D JEFFREYS *The Labour Market* (Collins)

CHAPTER 14
'The Way We Do Things Around Here'

Attention has recently been focussed on what is known as **organisational culture**. This is difficult to define except to say it is the beliefs, rituals and pattern of behaviour within an organisation. It affects everyone in the organisation and is alleged to have a marked bearing on its performance. This explains the attention paid by both academic theorists and business people to identifying (and if possible re-creating) the culture features considered conducive to success.

OBJECTIVES

1 To understand the concept of organisational culture.
2 To investigate styles of leadership.
3 To understand the role of communications within the organisation.
4 To investigate the nature of conflict.
5 To identify methods of successfully introducing change.

Organisational culture

Each organisation is unique. Even if two organisations are identical in size, formal structure and product range, they each have unique features. These intangible but nonetheless pervasive features of the organisation are known as the culture (or climate or personality) of the organisation. The easiest definition of organisational culture is simply 'the way we do things around here' and this in turn is influenced by:

1 the ENVIRONMENT in which the organisation operates.
2 the VALUES, BELIEFS and NORMS of people within the organisation but especially those of top management which are then communicated downwards.
3 the HEROES who personify the culture of the organisation.
4 the RITUALS that have to be performed and the behaviour expected of people within the organisation.

5 the NETWORK OF COMMUNICATIONS which disseminates the values, creates the heroes and unites the organisation.

By both formal means (training) and informal means (role models), the newcomer is introduced into the culture of the organisation. This is known as **socialisation**. Hence the attitudes, thoughts and behaviour of the individual are affected by the organisation. The opposite process is known as **individualisation** with the employee exerting an influence on the social system. Figure 14.1 depicts a matrix of individual acceptance or rejection of organisational values while exerting different degrees of influence on the organisation. From the organisation's point of view:
- rebellion is disruptive
- conformity suggests slavish devotion to existing procedures
- isolation leads to lack of co-ordination and integration
- creative individualism means a willingness to question, to challenge and to experiment while

not disrupting the organisation unduly. In a dynamic environment, creative individualism is important for the long-term success of the organisation.

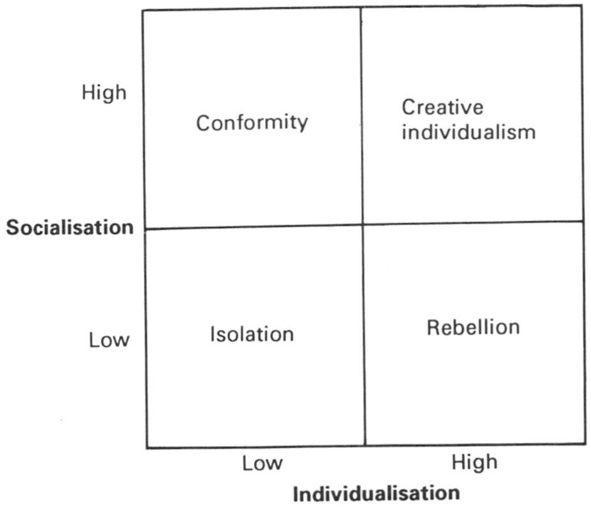

Fig 14.1 Socialisation-individualisation matrix (Adapted from Davis and Newstrom, *Human Behaviour at Work: Organisational Behaviour*, McGraw-Hill)

Organisational culture has a pervasive affect on those that come into contact with it. It affects employee morale, behaviour and productivity, and even affects the recruitment process with individuals being attracted to organisations with known cultural traits. It affects the way in which change is perceived. It is not surprising that both managers and academic theorists have tried to identify elements within particular organisational cultures that will contribute to enhanced performance. The most widely quoted book on excellent companies is *In Search of Excellence* by Peters and Waterman. The authors studied a number of top ranking American companies such as Boeing, Disney, IBM and 3m and concluded that there were eight features of 'excellent companies'. These are:

1 'BIAS FOR ACTION' with clear objectives and an absence of committees;

2 'CLOSENESS TO THE CUSTOMER';

3 'AUTONOMY AND ENTREPRENEURSHIP', meaning innovation and risk-taking as accepted features of the organisation;

4 'PRODUCTIVITY THROUGH PEOPLE' or worker participation and involvement;

5 'HANDS ON, VALUE DRIVEN'. By this they meant well-defined philosophies of senior management which remains close to the front line of action;

6 'STICK TO THE KNITTING' means a concentration on the organisation's strengths as opposed to the reckless pursuit of a diversified business;

7 'SIMPLE FORM, LEAN STAFF' is their answer to the complexity of classical hierarchies; and

8 'SIMULTANEOUS LOOSE-TIGHT PROPERTIES'. Decentralisation is necessary to allow for a healthy degree of autonomy but the centre should retain control over core decisions.

Leadership

Leadership is the art or process of influencing people so that they perform assigned tasks willingly and in an efficient and effective manner. Leadership is, therefore crucial in motivating and inspiring the workforce so it is not surprising that writers on management have addressed the question as to what makes a good leader.

Early studies of leadership attempted to identify traits common to leaders. Some studies concentrated on physical traits (e.g. energy, appearance) while others concentrated on intelligence or personality (e.g. aggressiveness, enthusiasm, self-confidence) or social characteristics (e.g. interpersonal skills). Unfortunately, this line of enquiry did not prove fruitful since there was an imperfect correlation between traits and leaders.

The trait approach was superseded by an analysis of behavioural patterns or styles of leadership. The main styles identified are:

1 THE AUTOCRATIC STYLE. The autocratic leader is authoritarian and assumes responsibility for all aspects of the operation. Communication is one-way with little or no scope for feedback. Within the autocratic style we can

style we can identify the 'tough' autocrat who demands total compliance from the workforce and the 'kindly' autocrat (or paternalist) who demands compliance on the basis that 'he knows best'. The autocratic style is seen as efficient and it is essential in some circumstances: for example, uniformed services (such as the Fire Service) have to be run on autocratic lines, and similarly, a symphony orchestra is conducted by an autocrat. However, the autocratic style can create frustrations and resentment. The work group becomes very dependent upon the leader and often will be unable to act independently. An autocratic style can and does work but much depends upon the qualities of the leader and compliance of the group. In most organisations today, employers demand greater participation in decision-making.

2 THE BUREAUCRATIC STYLE. The bureaucratic leader manages by the 'rule book' without exception. Subordinates are permitted little freedom or scope for initiative. There are advantages in terms of consistency and predictability with each person knowing exactly 'where they stand' but the bureaucratic leader tends to be inflexible and creates resentment in the workforce. When confronted with situations not covered by the rule book the bureaucratic leader is paralysed.

3 THE DEMOCRATIC STYLE. The democratic or participative leader seeks the opinions of subordinates and strives for mutual understanding. Democratic implies acceptance of group decisions, whereas most democratic managers consult but retain the ultimate responsibility for decision-making. Perhaps 'consultative' is a more apt description of this style of leadership. It is especially appropriate where experienced workers need to be fully involved in their work. Participation results in improved decision-making, higher morale and greater commitment. However, consultation is time-consuming and there is always the danger of loss of management control and an attempt to evade responsibility.

4 THE FREE REIN STYLE. The free rein leader sets goals for subordinates and clear parameters in which they should work. Once the objectives are established, the reins of control are dropped and the subordinate is left alone to achieve the objectives. This style works well when subordinates are willing and able to accept responsibility. The freedom of manoeuvre motivates the enthusiastic worker. However, there are risks associated with this style since success is dependent on the competence and integrity of subordinates.

In Rensis Likert's analysis of leadership, four systems are identified:

1 THE EXPLOITIVE-AUTHORITATIVE SYSTEM is characterised by threats, control and imposed decisions. There is little scope for teamwork and two-way communication.

2 THE BENEVOLENT-AUTHORITATIVE SYSTEM involves a paternalistic, master-servant relationship.

3 THE CONSULTATIVE SYSTEM motivates by rewards and by involving people in decision-making but consultation does not mean abdication of decision-making to the majority.

4 In the PARTICIPATIVE GROUP SYSTEM, which Likert regarded as the ideal, leaders have complete confidence in their sub-ordinates, participation is encouraged and employees become committed to achieving organisationalgoals.Likert'sempiricalresearchledhimto conclude that system four was the most effective system, but it is difficult to prove the line of causation from implementation of system four to achievement of goals, rather than the other way round. Likert's research is also disputed by those who argue that success today comes from quick action by those organisations dominated by a 'strong leader'.

Tannenbaum and Schmidt (1973) saw leadership in a continuum ranging from 'boss centred' to 'subordinate centred' (see Fig 14.2).

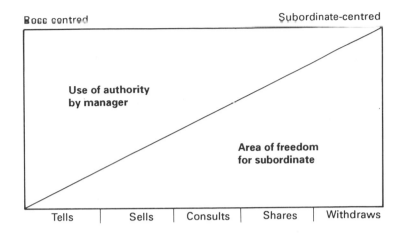

Fig 14.2 Continuum of leadership behaviour (based on Tannenbaum and Schmidt)

Communications

Managers devote a large proportion of the working day to communications. On average 66-75 per cent of managerial time is spent in talking to other people. At the highest levels of management this rises to 90 per cent. Effective communication is, therefore, vital to the success of the organisation. It is the process by which planning, organising, leading, directing and controlling are accomplished. Good communication will reduce conflict and prevent unnecessary misunderstanding. Some people would argue that communication is the solution to all conflict within the organisation: therefore, it is not only important for managers to be good communicators but also to understand the process of communication.

Communication can be defined as the process by which an idea is transferred from one mind to another. The purpose is to make the receiver understand what is in the mind of the sender. Communication can take a number of forms: the spoken and written word, figures, visual images, facial expressions or gestures. Body language (the conveying of a message in a non-verbal manner) can act as both a substitute for and a complement to verbal communication. The spoken word can be supported by non-verbal communication. On the other hand, one of the most difficult situations to handle in the workplace is where conflicting messages are received through the eyes and through the ears. Good communicators transmit a consistent message. The spoken word lacks the permanence of the written word, but it is more rapid and flexible. In speech we convey meaning both in the words we use and the way in which they are spoken. Hence, the same combination of words can be both a request or an order, a statement of fact or a question. A major problem for second language learners is to understand intonation in the spoken form of the English language. On the other hand, the written language is more accurate but is time consuming.

Communication can be classified as **formal** (meaning arranged, approved or official) and **informal**. The latter is unofficial, unplanned communication outside the organisation's formal channels. It is a mistake to equate formal communication with the written form and informal with the spoken and non-verbal forms. When a superior reprimands a subordinate by means of the spoken word it is a formal communication. A joke in written form passed around the office is informal communication. Small talk between superiors and subordinates may be informal, although it depends upon the circumstances and the individuals involved.

Deficiency in the formal channels of communication will lead to an increase in activity through informal channels. The **'grapevine'**, which is present in all organisations, is efficient at disseminating information, although there is a danger of distortion. Managers should beware of the disruptive effect of the grapevine. The surest way of reducing its activity is to be more open with employees in the formal communication channels. Some managers make use of the grapevine to selectively leak information but this is a high-risk strategy.

Communications can also be classified in terms of direction. **Downward** communication usually takes the form of instructions or directions and is, therefore, almost always formal. **Upward** communication takes the form of reporting back, complaints or suggestions. **Lateral** or **horizontal** communication refers to contacts (formal or infor-

mal) between people at the same level within the organisation. Where there is no facility for a reply (feedback) it is called **one-way** communication. An advertisement or information posted on a notice board are both examples of one-way communication. Such communication carries the danger of being misunderstood and/or causing resentment. Authoritarian leaders prefer one-way communications since their authority is preserved unchallenged. Feedback is built into two-way communication which is a feature of the democratic leadership style. The facility for feedback is important is ensuring that the message is fully understood and to enable subordinates to contribute to the process of decision-making. Feedback also binds the two sides closer together.

A model of the communications process is

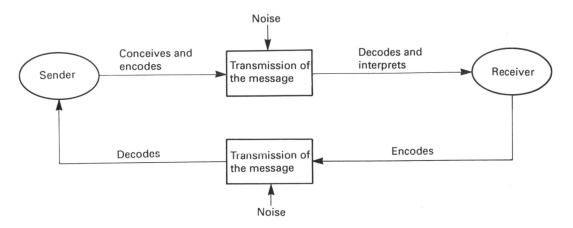

Fig 14.3   A model of communications

illustrated in Fig 14.3 and from this we can analyse the causes of communications failure. To accomplish communications it is necessary for the sender to encode a message in appropriate words, symbols or gestures. We must not be distracted by the word code which conjures up the image of spies. Language is a code: for example, the word 'cat' suggests a four-legged feline animal only because we have access to the code. To someone ignorant of the code of the English language the word 'cat' is a meaningless sound. The coded message has to convey the intended meaning and

be intelligible to the recipient. A common failing is to encode in an inappropriate way. Effective communicators will adjust their style of language to different situations but this must not result in 'talking down' to people since it will cause resentment. Technical jargon is common in most occupations and places of work as it serves as a shorthand form to speed the flow of communication. However, by its very nature, jargon refers to specialist vocabulary from which outsiders are excluded. Examples of jargon which are meaningless to the uninitiated are:

'putting the paper to bed' (newspaper production)
'a best boy and key grip' (jobs in film production)
'a return to Houghton' (teachers' pay)
'MO' (a measure of the money supply)
'a white knight' (in take-over battles)

In its place jargon is a valuable aid to communication but outsiders are excluded.

The message is then transmitted via a communication channel or medium. This can take various forms: sound, a sheet of paper, the telephone system, a television screen, film, a brochure or a VDU screen (another piece of jargon). Consider a telephone conversation: the speaker's words are converted into electrical impulses (i.e. encoded) and these are transmitted through the telephone lines. At the other end, the impulses are converted back into speech which is heard by the recipient (i.e. decoding). Senior government ministers use scrambler phones: the words are converted into a second code from which others are excluded. This prevents government secrets being revealed through phone tapping or accidentally crossed lines. Successful communication in this form requires access to a scrambler to decode the message.

The transmission can be affected by 'noise'. This is not confined to sound but refers to anything that distracts the recipient and causes either a failure to receive the message or a misinterpretation of the message. For instance, against a background of tension and disagreement within an organisation, a simple and polite request for information can cause resentment. The 1989 water privatisation compaign stressed the benefits of becoming an 'H$_2$ Owner'. The message was lost on people who did not know that H$_2$O was the chemical expression for water. Both are examples of noise.

The basic conclusion is that no matter how eloquent the speech or penetrating the analysis in a book, it fails to communicate if:

(*a*) the message is not received, or
(*b*) is not decoded in the manner intended.

Consensus v conflict

Within an organisation there is a community of interest on certain issues. Everyone from shareholders, directors, managers and manual workers has an interest in the survival of the organisation. In a capitalist system, profits are necessary for survival and, therefore, employees have an interest in ensuring that the business is successful and profitable. However, conflict is also present within an organisation. Employees may seek to maximise their earnings and minimise their effort. This is contrary to the goals of management which are to maximise output at the lowest cost. Even between shareholders and directors there is the potential for conflict over the relative sizes of distributed and retained profit. The main sources of conflict within organisations are:

- Personality differences
- Conflicting interests
- Communications failure
- Sense of territory
- 'Agitators' – the trouble-maker's view of conflict
- The alienating nature of the work environment
- Social class divisions reflected in the organisation, (e.g. the executive canteen)
- The failure of the organisation to satisfy the individual who then channels his or her energy to the alternative, informal system. Conflict is manifested in absenteeism, staff turnover, non-cooperation and low productivity as well as strikes and working to rule. In fact, overt conflict is easier to deal with than insidious, covert conflict which can cause the greater harm in the long run.

How should conflict be viewed and how should it be treated?

I THE TRADITIONAL VIEW (OR UNITARY VIEW) is that members of the organisation share common interests. Conflict is seen as harmful and a symptom of some failure within the organisation. Interestingly, both human relations and scientific management theories are consensus approaches. The interests of employees and management are not opposed and the task of management is to apply the correct principles to reconcile them.

2 THE PLURALIST VIEW stresses the plurality of interest groups within the organisation. Conflict is inevitable but can be controlled and channelled into institutional mechanisms (e.g. collective bargaining). Conflict can actually be beneficial in stimulating ideas, identifying inadequacies in original proposals and generally acting as a catalyst. The pluralist notion of an optimum level of conflict is illustrated in Fig 14.4 and the traditional and pluralist views are contrasted in Table XXXIV.

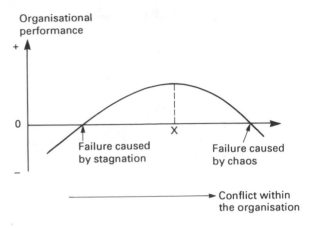

Fig 14.4   Optimum level of conflict (x)

Table XXXIV   Two views of conflict

Traditional/unitary view	*Pluralist view*
1 Avoidable, unnecessary	1 Inevitable, often necessary
2 **Causes:** (a) Management failure (b) Communication problems (c) Trouble-makers	2 **Causes:** Numerous, but especially conflicts of interests
3 Conflict is harmful	3 Conflict is both harmful and beneficial.
4 Management's task is to eliminate conflict	4 Management's task is to manage the level of conflict for optimal organisational performance.

3 THE MARXIST OR CLASS CONFLICT VIEW. Marxists believe that conflict is inevitable since it reflects contradictions within a capitalist system which is inherently exploitative. Unlike the pluralists, they do not believe that conflict can be institutionalised or resolved. Instead, it will result in the inevitable collapse of the capitalist system of production.

Managing change

A major challenge facing management is the need to manage change in response to the changing environment. The changes may involve new technology, new methods of working and new ways of organising. Continued success of the organisation depends upon changing with the environment but at all levels within the organisation change is feared and resisted. The resistance is sometimes in an institutionalised form via the trade union movement. This can take the form of recourse to law, strikes, a refusal to accept new work practices, working to rule or an insistance on previous manning levels. In many other cases the resistance takes the form of individual non-cooperation. Low morale, a lethargic attitude to work and a high turnover of labour will result in low productivity. In the long run this insidious form of resistance may prove more harmful than union action. The task for management is to understand why people resist change and to devise strategies to make change more acceptable to the workforce.

Change is resisted for a variety of reasons but for convenience we can group them as economic, social and psychological:

1 ECONOMIC REASONS. These include fears about job losses, loss of earnings or reduced promotion prospects. Alternatively, change might be resisted because employees fear that it will involve an increase in work load.

2 SOCIAL REASONS. Change at work might cause the break-up of the work group and a change in social relationships with colleagues and superiors. We know from Mayo's work that the cohesiveness of the work group plays an important role in determining output.

3 PSYCHOLOGICAL REASONS. People fear the unfamiliar and are afraid that they will be unable to cope in the new situation. Moreover, they fear loss of status and self-esteem. This fear will be accentuated if change is imposed from the top with the future of the individual being decided by unknown and remote people. This suggests that sometimes it is not the change itself which is resisted but the manner in which management attempts to implement it.

In implementing change, management's first task is to discover the root cause of opposition and to devise strategies to overcome it. These strategies can be categorised as

(a) *Education and communication*. This involves informing and reasoning with the workforce so that the reasons for change are understood and accepted.

(b) *Participation*. Here the workforce is brought into the process of planning change. Workers who are able to participate in planning change (or are persuaded of the need for change) will be more enthusiastic about implementing it. It is important for management to appreciate that workers have something to contribute. They may be able to improve the proposal.

(c) *Support and training*. If resistance is the result of temporary adjustment problems then the solution is to help workers to adjust to the new situation.

(d) *Negotiation*. This involves the search for a compromise. Employees may be willing to accept change in return for improvements in pay or conditions. Alternatively, the compromise might mean a partial or phased implementation of the change.

(e) *Manipulation*. A Machiavellian strategy is to 'buy-off' potential leaders of resistance.

(f) *Threats and coercion*. Like manipulation, threats of dismissal might be sufficient to end resistance but on the other hand could result in a major dispute, and low morale among workers.

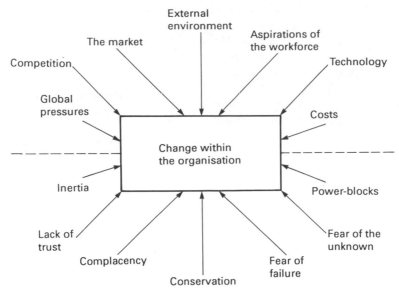

Fig 14.5 Forces causing change within an organisation

Conclusion

The major theme of both this textbook and 'A' Level syllabuses in Business Studies is the process of decision-making within the business organisation set against the context of a dynamic environment. Decision-making is seen as a rational process involving the gathering, the presentation, the interpretation and analysis of data. This is the basis of decision-making in each of the inter-related functional areas of the organisation.

Decisions relating to people in organisations can also be approached in the same way even though people, as a resource, have distinctive characteristics setting them apart from inanimate resources. In the past the emphasis was placed on order, control, division of work and clear lines of responsibility and authority. Apart from a tiny proportion of people at board and top management level, organisations sought to employ functionaries who would carry out procedures.

Today there is a greater emphasis on leadership rather than control and releasing the talents of people for the benefit of the organisation as well as their own self-fulfilment. How people respond will depend upon the beliefs, values, the history, communication system and the inter-action between leader and led: in short, it is the intangible concept of the culture of the organisation. That culture has a profound and pervasive affect on the behaviour of people. People perform in the manner expected of them and, therefore, the most important task for top management is to create and manage the culture of the organisation. In today's environment, that means participation, greater autonomy in the work place, and the encouragement of initiative.

CASE STUDY 1
Organisational culture

The economic success of Japan has led to intense interest, in both academic and business circles, in Japanese styles of management and the organisational culture of Japanese firms. To what extent is Japanese economic success the result of cultural factors and to what extent are they exportable?

As a nation, the Japanese generally place great emphasis on:

- cultural cohesiveness;
- respect for authority;
- group behaviour, as opposed to individualistic behaviour;
- duty and obligations;
- education; and
- national pride.

These national characteristics are reflected in the organisational culture of Japanese corporations. Management fosters a climate of corporate community by:

- a 'flat' organisational structure;
- life-time employment of key workers (both manual and white collar);
- payments linked to length of service;
- welfare provision;
- commitment to the company;
- rigorous selection;
- consultation and explanation;
- classlessness in the form of integrated facilities and company uniforms; and
- stress on quality.

Komatsu is a Japanese multinational company producing construction equipment on Tyneside. The twin Komatsu principles are quality and employee involvement. Each worker is expected to perceive the next worker in the chain of production as his customer who desires work of a high standard. This is part of Komatsu policy of total quality control which is also seen in the establishment of quality circles.

Each worker is fully informed about the performance of the company and any proposed changes. Participation is encouraged by the establishment of a council. Two-way communication is encouraged throughout the organisation. Like other Japanese multinationals, it insists on a single union agreement, pursues a paternalistic welfare policy and has a common working week for all, irrespective of position held.

'Komatsu can be quite a culture shock. Tyneside was notorious for its prehistoric industrial relations. Stepping into single-status, communicative, highly informed, opinion-seeking and, above all, quality-seeking Komatsu with a traditional attitude could be surprising'
(B Reynolds in *The 100 Best Companies to work for in the UK*).

1 What do you understand by:
    (*a*) paternalistic;
    (*b*) organisational culture; and
    (*c*) flat organisational structure?
2 Why was Tyneside 'prehistoric' in terms of industrial relations?
3 Why is 'single-status' seen as important in the success of Japanese companies?
4 Explain quality circles and total quality control.
5 Are Japanese styles exportable?
6 Why is participation regarded as important to organisational success?

CASE STUDY 2
The Body Shop

'Body Shop' was started with the aid of a £4000 loan which enabled its founder and Managing Director, Anita Roddick, to establish a retail outlet in Brighton. Ms Roddick combined an attractive and highly marketable concept (selling herbal and plant-based cosmetics) with great entrepreneurial drive and qualities of leadership that have inspired others in her expanding business. Body Shop now has an annual turnover of £30 million with pre-tax profits in 1987 of £6 million.

Body Shop International owns:
- production facilities in Littlehampton
- 11 principle shops
- headquarters and training facilities in Littlehampton and London.

The 11 shops owned by Body Shop International are seen as the flagships of the company, setting the style, fostering the image and test marketing new products before they are released to the 300 other Body Shop branches that exist in 30 different countries. Body Shop is, therefore, a franchise operation. The right to trade under the Body Shop name and to sell its products is purchased by local entrepreneurs. Body Shop franchises are very expensive but are much sought after because of the image, the name and the high quality of Body Shop products. Franchising is a mutually beneficial arrangement with the franchisee benefitting from a famous name and well developed products and the franchiser benefitting from the locally based enthusiasm and commitment. Franchisees are carefully selected and trained: Ms Roddick looks for people who share her ideals, her commitment and enthusiasm for selling Body Shop products. It is because the franchises are so keenly sought after that Ms Roddick can be very selective in the choice of franchisees.

One reason why Body Shop is included in a list of the *100 Best Companies To Work for in the UK* (B Reynolds) is that is has a highly developed system of two-way communications which reflects the managerial style of its Managing Director. The bi-monthly *Talk Sheet* produced for staff encourages job swaps on an international as well as national basis. The monthly 'Talk Shop' video magazine includes reports on community projects sponsored by Body Shop as well as skin and hair care in different cultures. Staff are fully briefed about new products and in handling customers, and in turn, they are encouraged to voice their opinions. Communication with customers is also considered a key to the organisations success. Body Shop produces explanatory leaflets on products, has suggestion boxes in its stores for customers comments and organises exchanges of views about skin care.

Body Shop has a well-developed, positive organisation culture with an emphasis on:
- commitment to its principles;
- the right to speak out;
- training;
- enthusiasm; and
- care for the community, the third world and the environment.

The development of this culture has been crucial in Body Shop's success.

1 Why do you think Ms Roddick chose to organise Body Shop on a franchise basis?
2 What are the advantages of obtaining a franchise rather than being a branch manager of a chain store? Are there any drawbacks?

3 Why is it essential to carefully select and train franchisees?
4 Why do you think Body Shop places great emphasis on the swap-a-job scheme?
5 Why is it essential to develop a good system of communication?
6 Organisational culture has been crucial to the success of Body Shop. Explain why, and what are the features of its organisational culture?

EXERCISE ● ● ●

● 1 Read *The Guardian* article on 'old Spanish practices' and answer the questions that follow:

Barcelona's old Spanish practices

John Hooper reports the culture clash when VW took over SEAT

"YOU CAN offer any money you like but they won't accept it," Mr Joachim Herrmann, one of the German Vice-Presidents of the SEAT car company, said with a bemused air. A few floors and a few minutes later, Mr Adelino Bonet, a factory leader of the Communist trade union, Workers' Commissions, leant forward and declared with satisfaction: "There are things that we say 'no' to however much they offer to pay us."

At SEAT's main car plant, a stalemate has been reached in a trial of strength between two cultures.

In 1986, when Volkswagen started buying into the state-owned Spanish car manufacturers, they were, according to trade union representatives, welcomed with enthusiasm. SEAT had not shown a profit since 1977 and its losses were mounting. "From the Government's point of view, it would have made sense to close down the company altogether," acknowledges Mr Jose Miguel Perez Villanueva of the socialist General Workers' Union.

Three years on, VW has a controlling interest. It has put SEAT back into profit – and stirred up anti-German feeling in the process.

A lot of Spanish middle managers were demoted to make way for

West German appointees at the beginning, although Mr Herrmann says that "many of the Germans have been returned to Germany and the Spaniards re-promoted."

The firm says that there are now 118 Germans out of a total staff of more than 17,000. Mr Herrmann, though, admits that the Spaniards "feel the merger like a kind of conquest" at least at the middle-management level.

It seems to go further. Mr Jose Luis Estrach, a draughtsman, said relations between the Germans and Spaniards were zero. He is one of 52 in a department which was put under a German executive three years ago. He had never talked to the German and thought it would be difficult anyway since his boss appeared to speak only the most rudimentary Spanish.

"In the canteens, you will never see the Germans and Spanish together," says Mr Bonet. "On the shop floor, if you were to shout out an anti-German slogan, you'd get an enthusiastic reception."

This kind of sentiment appears to be making it difficult for VW to solve problems that would have faced whoever took on SEAT – problems rooted in deep-seated cultural peculiarities.

The management's difficulty, as

explained by its Director of Communications, Mr Enrique Zorzano, is this: VW has committed itself to spending £3 billion over the next five years on a company which is currently producing barely more than half as many cars per worker per day as General Motors in Spain. Having ruled out a cut in the workforce, the company's only way ahead is to improve productivity per worker.

Japanese-inspired "quality circles" have been introduced and, according to Mr Herrmann, they have attracted more members in Spain than in Germany. But Volkswagen is also engaged in the thankless enterprise of trying to impose German order and discipline on a firm whose main workforce, at its plant in the Zona Franca in Barcelona, recently turned to the anarchists for leadership.

Last year, the workers there made history by becoming the first in Spain to throw out their elected works committee. The law makes this almost impossibly difficult to achieve. Yet the anarchist General Workers' Confederation not only succeeded in getting the necessary signatures of a third of the workforce and more than half the votes of the workers in an assembly, but also came out top in the new elections convened as a result.

The outcome is that VW, a corporate expression of suit-and-briefcase Europe if ever there was one, finds itself having to negotiate with a works committee headed by a libertarian with punk-style ear rings. This year's deal on pay and conditions is currently deadlocked because of the refusal of the anarchists – and Communists – to agree to further changes in the working calendar.

If it is true that northern Europe lives to work whereas southern Europe works to live, then the difference is nowhere clearer than in Spain where the word for "business" is made up of those for "denial" and "leisure." Spain is also a country in which, because of the importance of family and community activities, it is regarded as crucial that society's leisure time should coincide.

The Zona Franca plant has traditionally closed down completely for the weekend and for the whole of August. Over the past two years, the management has succeeded in getting the working year extended by a total of eight days, so that there are now 2,000 workers whose days off do not necessarily fall on Saturday and Sunday.

But for Mr Francisco Selas, the CGT head of the works committee, this represents "an erosion by leaps and bounds of what we had struggled to achieve." He is determined that an adequate price be put on any further moves in this direction.

In the background lurks the management's stated intention of introducing productivity bonuses calculated by reference to measurement, time, and methods.

It is hard to think of anything more alien to the Latin soul than this US-devised system in which workers are filmed and their movements analysed in detail to determine how quickly each action can be performed.

So far this work study is a prospect rather than a reality, but, according to Mr Emilio Cortavitarte, the CGT's General Secretary in Catalonia, the management has already imposed restrictions aimed at boosting output. With horror, he recounts that workers have been prevented from smoking in some areas of the factory because they say it makes it more difficult for them to monitor the machines.

(Source: *The Guardian*, 20 December 1989)

(a) Mrs Thatcher referred to British television as the 'last bastion of Spanish practices'. If 'Spanish practices' occur outside Spain, what are they?

(b) What is meant by (i) 'problems rooted in deep-seated cultural peculiarities'; and (ii) a corporate expression of 'suit and briefcase Europe'?

(c) What do you understand by 'Japanese-inspired 'quality circles"?

(d) Why is the 'working calendar' the cause of a dispute?

(e) Explain the sentence: 'Having ruled out a cut in the workforce, the company's only way ahead is to improve productivity per worker.

(f) What conclusions can be drawn about the problems of international mergers?

2   Read the article opposite on privatisation taken from *The Guardian* and answer the following questions.

(a) Define and explain the following terms:
privatisation; market leader; contract hire; participation.

(b) What does the author mean when he writes that NFC is a 'rogue among the 1980s herd of quick-buck, knock-down sales'?

(c) How do we measure success in conventional business terms and why are the figures quoted rather deceptive?

(d) What is a mission statement? Are the two elements of the NFC mission statement compatible?

(e) Business is not just about profits. It is about how you share them and who does well out of them. Does Sir Peter Thompson's comment reflect socialist sentiment, or a modern form of capitalism?

Privatisation that got away shows how to share the corporate bounty

Outlook

Roger Cowe

NFC stands as a monument to the irrelevance of both nationalisation and denationalisation; as a monument to the vision of Sir Peter Thompson and his colleagues whose commitment to employee involvement has made the transport group, which was floated in February, the one privatisation that got away.

But only a hiatus at National Carriers caused by the closure of British Rail's door-to-door parcels service in 1980 stopped NFC going the way of other privatisations – into the pockets of disinterested individuals and institutions. The resulting delay allowed Sir Peter to develop and lead the employee buy-out of the Pickfords and BRS group.

As a company with a heart and a determination to maintain employee control it is clearly a rogue among the 1980s herd of quick-buck, knockdown sales. But it remains to be seen whether NFC is a throwback to the 1970s or a model for the 1990s.

Whatever else it is, though, it has been successful in conventional business terms, although not as successful this year as the table suggests.

Reported profits soared by a third. But the profits increase was helped by a suspension of pension fund contributions (shared with employees, unlike most companies) and other special effects.

	1989	1988	%
Sales	£1494m	£1255m	+19
Profits	£90m	£67m	+34
Earnings	18.3p	14.2p	+29
Dividends	7.5p	5.7p	+31

Without those benefits the profits would have been lower than last year, although the core transport and distribution divisions did much better. But the property profit is expected to continue growing. Similarly the pensions holiday will continue for several years.

At any rate NFC (unique among public companies in giving a profits forecast) believes profits will grow by another 10 per cent in the current year.

That is good news in the light of worsening market conditions for the removals and holiday businesses.

The travel agency business has slumped into loss in the face of disappearing package holidays and market leader Lunn Poly's price-cutting tactics. The worst is unlikely to be over yet.

NFC's caring approach makes it more reluctant than most companies to show employees the door. But Sir Peter and his colleagues have also demonstrated their commitment to what the mission statement describes as "a participative *and* results-oriented management style" (my italics). Staff in the travel business have already been cut by 15 per cent. And the crunch comes next month when the company has to face the possibility of closing down or selling off the whole business – although this will be a last resort and an acquisition or joint venture may be more likely.

Such hard decisions must be made easier by the better outlook elsewhere in the group. Contract hire and the managed distribution business known as "logistics" have both done well. And the property development operation more than doubled profits.

That does not prove that Sir Peter's participative style is responsible, but it does prove that it is not irresponsible – as many bosses would claim.

The style includes a consultation exercise on future strategy, culminating in endorsement (presumably) at the annual meeting. Objectives include "seeking improved employment opportunities". Sir Peter even suggested yesterday that business was not just about making profits. "It is about how you share them and who does well out of them."

Many of Sir Peter's fellow company chairmen will scoff at such social sentiments. But they might ponder whether such sentiments are more in line with the German and Japanese approaches that will probably dominate the 1990s rather than are their traditional capitalist values that have dominated the 1980s.

(Source: *Financial Times*, 16 February 1989)

● 3   Study the article on satisfaction and productivity and answer the following questions:

When satisfaction does not equate with productivity

By Michael Dixon

Are people who feel satisfied in their jobs more productive than those who do not? The consensus view among managers seems to be that the answer is yes. But the known facts contradict that commonsense belief.

Certainly, studies of various types of worker have found that the highly productive are often satisfied in their work. On the other hand research has also shown that people low in individual output often feel similar satisfaction, perhaps because they like the easy life their bosses allow them.

So productivity can hardly be caused by job satisfaction; the connection is, if anything, the other way round. What ultimately accounts for unusually high individual performance remains obscure even though there has long been a word for it – "motivation".

Some fresh light on the mystery has been provided by Nigel Nicholson of Sheffield University's Social and Applied Psychology Unit. He has studied nearly 4,000 workers in seven different organisations, although six belong to the same parent company. And one of his questions is: "Of the various things your managers do, which make you feel motivated?

The answers can be related to a classification of the whole gamut of managerial activities which divides them into five categories, ranging between two extremes. At one end are activities focused on workers' human needs. At the other are those centred on the objective demands of the task for completion of which the manager is responsible.

The human-focused kind are called "nurturing". The next set are "guiding", followed by "democratic". Then come activities which are "upwardly influential" in being aimed at gaining approval and support from the manager's superiors, and finally the task-centred variety.

While commonsense may suggest that nurturing activities have the greatest effect in making managers popular with their subordinates, earlier research indicated that the upwardly influential kind are the most decisive. It seemed that the generality of employees most likely to work for someone with political clout in the organisation.

But the Sheffield University researcher has probed beyond popularity into the underlying factors which account for it. One of them, for example, is the extent to which people feel relaxed and comfortable working for their managers. According to his analysis, the activities mainly linked with such feelings are nurturing, guiding, and democratic – the three groups clustered at the human end of the scale.

The pattern is markedly different when the question is what makes workers feel well motivated. The activities most strongly linked with that kind of feeling are the two at the opposite extremes: nurturing and task-centred.

Nicholson told the British Psychological Association's recent conference in Windermere that his findings gave practical-trial support to a pair of decades-old framework theories about management. They are the two-dimensional managerial grid developed by Robert Blake and Jane Mouton, and the three-dimensional grid produced by Bill Reddin.

These suggest that it is not enough for managers to be single-minded, concentrating *either* on the human wants of their subordinates *or* on the objective demands of the task in hand. Nor is it enough for them to split their attention between those two elements, devoting perhaps half of it to the one and the remaining half to the other. If managers are to get the best out of the human and other resources entrusted to them, they must find ways of concentrating on both elements at the same time.

Nicholson's results do not stop at supporting that view; they suggest that the theories understate the problem. While the nurturing and task-centred activities had the strongest links with motivation, it was also linked pretty strongly with the other three. So it seems that the job of motivating staff calls for managers who are not just good, but excellent all-rounders.

(Source: *The Financial Times*, 17 January 1989)

(*a*)   Consult more advanced books (e.g. L Mullins, *Management and Organisational Behaviour*, Pitman) to investigate the work of (i) Blake and Mouton and (ii) Reddin. What do Blake and Mouton mean by

- country club management
- impoverished management
- team management
- authority-obedience
- organisation man management.

(b) What is meant by 'correlation' and 'line of causation'. What correlation and line of causation is being questioned in the article?

(c) In your own words explain the 'human focussed activities'?

(d) Why do you think 'nurturing' and 'task-centred' activities have the strongest links with motivation?

(e) In what way does Nigel Nicholson's work suggest the job of managing is even more difficult than previously imagined?

EXAMINATION QUESTIONS ■■■

1 (a) Distinguish between *autocratic* and *democratic* styles of management.
   (b) Why is 'span of control' relevant in any discussion of management style?
   (c) Compare and contrast the advantages and disadvantages of the following methods of communication, and say to which management style they might be appropriate:
       (i) letters;
       (ii) notice boards;
       (iii) telephones;
       (iv) meetings.

(Cambridge, June 1987)

2 How far does the style of leadership adopted by management make any significant difference to the way people work?

(AEB, June 1988)

3 Examine the barriers to effective communication in a large company.

(AEB, June 1986)

4 Are all attempts to motivate workers merely gimmicks or are they based on established motivational theories?

(AEB, June 1989)

5 'Appropriate leadership styles depend upon circumstances and personalities.' Discuss.

6 'Conflict within an organisation is the result of failure of communications.' Discuss.

7 'Japanese management techniques are inappropriate and unworkable in Britain.' Discuss.

8 'Improvements in communication technology will eliminate all communications problems.' Discuss.

FURTHER READING

ORGANISATIONAL CULTURE

Most of the works mentioned at the end of Chapter 12 are relevant but the following are particularly useful:

L MULLINS *Management and Organisational Behaviour* (Pitman)

D NEEDLE *Business in Context* (VNR Int.)

K DAVIS AND J NEWSTROM *Human Behaviour at Work: Organisational Behaviour* (McGraw-Hill).

Index